GENDER IN HISTORY

Series editors:
Lynn Abrams, Cordelia Beattie, Pam Sharpe and Penny Summerfield

The expansion of research into the history of women and gender since the 1970s has changed the face of history. Using the insights of feminist theory and of historians of women, gender historians have explored the configuration in the past of gender identities and relations between the sexes. They have also investigated the history of sexuality and family relations, and analysed ideas and ideals of masculinity and femininity. Yet gender history has not abandoned the original, inspirational project of women's history: to recover and reveal the lived experience of women in the past and the present.

The series Gender in History provides a forum for these developments. Its historical coverage extends from the medieval to the modern periods, and its geographical scope encompasses not only Europe and North America but all corners of the globe. The series aims to investigate the social and cultural constructions of gender in historical sources, as well as the gendering of historical discourse itself. It embraces both detailed case studies of specific regions or periods, and broader treatments of major themes. Gender in History titles are designed to meet the needs of both scholars and students working in this dynamic area of historical research.

Gender, rhetoric and regulation

MANCHESTER
1824
Manchester University Press

Love, intimacy and power: marriage and patriarchy in Scotland, 1650–1850   Katie Barclay
(Winner of the 2012 Women's History Network Book Prize)

Modern women on trial: sexual transgression in the age of the flapper   Lucy Bland

The Women's Liberation Movement in Scotland   Sarah Browne

Modern motherhood: women and family in England, c. 1945–2000   Angela Davis

Jewish women in Europe in the Middle Ages: a quiet revolution   Simha Goldin

The shadow of marriage: singleness in England, 1914–60   Katherine Holden

Women, dowries and agency: marriage in fifteenth-century Valencia   Dana Wessell Lightfoot

Women, travel and identity: journeys by rail and sea, 1870–1940   Emma Robinson-Tomsett

Imagining Caribbean womanhood: race, nation and beauty contests, 1929–70   Rochelle Rowe

Infidel feminism: secularism, religion and women's emancipation, England 1830–1914   Laura Schwartz

Being boys: working-class masculinities and leisure   Melanie Tebbutt

Queen and country: same sex desire in the British Armed Forces, 1939–45   Emma Vickers

The 'perpetual fair': gender, disorder and urban amusement in eighteenth-century London   Anne Wohlcke

GENDER, RHETORIC AND REGULATION

WOMEN'S WORK IN THE CIVIL SERVICE AND THE LONDON COUNTY COUNCIL, 1900–55

⇥ Helen Glew ⇤

Manchester University Press

Published by Manchester University Press
Altrincham Street, Manchester M1 7JA, UK
www.manchesteruniversitypress.co.uk

British Library Cataloguing-in-Publication Data is available

ISBN 978 0 7190 9027 1 hardback
ISBN 978 1 5261 4663 2 paperback

First published by Manchester University Press in hardback 2016

This edition published 2020

Typeset by Out of House Publishing

Dedicated to the memory of my grandfather, Gordon Glew (1925–2013), whose enthusiasm for life and learning I miss. I hope he would have enjoyed this book.

Contents

Figures

Credits for all figures: © Royal Mail Group Ltd 2015,
courtesy of The British Postal Museum & Archive

Tables

Acknowledgements

This book has been a long time in the making. Parts of it started life as an AHRC-funded PhD thesis undertaken collaboratively at the Institute of Contemporary British History (now at Kings College, London) and the British Postal Museum and Archive. I benefited enormously from the support of Pat Thane, whose practical, calm and wise guidance was always helpful. Thanks also to Michael Kandiah and Virginia Preston for their help and support. Sally Alexander and Martin Daunton examined the thesis and offered generous comments and insights into my work. It was Martin who first suggested that I expand my research to look at women working in the LCC and I am grateful for the new direction this offered me. I hope this book does his idea some justice.

My colleagues in the Department of History, Sociology and Criminology at the University of Westminster always took an interest in this project and offered guidance throughout. In particular, Mark Clapson, Peter Catterall, Martin Doherty, Anthony Gorst and David Manlow were always willing to discuss ideas and the progress of my work and I am grateful for their support. I would also like to thank the students who have taken 1HIS658 Women and the Women's Movement, 1918–70, with me over the years. Sharing elements of my research with them and hearing their questions helped me to think in new ways about what I was writing.

In the course of my research I have drawn on bodies of material held at a large number of institutions and I am grateful to the assistance given to me by so many members of staff. First and foremost, the British Postal Museum & Archive's staff have been there from the very beginning of this project and have always been supportive, ready with encouragement, suggestions of new sources or just positivity on the days when I wondered where the research was going. I would particularly like to thank all of the archivists and cataloguers past and present, all the members of the search room team, Libby Buckley and Adrian Steel for their supervision and support and Martin Devereux for his good humour and his help preparing the photographs that appear in this publication. Thanks also to all of the staff at the following: the London Metropolitan Archives (especially Bridget Howlett who patiently answered a number of lengthy queries), the National Archives, the Modern Records Centre at the University of Warwick, the Women's Library, the Wellcome Library, the Imperial War Museum Sound Archive, the British Library and BT Archives.

I would like to thank everyone at Manchester University Press for their help, for all they have done to bring this book to completion and most of all for their patience. I received excellent feedback and critique from the anonymous peer reviewers at both the book proposal stage and on completion of the draft manuscript. A number of fellow scholars have offered useful critiques or suggestions for sources or read sections of the draft manuscript. In no particular order I would like to thank Lucy Delap, Sonya Rose, Adrian Bingham, Claire Langhamer, Helen McCarthy and Selina Todd. As with any project, any errors or omissions that remain are my responsibility.

Researching and writing a book, as all those who have done it know all too well, takes a huge amount of perseverance, belief, energy and sheer hard work. I would hereby like to apologise to all those who received an eye-roll or a sigh whenever they well-meaningly asked how the book was going and happened to ask at a time where things seemed more difficult. Completing the book would have been immeasurably harder without the support of a huge number of people who have been there along the way to offer encouragement, advice or commiseration or to remind me that there was a world beyond the book. In no particular order I would like to thank Liza Filby, Kath Sherit, Jennifer Pecho, Emma Vickers, Charles Sandeman-Allen, Julie Hipperson, Cath Feely, Lucie Matthews-Jones, Kate Bradley, Jodi Burkett, Mark Freeman, Peter Sutton, Mark Crowley, Suzanne Davis, Gareth Stockey, Steve Dempster, Alex Warwick, Lucy Bond and Georgina Colby. Tanya Symington and Rae Ritchie commented on early drafts and have been great, supportive friends. I am grateful to Daniel Grey for his friendship, encyclopaedic knowledge of useful secondary reading on so many topics and his encouragement to me to finish the book because he needed to read it. Mari Takayanagi and I were PhD students at the same time working on cognate topics and we usefully shared ideas and sources. I am grateful to her for her help, her willingness to share her knowledge of parliamentary procedures with me and her comments on several draft chapters. Having Hannah Elias as a friend has done more than she probably realises to help the process of finishing this book. Anthony Gorst has been an unfailingly supportive friend and colleague who read and commented on much of this book in its final stages. I am so grateful to Simon Avery for critique of several chapters but even more so for his positivity, friendship and constant encouragement. Corinna Peniston-Bird has been a mentor and friend for many years and her support of me and my work is impossible to quantify. My parents, Pam and Ray, have helped me in more ways than I can explain and I would like to thank my sister, Louise, for her enthusiasm for this project and the perspectives she has offered.

I met Patrick Stribley three months before I began this project. The part he has played in helping me complete this is impossible to put into words. I thank him for his love, encouragement and belief in me.

Abbreviations and terms

APOWC	Association of Post Office Women Clerks. Formed 1901; later a constituent association of the Federation of Women Civil Servants and merged to become part of the National Association of Women Civil Servants from 1931.
AWCS	Association of Women Clerks and Secretaries. Had a dedicated Civil Service section and specifically represented women employed temporarily.
BMA	British Medical Association
BPMA	British Postal Museum & Archive
CAB	Conciliation and Arbitration Board
CC&T	Counter Clerk and Telegraphist. London-only grade in the GPO. The provincial equivalent was SC&T.
CSCA	Civil Service Clerical Association. Female clerical officers and writing assistants admitted 1921.
CSEPC	Civil Service Equal Pay Committee
CTO	Central Telegraph Office (GPO)
CWCS	Council of Women Civil Servants
EPCC	Equal Pay Campaign Committee
FWCS	Federation of Women Civil Servants, formed 1913.
GPO	General Post Office
IWMSA	Imperial War Museum Sound Archive
Joint Committee of Members and Staff	The employer/employee negotiation machinery in the LCC.
Joint Committee on Women in the Civil Service	A loose alliance of women's organisations and allies who campaigned for women's rights in the Civil Service.
LCC	London County Council

London County Council Staff Gazette	The journal of the London County Council Staff Association. Replaced by *London Town* from 1929.
London Town	The journal of the London County Council Staff Association from 1929.
LMA	London Metropolitan Archives
LNSWS	London & National Society for Women's Service
MacDonnell Commission	See Royal Commission on the Civil Service (1912–14)
MRC	Modern Records Centre, University of Warwick
MWF	Medical Women's Federation
NALGO	National Association of Local Government Officers
NAWCS	National Association of Women Civil Servants. Formed 1931–32.
NUSEC	National Union of Societies for Equal Citizenship
Opportunity	The journal of the FWCS and later the NAWCS.
P&TCA	Postal & Telegraph Clerks' Association. Founded 1914.
PF	Postmen's Federation. Merged with other unions to form the UPW in 1919.
Red Tape	The journal of the CSCA.
Reorganisation Report (1920)	Post-First World War restructuring of the Civil Service negotiated through Whitleyism.
Royal Commission on the Civil Service (1912–14)	Royal Commission appointed to examine a wide range of issues in the Civil Service. Chaired by Lord MacDonnell.
Royal Commission on the Civil Service (1929–31)	Royal Commission appointed to examine a wide range of issues in the Civil Service. Chaired by Lord Tomlin.
SBD	Savings Bank Department (GPO)
SC&T	Sorting Clerk and Telegraphist (GPO)

SJCIWO	Standing Joint Committee on Industrial Women's Organisations
Tomlin Commission	See Royal Commission on the Civil Service (1929–31)
TUC	Trades Union Congress
UPW	Union of Post Office Workers. Formed 1919. Represented around 100,000 GPO workers on major grades such as CC&T, SC&T, postman, telephonist, telegraphist.
WFL	Women's Freedom League
Whitleyism/Whitley Committees	Employer/employee negotiation mechanism in the Civil Service.

Introduction

This book opens just after the emergence of the first female professionals and amidst a growing discourse about careers for women, as well as growing social anxieties about the 'new woman'. In the later nineteenth century, female specialists had emerged in key areas such as nursing and public health, carrying out work in particular for fellow women and children, and the period also saw growing numbers of women in clerical work in its myriad forms. The Civil Service and the London County Council (LCC) both began employing women in this period. Each employer encompassed a huge range of professions. The Civil Service, a loose federation rather than a monolith, began employing women in the Post Office in the early 1870s, once it took over the nationalised telegraph service, and gradually women's employment was increased both in other Post Office sections and other Civil Service departments. The Metropolitan Board of Works, the LCC's predecessor, employed a handful of women. Though it had no specific stipulation against women's employment, it also did not actively seek it.[1] When the LCC was brought into being in 1889, it employed mainly female typists, as well as women in the specialist female welfare roles. At the turn of the century, the ideas of sensible and suitable careers for women were by no means fully formed, however, and it is in the first quarter of the new century that we see these become more cemented.[2] This book allows us to look at these key developments through the lens of the officials at the heads of two public bodies, as well as through responses of the women employees themselves and reactions amongst the wider public. In particular, this book is concerned with exploring three key facets of women's employment in the public service: the marriage bar, the long campaigns for equal pay, and the particular brand of occupational segregation that was present in the public service. In so doing, it illuminates the highly gendered nature of public service employment, the ways in which public service was conceived, and also provides a significant contribution to our understanding of the operation of such gendered working practices in the past, which private employers often mirrored. In a time period which encompassed the enfranchisement of women, the right of women to become MPs and to enter public life more broadly, a thorough examination of the state's conceptualisation of women public servants and the way that it created and upheld specific policies relating to women's work is important.

There has been considerable historical writing on women in the public sphere in terms of either voluntary work or public office.[3] By contrast, little comprehensive work has hitherto been conducted on women (or, for that matter, men) as public service employees, perhaps in part because working in national and local government encompassed such a huge array of roles. Indeed, despite the volume and breadth of jobs it provided, historians have paid scant attention to the LCC as an employer. This is particularly surprising as it was the largest employer in London in 1914.[4] Susan Pennybacker's broader work on the LCC in the earlier period of its existence describes some facets of the Council as an employer for women. In particular, she focuses on employment culture and the wider cultural meanings of the marriage bar. For example, she asserts that '[t]he concepts of "patriarchy" and of "gendered work" are also not specific or accurate enough to address the nature of women's LCC employment' and though she suggests that the concept of the "new woman" is useful in understanding employers' perceptions of young female LCC employees, she does not offer a comprehensive analysis of the perceptions and significance attached to women's work, in part because the focus of her work lay elsewhere.[5] Although concerns about the "new woman" had metamorphosed into concerns about the "flapper" by the 1920s, it is argued here that gender stereotypes and patriarchy were indeed often central to understanding LCC and Civil Service attitudes to women's employment in the first half of the twentieth century. Therefore, although studies such as Pennybacker's and Dina Copelman's comprehensive *London's women teachers* have drawn on some of the aspects of women's LCC employment, the full complexity of the regulations and culture surrounding their roles has not yet been understood.[6] For example, they were employed plentifully as typists and clerks in various, quasi-autonomous, sections of the LCC and in a number of areas of "feminine expertise" such as those in medical and health departments, school inspectorates and childcare departments. They also worked as cleaners, kitchen and domestic staff. However, in the period under discussion here, women were also able to make considerable strides into the LCC hierarchy and into more "gender neutral" posts. These were seen as particularly important by an interwar feminist movement which, in part, wished to see women employed in all levels of work without regard to their gender.[7] These women were public servants serving the ever-growing London, and were also in roles akin to, or surpassing, the various grades of the Civil Service with which their contemporaries were more familiar.

There is more existent work on women civil servants compared to work on the LCC, but none which has offered a comprehensive picture of the complexities of the state as an employer for women at both service-wide and departmental levels. This book focuses on key departments and service-wide policies in the non-industrial, "home" Civil Service.[8] The General Post Office (GPO), examined here in detail, was the nation's largest single employer at the start of the interwar period and employed 43,850 women by 1938.[9] Despite its significance, it has received little attention from historians of the twentieth century. Indeed, many of the histories which include the Post Office at any period in time are institutional histories.[10] The three substantial works on the Post Office which cover the period under investigation here included only brief discussions of women's employment because their focus lay elsewhere.[11] When historians have examined women's work in the Post Office and its implications for women's work more widely, it is almost exclusively for periods earlier than that considered here. Histories of women's clerical employment in the late nineteenth century cite the GPO as an important case study in the establishment of conditions of employment for middle-class women.[12] There has been some work on women's employment as civil servants in other departments in the early twentieth century, such as Meta Zimmeck's important work on women clerks.[13] Sociological work has also considered the employment of women in the Post Office in various ways.[14] However, there has yet to be a study which considers the range and complexity of women's work and the ways in which the Civil Service sought to circumscribe it. Helen Jones' *Women in British public life, 1914–1950* provides a broad overview of women in policymaking, Parliament and the Civil Service in the period and her work offers some brief discussion of women civil servants. However she overwhelmingly concentrates on the "exceptional" women civil servants – the handful of women who were able to break through to senior positions.[15] The lessons, examples and experiences of these women are of course important, but the current study examines the struggles and experiences of women in public sector employment at all levels as far as archival records allow. It is only by taking a broader view of the public service that we can gain a deeper understanding of how the status of women public servants was conceived by those in charge. The very exceptional women who rose to prominence are thus well known amongst historians of women – Frances Durham, Maude Lawrence, Hilda Martindale, to name just three – but not since Martindale's own history of women civil servants has there been a comprehensive account of the constraints on, and expectations of, women civil servants as a whole and the ways in which their work was understood by officials and policymakers.[16]

The comparison between the Civil Service and the LCC is mutually illuminating because the broad aims and *raison d'être* of each organisation were the same. The inter-relationship between the two organisations is also important because in some cases the tendency for one organisation to consult the other solidified a decision; in other cases, where policies remained different, this highlighted the sometimes more contentious issues or even lines which one organisation was not prepared to cross. This cross-fertilisation of policy is illuminated throughout this book. In particular, the LCC looked to the Civil Service to inform its own employment policy, but at times was also prepared to disregard this and make its own. It also offered positions, on occasion, to successful candidates in Civil Service examinations who were surplus to Civil Service vacancies. In addition, a number of individuals had both Civil Service and LCC connections and brought their expertise and experience from one to the other. At decision-making levels, the personal connections or transfers between one organisation and another were often men, which also serves to underline how male the institutional elite remained and how so often policy affecting women was made by men. For example, Kingsley Wood was elected LCC Municipal Reform member for Woolwich in 1911, and thus was involved in decisions affecting female employees of the Council. He became Member of Parliament for West Woolwich in 1918 and, by 1931, he was Postmaster General, remaining in post until the 1935 general election and overseeing changes to women's employment in the GPO.[17] But women who served in both institutions did exist: Maude Lawrence served on the London School Board – subsumed into the LCC in 1904 – and by the early 1920s was appointed as Woman Establishment Officer at the Treasury, though as a woman she held less power than her position might have suggested. Frances Durham held inspector positions in the LCC followed by the Civil Service, rising throughout a long career to the rank of Assistant Secretary in the Ministry of Labour and also helping to make policy for women's employment. The transfers from one institution to the other between junior members of staff are harder to trace but nonetheless would have existed due to the large number of temporary clerical workers in London. Philippa Fawcett worked for the LCC in a senior role in its education department and joined the First World War effort as a relief postwoman.[18]

The shared location of these two institutions was also hugely important. From 1922, when County Hall was built, the central powers of the LCC were located there, on the south bank of the Thames, more or less opposite Parliament. Near Parliament was of course Whitehall, which (amongst other departments) housed the Treasury, which as budget-holder made significant decisions about the staffing of the Civil Service. Before County Hall as an institution there was Spring Gardens, the street which housed the central functions of the LCC, tucked north of the Thames near Whitehall. Whilst both the Civil Service and the LCC had headquarter departments stationed in other London districts or suburbs – and so their workers populated myriad parts of London – there was a concentration of local and national government activity in a relatively small area, thus creating ideal conditions for networking and informal discussion between members of each organisation. At the same time, the reach of the Civil Service – and therefore of this book – was not just metropolitan London: the Ministry of Labour and the GPO, to name just two, employed men and women around the country in larger and smaller communities. Therefore the experiences of working conditions discussed here include those of individuals in rural and provincial communities too.

Women civil servants adopted the common cry of the era, 'a fair field and no favour', to describe the environment that they wished to work in: one in which they had equal opportunity and no special or different treatment just because they were women. This book thus explores the policies formulated for women's employment in both the Civil Service and the LCC and considers their inter-relationship with wider social attitudes and cultural notions of both women and paid work. With the exception of equal pay, which was deemed a matter for the government only, questions affecting staff were addressed by the Whitley Council in the Civil Service after the First World War. This comprised a staff side and an official side, the latter being controlled, in practice, by the Treasury – and the Treasury was ultimately controlled by the government of the day. The work of the Whitley Council was also influenced – and ultimately circumscribed – by legislation, and also by non-binding recommendations of Royal Commissions. High-ranking civil servants tended to have long tenure, be part of the educated elite and were therefore often politically conservative, as Gail Savage has explored.[20] In the LCC, major decisions affecting staff had to be passed by the Council, so whilst the joint body – the Joint Committee of Members and Staff – could formulate decisions, it was the elected members who had the final decision-making powers. This meant, therefore, that the Civil Service and LCC had slightly different power structures in terms of formulating policy about women's employment, whilst also clearly keeping an eye on one another.

The First World War and interwar periods are critical moments to examine in terms of both gender and employment. This book begins at the turn of the century, where it outlines the position of women in both organisations. The First World War marked the first national emergency of the modern era and the point at which employers' carefully laid plans for women's employment had to be disrupted, with women employed in roles previously performed only by men. The First World War was seen by contemporaneous commentators and sometimes by historians as a "watershed" in women's lives.[21] In taking on "men's jobs" for the duration of the war, women were entering new workspaces or roles in the workplace, and many felt that the war constituted an opportunity for them to prove themselves. Over the last thirty or so years, the war's effects on women's employment during the conflict and after have formed the subjects of in-depth studies, many of which oppose the view that the war was a watershed in societal attitudes to women.[22] Broadly, the historical consensus is that the First World War did not, in fact, materially advance women's employment, and it is important to add the insight gained from a study of the Civil Service and the LCC to this debate. This is explored in particular in the first three chapters of the book.

After – and in part because of – the war, women's employment was re-examined in both the Civil Service and the LCC. It is precisely these debates which are so important for assessing the conceptualisations of women as workers as well as the effects of the women's movement on established institutions. The Civil Service underwent considerable scrutiny in this period in terms of its employment practice and the immediate post-war period saw significant reorganisation and restructuring via numerous committees. Such organisational change, against the backdrop of the experience of new roles for women in the First World War, constituted an opportunity for conditions to change for women public servants. The fact that change was slow and incremental contributed to the feeling among women civil servants – in particular – that the interwar years comprised stagnation, frustration and continuity with earlier periods. Arguably, women's employment in the LCC underwent a more dramatic shift after the First World War, though it started from a less solid foundation. The climate of interwar society, in which women public servants and their supporters and detractors operated, is the backdrop to much of this book.

This book examines, first and foremost, top-level decisions and negotiations with regard to women's employment. The staff records of the LCC, though less complete than those for the Civil Service, have remained largely untouched by historians and so provide a new comparative perspective on the debates about the role and place of women in public service. Similarly, the completeness of the GPO's staff records allows a second detailed case study of its approach to women's employment nationwide. This is particularly important as the GPO employed by far the largest number of women in the Civil Service. Records for other Civil Service departments are less extensive, but these and other Civil Service staff establishment and policy records each inform and contribute to perspectives on women's employment in this period. Complementing these are the Treasury records at the National Archives and the records of the Civil Service Commissioners, the Civil Service Conciliation and Arbitration Board (and its later incarnations) and the various Civil Service Whitley Councils. Though there was an ongoing debate about how far the public service – and in particular the Civil Service – could or should be considered a model employer, a detailed examination of such processes and negotiations can assist our interpretation of the realities of, and attitudes towards, women's employment more widely in this period.[23] Although the Civil Service and LCC were both employers which imposed a significant number of regulations on their employees, policy and practice could be two different things. Similarly, analyses of numerous memoranda, journals, petitions and campaigns by unions and associations representing female public servants enable an understanding of women and men as agents of change and of the manner in which these campaigns were framed and contextualised. The book situates the sustained activity for women's workplace equality in the two institutions in the context of both the women's movement and the trade union movement. There was, however, a specific context to unionisation as the LCC Staff Association was prevented from joining outside organisations in 1915 and civil servants were not supposed to strike and could not join the Trades Union Congress after the Trade Disputes and Trade Unions Act of 1927. The backdrop of the partial enfranchisement of women in 1918 and the granting of equal suffrage in 1928, as well as the gradual opening of wider employment opportunities to middle-class women in particular, were amongst the important focal points for those campaigning for improvements to women public servants' employment. Again, whilst a number of publications on trade unionism and the women's movement make reference to campaigns for women's equality in the Civil Service,[24] the extent and significance of such campaigns have not been fully explored hitherto and remain unexplored for the LCC.

It is contended here that, although Civil Service officials broadly viewed women's employment favourably because women were cheaper to employ than men, there were very specific limits within which they perceived women's employment to be permissible. There was systemic prejudice against women employees, and definite limits placed on women's advancement. The exact nature of these limits and prejudice will be delineated throughout the book. The conditions under which women were employed were not so different from other occupations. However, the longevity of these conditions, the fact that they were maintained by successive governments despite parliamentary promises otherwise, and the justifications used to underpin them, reveal much about attitudes to women's employment and womanhood more generally. The fact that the Treasury controlled Civil Service staffing arrangements and that all civil servants were government employees was also an important factor: time and again in this study, both government officials and the female employees express awareness that the government's treatment of its own employees would be used as a barometer by employers everywhere.[25] There are parallels in the LCC. Although the LCC was famously progressive in parts of this period, there were still tussles over women's employment questions between elected officers, high-ranking officials and the staff and, by often using the Civil Service as a starting point for its own policy, the LCC often became caught up in many of the same discourses and patterns of thinking.

Although this volume is concerned with top-level policy towards women's employment and reactions to and campaigns against such policy, and though it records disappointment and frustration among the women involved, it is important to point out that such feelings were not necessarily uniform, universal or unchanging. Especially given that the full experiences of many of these women can no longer be adequately accessed, we need to acknowledge that women would have had varying and wide-ranging experiences throughout their working lives in the public service. The experience, for example, of a woman clerk in the LCC or a London Civil Service department continually working overtime might differ greatly from a sorting clerk and telegraphist in a provincial post office, who worked in a small team of people who were all often long-standing members of the same community. For a number of women, as for some men, work might simply have been a way to earn money; others viewed it as a career and carried with them aspirations and expectations. Though this book is very much concerned with women's employment conditions and the ways in which these were largely maintained throughout this period, owing to their numbers it cannot, and does not claim to, speak comprehensively for all of the women employed. The methods of compilation of institutional records often render it impossible to trace individual careers, unless these were also traced by the original policymakers. Thus, many of the individual stories mentioned here have only been possible through extensive cross-referencing and a little good fortune favouring the researcher. Additionally, little is known in particular about temporary or part-time women employees (especially outside of the First World War period) – and what does survive in this regard has largely done so by chance rather than design. Therefore, this study by default concentrates largely on the women who were in what was known as 'established employment' – that is, permanent and usually full-time positions with pension rights.[26] Such employment was organised in a complex but occasionally fluid way. As indicated already, a large number of those employed performed clerical or quasi-clerical work, a traditional middle-class employment for men and a growing source of employment for middle-class women from the later nineteenth century.[27] Other women, however, working as postwomen, maids or cleaners, carried out work more akin to traditional working class employment, and others still were qualified professionals in the sense of having university degrees or other equivalent, specialist training. Therefore, the public service was constituted by individuals from a range of social class backgrounds as well as ages, though there was a caveat in the Civil Service that applicants had to be natural-born British subjects and daughters of fathers who met the same qualification, and in the LCC that they be natural-born or naturalised British subjects.

As much as certain of its working conditions – and its continued differentiation of workers along strongly gendered lines – exasperated large numbers of women, the public service was not, by comparison with a number of other employment options for women, a bad place to work. For women with the requisite education, the service offered a job for life once an officer was established and a pension with retirement at sixty. On the other hand, the price women paid for this – as in a considerable number of other interwar occupations – was remaining single. For women with aspirations to reach the higher echelons of the Civil Service or the LCC and to do something other than routine work, life in certain departments could become frustrating because of the relative lack of opportunities they offered to women. However, it should also be remembered that women were not the only group who were marginalised or discriminated against. Certain grades of men's employment – postmen and other manual, semi-skilled workers in particular – often felt the social divisions between themselves and their "indoor" counterparts, and prospects and conditions were not always favourable for those under eighteen, or, in a number of cases, those at the latter stages of their careers.[28] One study can only cover so much, but by focusing solely on women it is in no way contended that women were the only group treated unfavourably. Furthermore, women public servants had luxuries – a longer holiday allowance, and, variously, better working hours or the right to a pension – that many women in private employment just did not have. However, being employed by the state meant that women's employment could also be more restricted – or subject to more rules than the more ad-hoc arrangements in private employment – as a means of dictating state policy. Arguments over changing the terms on which women were employed were also public, wide-ranging and were often a challenge to the state's concept of womanhood.

The book is divided into three thematic sections, each of which explores a different aspect of women's employment. The first documents the work women did and their place in the hierarchies of each organisation. Chapter 1 thus examines the roles which women typically undertook, exploring the justifications offered for work designated as "women's work" and for keeping women's work largely segregated. The justifications for employing women often on routine work were social as well as economic, and were also constructed with prevailing ideas about physiology and women's intellectual capabilities in mind. The chapter considers the First World War and the resultant need for women to take on work ordinarily designated as men's within each organisation, arguing that the war should be considered an aberration rather than offering a drastic break and new opportunities in the long term within the Civil Service. For the LCC, the war played more of a distinctive part in widening their opportunities to more or less equivalency with the Civil Service, but again some of the wartime opportunities were not carried into peacetime. Chapter 2 examines the challenges mounted by women employees and their supporters to regulations and barriers to women's advancement and in particular addresses the question of promotion to the highest grades in each organisation. Such challenges reveal not only how women, their work and its limits were conceptualised by officials and the wider public, but also show the extent to which campaigns for equal opportunity were rooted in the wider interwar movement for greater roles for women in public life.

The next three chapters provide a chronological exploration of the campaigns for equal pay. In the interwar period, women civil servants were one of very few groups of women who were regularly employed on the same or very similar work to men. Thus the Civil Service campaign for equal pay was vociferous, long-term and prominent, not least because it was repeatedly debated in Parliament. There had been calls for equal pay for a number of years before the First World War and the experience of war only intensified such calls. Equal pay was demanded for a number of reasons, particularly on equality grounds and to protect male wages. It also had its detractors, including those who questioned women's abilities and those who believed in a 'family wage' for men. The chapters explore these and other discourses in depth as well as charting the successive campaigns. The position in the GPO was more complicated than that in a number of other departments owing to the need for employees to work overnight and the fact that labour legislation, and social protocol, prevented this for women. Although the principle of equal pay was affirmed by Parliament early in the interwar years, a range of reasons was given for not implementing it which included finance but also, and more prominently, encompassed gendered assumptions about women. There were, however, important moments and moral victories which provided a significant foundation for the rest of the campaign. After the Second World War, there was more detectable sympathy for the equal pay cause among MPs and others and so Chapter 5 interrogates how and why such a change in attitude came about. The LCC's position on equal pay adds various dimensions to the early struggle for equal remuneration. When women were admitted, in small numbers, to the major establishment – home to some more senior positions – in 1919 they were paid on the existing men's scale. Though the disparity between this and the pay policy for women in other sections of the LCC was noted, it did not, remarkably, form the bedrock of a wide and sustained campaign. Equal pay was granted finally and with relatively little fanfare in 1952, three years before the Civil Service. These chapters thus narrate these twin stories of the LCC and the Civil Service, and show the ways in which officials and campaigners looked from one employer to the other throughout these events.

The final two chapters of the book evaluate the marriage bar, its implementation and operation and the limits it placed on women's opportunities. In short, officials wanted it both ways: there was often much mumbling and grumbling that women left soon after being trained for their jobs whilst such complaints ignored the fact that women were compelled to leave on marriage. Chapter 6 examines the social, ideological and economic bases for the bar in amongst interwar gendered expectations of women and marriage, and compares the evolution of marriage bar policy in both the LCC and the Civil Service. In particular, the LCC's lifting of the marriage bar for women teachers, its largest group of female employees, in 1935 changed the landscape of married women's work considerably, as the Second World War also would. The chapter also examines the varying attitudes to the bar of the numerous unions and associations in the Civil Service, and by extension discusses the sometimes contrasting attitudes to it on the part of women civil servants. By looking, as Chapter 7 does, at case studies of women who did not fit neatly into either the 'married' or 'single' categories – women separated from or deserted by their husbands; divorcees; women whose engagements were broken – we can gain an insight not only into the changing conceptualisations of marital status and divorce law but also into the pervasiveness of the male breadwinner model and the vulnerable position in which women experiencing marital breakdown often found themselves. In many ways, then, this is a study of the relationship and interplay between rhetoric, policy and broader social attitudes and serves to highlight the working experiences of working-, lower middle- and middle-class women in the early twentieth century. In considering the LCC and key Civil Service departments, this book provides a sustained analysis of the ways in which women were employed in public service roles, the policies governing this employment and the ramifications of these policies.

Notes

1 Gloria Clifton, *Professionalism, Patronage and Public Service in Victorian London* (London: The Athlone Press, 1992), p.53.

2 The proliferation of contemporaneous literature on careers for girls is testament to this. See, for example, *The Times*, 'Careers for Girls I – The Probation Officer', 12 October 1938; *The Times*, 'Careers For Girls XV: The Hospital Almoner', 1 May 1939 and also published guides: Margaret Cole (ed.), *The Road to Success: Twenty Essays on the Choice of a Career for Women* (London: Methuen & Co., 1936); Dorothy Evans, *Women and the Civil Service: A History of the Development of the Employment of Women in the Civil Service, and a Guide to Present-Day Opportunities* (London, 1934). Though it was, first and foremost, a history of women in the Civil Service, Martindale's *Women Servants of the State* also included a section on how girls and young women could become civil servants. Hilda Martindale, *Women Servants of the State, 1870–1938: A History of Women in the Civil Service* (London: Allen & Unwin, 1938).

3 Patricia Hollis, *Ladies Elect: Women in English Local Government, 1865–1914* (Oxford: Oxford University Press, 1986); Helen Jones, *Women in British Public Life, 1914–50: Gender, Power and Social Policy* (Harlow: Pearson Education, 2000); Helen McCarthy, *Women of the World: The Rise of the Female Diplomat* (London: Bloomsbury, 2014); Pamela Brookes, *Women at Westminster: An Account of Women in the British Parliament, 1918–1966* (London: Peter Davies, 1967); Elizabeth Vallance, *Women in the House* (London: Continuum, 1979); Martin Pugh, *Women and the Women's Movement in Britain, 1914–1959* (London: Macmillan, 1992); Brian Harrison, 'Women in a Men's House: The Women M.P.s, 1919–1945', *The Historical Journal*, vol. 29, no. 3 (September 1986), pp.623–654; Martha Vicinus, *Independent Women: Work and Community for Single Women, 1850–1920* (London: Virago, 1985).

4 Susan Pennybacker, *A Vision for London: Labour, Everyday Life and the LCC Experiment* (London: Routledge, 1995), p.93. For an account of the early LCC, see Gwilym Gibbon and Reginald W. Bell, *History of the London County Council, 1889–1939* (London: Macmillan & Co., 1939).

5 Pennybacker, *A Vision for London*, pp.64–65.

6 Dina Copelman, *London's Women Teachers: Gender, Class and Feminism, 1870-1930* (London and New York: Routledge, 1996).

7 Alison Oram, *Women Teachers and Feminist Politics, 1900-39* (Manchester: Manchester University Press, 1996); Cheryl Law, *Suffrage and Power, The Women's Movement, 1918-1928* (London: I. B. Tauris, 1997), pp.63-93; Pugh, *Women and the Women's Movement in Britain*, pp.90-100. For a discussion of women university students see Carol Dyhouse, *No Distinction of Sex? Women in British Universities, 1870-1939* (Oxford: Routledge, 1995).

8 This is distinguished from the Diplomatic and Consular Services and the Foreign Office which did not admit women until much later. For a discussion of this, see Helen McCarthy, *Women of the World* and 'Petticoat Diplomacy: The Admission of Women to the British Foreign Service, c.1919-1946', *Twentieth Century British History*, vol. 20, no. 3 (2009), pp.285-321.

9 G. E. P. Murray, *The Post Office* (London, 1927), p.190. Murray argues that by the late 1920s, the amalgamation of some of the railway companies had formed the nation's largest employer. Figure for 1938 in British Postal Museum & Archive [hereafter BPMA], POST 59/171, GPO Establishment Book, 1939.

10 See, for example, C. F. D. Marshall, *The British Post Office from its Beginning to the End of 1925* (London, 1926); Murray, *The Post Office*; Howard Robinson, *Britain's Post Office: A History of Development from the Beginnings to the Present Day* (Oxford: Oxford University Press, 1953).

11 Martin Daunton, *Royal Mail: The Post Office Since 1840* (London and Dover, NH: Athlone Press, 1985); Alan Clinton, *Post Office Workers: A Trade Union and Social History* (London and Boston: Allen & Unwin, 1984); Duncan Campbell-Smith, *Masters of the Post* (London: Penguin, 2011).

12 See, for example, Lee Holcombe, *Victorian Ladies at Work: Middle-Class Working Women in England and Wales, 1850-1914* (Newton Abbot: David & Charles, 1973); Ellen Jordan, *The Women's Movement and Women's Employment in Nineteenth Century Britain* (London and New York: Routledge, 1999); Ellen Jordan, 'The Lady Clerks at the Prudential: The Beginning of Vertical Segregation by Sex in Clerical Work in Nineteenth Century Britain', *Gender and History*, vol. 8, issue 1 (April 1996), pp.65-81; Jane E. Lewis, 'Women Clerical Workers in the Late Nineteenth and Early Twentieth Centuries' and Susanne Dohrn, 'Pioneers in a Dead-End Profession: The First Women Clerks in Banks and Insurance Companies' in Gregory Anderson (ed.), *The White-Blouse Revolution: Female Office Workers since 1870* (Manchester: Manchester University Press, 1988), especially p.55. For a discussion of why clerical work was particularly attractive to single, middle-class women in the late nineteenth century, see, amongst others, Meta Zimmeck, 'Marry in Haste, Repent at Leisure: Women, Bureaucracy and the Post Office, 1870-1920' in Mike Savage and Anne Witz (eds), *Gender and Bureaucracy* (Oxford and Cambridge, MA: Blackwell Publishers, 1992), pp.76-77 and Anna Davin, 'City Girls: Young Women, New Employment, and the City, London, 1880-1910' in Mary Jo Maynes, Birgitte Soland and Christina Benninghaus (eds), *Secret Gardens, Satanic Mills: Placing Girls in European History, 1750-1960* (Bloomington: Indiana University Press, 2005), pp.209-223.

13 Meta Zimmeck, 'Jobs for the Girls: The Expansion of Clerical Work for Women, 1850–1914' in Angela V. John (ed.), *Unequal Opportunities: Women's Employment in England, 1800–1918* (Oxford and New York: Basil Blackwell, 1986); Meta Zimmeck, '"Get Out and Get Under": The Impact of Demobilisation on the Civil Service, 1918–1932' in Anderson, *The White-Blouse Revolution*; Meta Zimmeck, 'The New Woman in the Machinery of Government: A Spanner in the Works?' in R. Macleod (ed.), *Government and Expertise in Britain, 1815–1919: Specialists, Administrators and Professionals* (Cambridge: Cambridge University Press, 1988), pp.15–202; Zimmeck, 'Marry in Haste'; Meta Zimmeck, 'Strategies and Stratagems for the Employment of Women in the British Civil Service, 1919–1939', *The Historical Journal*, vol. 27, no. 4 (1984), pp.901–924.

14 Samuel Cohn, *The Process of Occupational Sex-Typing: The Feminisation of Clerical Labour in Great Britain* (Philadelphia: Temple University Press, 1985) and Keith Grint, 'Women and Equality: The Acquisition of Equal Pay in the Post Office, 1870–1961', *Sociology*, vol. 22, no. 1 (1988), pp.87–108.

15 Jones, *Women in British Public Life*.

16 Martindale, *Women Servants of the State*.

17 G. C. Peden, 'Wood, Sir (Howard) Kingsley (1881–1943)', in *Oxford Dictionary of National Biography* (Oxford University Press, 2004), online edn, January 2011 [www.oxforddnb.com/view/article/37002, accessed 12 October 2011].

18 Rita McWilliams Tullberg, 'Fawcett, Philippa Garrett (1868–1948)', in *Oxford Dictionary of National Biography* (Oxford University Press, 2004) [www.oxforddnb.com/view/article/39169, accessed 1 October 2011].

19 London Metropolitan Archives [hereafter LMA], LCC CL/ESTAB/1/3, case of Irene Pearson.

20 Gail Savage, *The Social Construction of Expertise: The English Civil Service and Its Influence, 1919–1939* (Pittsburgh: Pittsburgh University Press, 1996).

21 Perhaps the greatest proponent of this view is Arthur Marwick. See Arthur Marwick, *The Deluge* (Basingstoke: Macmillan, 1991), pp.333–334.

22 See, for example, Deborah Thom, *Nice Girls and Rude Girls: Women Workers in World War I* (London: I. B. Tauris, 2000), esp. p.45; Gail Braybon and Penny Summerfield, *Out of the Cage: Women's Experiences in Two World Wars* (London and New York: Pandora Press, 1987), pp.131–132; Gail Braybon, *Women Workers in the First World War* (London and New York: Routledge, 1989), esp. pp.216–232.

23 Other important work looking at aspects of women and employment includes Copelman, *London's Women Teachers*; Louise A. Jackson, *Women Police* (Manchester: Manchester University Press, 2006); Oram, *Women Teachers*; Selina Todd, *Young Women, Work and the Family, 1918–1950* (Oxford: Oxford University Press, 2005); Selina Todd, 'Domestic Servants and Social Relations in England, 1900–1950', *Past and Present*, vols 2–3, no. 1 (2009); Helena Wojtczak, *Railwaywomen: Exploitation, Betrayal and Triumph in the Workplace* (Hastings: The Hastings Press, 2005); Nicola Verdon, 'Agricultural Labour and the Contested Nature of Women's Work in Interwar England and Wales', *Historical Journal*, vol. 52, no. 1 (March 2009), pp.109–130.

24 Sarah Boston, *Women Workers and the Trade Unions* (London: Lawrence & Wishart, 1987); Pamela M. Graves, *Labour Women: Women in British Working-Class Politics, 1918-1939* (Cambridge: Cambridge University Press, 1994); Law, *Suffrage and Power*; Sheila Lewenhak, *Women and Trade Unions* (London and Tonbridge: Ernest Benn, 1977).

25 See, for example, *Report of the Royal Commission on the Civil Service* (1931) [hereafter Tomlin Commission, *Report*] (London: HMSO, 1931), para. 465, and BPMA, POST 115/86, *Opportunity*, Mrs Oliver Strachey [Ray Strachey], 'Women in the Civil Service', January 1921, p.5.

26 For a discussion of the significance of established employment, see Daunton, *Royal Mail*, pp.237-259.

27 See, for example, Holcombe, *Victorian Ladies at Work*, pp.141-193; Jordan, *Women's Movement and Women's Employment*, pp.179-197.

28 Daunton, *Royal Mail*, p.214; p.202.

1

Work for women? Challenges to the gendering of routine work in the LCC and the Civil Service

> At any moment of time there is strong resistance to allowing women into any occupation which they have not already entered.
>
> Dame Anne Loughlin, Dr Janet Vaughan and Miss L. F. Nettlefold, 'Memorandum of Dissent', *Report of the Royal Commission on Equal Pay* (London: HMSO, 1946), p.191

I t is impossible to understand women's public service employment in the early twentieth century without examining first the work that they were permitted to do as well as the work that they were barred from doing. This chapter discusses the changes and continuities in conceptions of women's routine work in the Civil Service and the LCC until the outbreak of the Second World War. The following chapter will examine the campaigns for, and changing attitudes towards, greater opportunities for women in the higher echelons of the public service. Each of these chapters thus addresses a form of occupational segregation: this chapter discusses horizontal segregation by job task, with the following chapter looking at vertical segregation and the construction of a gendered hierarchy in the workplace. Separately and together, these chapters reveal the highly gendered nature of public service employment, the roots and continuation of this, and how the gendering of this work reflected wider cultural assumptions whilst also in some ways providing a standard for private employment.

Ideas about the routine work that middle-class women could do were shaped and circumscribed by dominant perceptions of femininity. Such ideas shifted, of necessity, in the First World War and there were post-war reorganisations in both the LCC and the Civil Service. In some cases a wider range of work was opened to women, but attitudes regarding what was truly acceptable as "women's work" remained largely unchanged. The expectation that women would leave public service employment on marriage also helped to determine their concentration at the routine level of work: as will be demonstrated here, although the Treasury itself imposed the marriage bar in the Civil Service, the assumption that women would all marry and therefore all leave the Service was so strong as to mean that officials could use this as an excuse to confine women to the routine work. The belief that middle class women in particular were short-term workers only was not something that was unique to the public service, and indeed social expectations of women's roles as wives and mothers played an important part in shaping this perception both inside and outside public service employment. However, this chapter argues that because the public service constituted such a huge operation, clear and defined roles had to be carefully but publicly demarcated for women, and the marriage bar and other ideas about femininity could easily be used as a justification for confining women's opportunities. However, as I will demonstrate, such employment practices were challenged by many women and their supporters throughout the interwar period and the idea of "women's work" could also be challenged and contested by external circumstances.

Although the work of Meta Zimmeck is particularly important in understanding women's opportunities in some grades in the Civil Service before and immediately after the First World War, this chapter intends to lengthen and broaden her discussion to examine the developments in the interwar years and the forces shaping them as well as exploring grades other than the clerical which were Zimmeck's chief focus.[1] There is some brief discussion of women's opportunities in the LCC offered by Susan Pennybacker for the period before 1914 and Gloria Clifton has broadly surveyed elements of working conditions for women staff for the lifetime of the LCC (1889–1965).[2] The present study will therefore provide a comprehensive assessment of women's opportunities and attitudes to women as workers in the LCC, comparing these to the Civil Service. Occupational segregation by sex has been the subject of much research by sociologists, in terms of both horizontal and vertical segregation.[3] However, such work which addresses the Civil Service tends to be overly concerned with theorising the structures and mechanisms of the segregation process, rather than examining the wider social context and the specificity and distinctiveness of Civil Service employment, which are both crucial to understanding the policies of public service employers and women's experiences.[4] Samuel Cohn has examined the sex-typing of some routine work in the Post Office for this period but as his is a quantitative study he also does not explore fully how the demarcation of posts between men and women came about, or give sufficient attention to the action of unions or the wider social context.[5] This chapter therefore explains and analyses the factors affecting the demarcation of routine work and the ways in which this was challenged and reaffirmed.

Women's employment in the Civil Service before 1914

Throughout the period this book considers, the majority of women civil servants were employed in the GPO, and female employment had the longest history there. The story of how women came to be employed in the GPO has been recounted in detail by historians of white collar work for women in the late nineteenth century.[6] Women's GPO employment also helped to propel a general expansion of employment opportunities for middle-class women in the metropolis.[7] Although there had been some ad-hoc employment of women before this point, the wholesale employment of women civil servants began when women telegraph operators were transferred to the Post Office in 1870 when the telegraph service was put under GPO control. This effectively led to the growth of the female civil servant. The extension of women's employment in the Post Office and other departments was recommended in a now-infamous 1871 report by Frank Scudamore to the Postmaster General. Women's supposed natural aptitude for working in one place and on one specific task, and the fact that women could be employed for lower pay than men, were highlighted as reasons for increasing women's employment.[8] Accordingly, lower middle class women were employed in the headquarters of several GPO sections throughout the 1870s and into the 1880s and were assigned specific duties, many of which were similarly justified by condescension towards women's abilities or by concern for their supposed delicate sensibilities or moral well-being.[9] These certainly patronising and paternalistic attitudes amongst Treasury officials were of course also in keeping with wider *fin de siècle* social attitudes to the capabilities of middle-class women in the workplace.[10] Thus, by the end of the 1880s, women were employed as clerks in the headquarters of various GPO departments, on telegraphic work and, gradually, in post offices of various sizes around the country.

The differences between perceptions of women's GPO work in cities compared to rural areas were important and will be discussed later in this chapter. Women clerks in headquarter departments, undertaking the best-paid and best-regarded work, were often physically segregated from men and were given what were termed "blocks" of work to themselves which ensured that they could be supervised by women. This concern about women supervising any men or being near men of a lower social class continued through the period: women were never employed in the headquarters of the London Postal Service between 1870 and 1939 (except during the First World War).[11] This effect of segregating the work was two-fold: the work was seen as less-important work, simply because it was done by women, and it was also used as a means to pay women less. They were technically doing blocks of work different to men's, though of equivalent complexity, but as it was not the same work, different pay was justified by officials.[12] Although the static position of the technology meant that women on telegraph work often worked in the same room as men but in physically segregated sections, they did the same work.[13] The same was also true of women employed on post office counters, particularly in the provinces, and as telephonists: they did the same or very similar work to men (although women were banned by international legislation from working at night) and often worked alongside men, but they were paid less and had fewer promotion opportunities.

In the GPO there was a hierarchy of "women's work". Women were required to have greater education – and therefore to be from the more "genteel" sections of the middle classes – to be clerks, and a little less education was required for telegraph and post office counter work.[14] This mirrored the requirements for male staff. Postwomen existed only in rural areas where their labour was needed often on a part-time or ad-hoc basis and thus there were few formal entrance requirements. This was also the case for "charwomen" (known as cleaners by the interwar years) who were also often employed on part-time or temporary contracts without benefits throughout the Civil Service.[15] When the GPO began taking over the telephone service from 1900 it acquired a large female staff who operated switchboards and transferred calls. The educational requirements were similar to those for telegraphists and counter clerks.

This hierarchy, dictated by education levels – and thus class – at the point of entry, was replicated in other Civil Service departments. After what officials referred to as the GPO "experiment", the Board of Education began employing women clerks in 1899 to do similar work to women clerks in the GPO. In 1910, female registration clerks and supervisors were instituted in the Board of Trade (and later transferred to the Ministry of Labour) initially on a temporary basis. Those appointed to these roles were generally given positions because of social work qualifications or knowledge of local industrial conditions and worked for the women's section of the labour exchange only. This therefore initiated a tradition of gender-divided labour exchanges.[16] The National Health Insurance Commission also began employing women clerks around this time, many of whom were transferred or in some cases promoted from the Post Office.[17]

In 1911, a women-only grade of female assistant clerks was instituted below the woman clerk grade, in which women would do the most routine of clerical duties such as filing, basic form-filling and elementary ledger preparation. This further relegated women to routine work on lower pay and left women clerks with only the more complicated tasks from their original workload without any change to their pay.[18] In 1915, the female assistant clerk grade was amalgamated with the girl clerk grade and renamed the "writing assistant" grade.[19] This grade continued to be viewed as problematic throughout the interwar years as it was seen as a blatant attempt to keep women on the most routine work and was taken as a wider symbol of what the Treasury thought about women's employment. Although this was not necessarily markedly different from women's office work in private businesses in this period, this use of women by the state sent a message to these employers and also left some women feeling that the Civil Service should offer them more.[20] Also of significance in the wider story of the gendered demarcation of jobs was the role of the typist. As Meta Zimmeck has explored, this role originated in the late nineteenth century as a male occupation as it involved the skilled use of a machine. She documents how it quickly and definitively became a women's occupation at the turn of the century, in part because of the Treasury and GPO's compartmentalisation of it as "women's work".[21]

Table 1.1 gives an indication of the types of work on which women were employed in the Civil Service in 1914. Given the vagaries of compilation methods for staff data, some numbers are clearly estimates and categories are used fairly loosely: we know, for example, that there were typists in the GPO but they are clearly included in another category. It is also likely that temporary staff were not included in the original gathering of the data. Nevertheless, this is a useful snapshot of the distribution of women in the service and the ways in which they were employed. The fact that there are no columns for work higher than the clerical grade, save for the specialised female inspector grade (to be discussed in more detail in the next chapter), is particularly revealing.

As the GPO employed so many women in comparison with the other departments Table 1.2 shows approximate numbers of women employed in each grade of the GPO, and women employees as a percentage of each grade (where they could be said to be on a quasi-parallel grade to men). GPO staff figures are notoriously difficult to work with because they changed so often and the method of compilation changed over time. Moreover, it should be borne in mind that the figures in the table include only established positions – that is, full-time work with benefits and pensions – except when otherwise stated.

Table 1.1 Women's employment in the Civil Service, 1914

Department	Girl clerks	Woman clerks	Female inspectors	Typing grades	Domestic workers, matrons, nurses etc	"Special situations"	Manipulative grades* – established	Manipulative grades* – unestablished
General Post Office	250	2,750					21,000	37,100
Board of Education		19						
Registrar General		2						
Public Trustee		70						
Labour exchanges and National Health Insurance Commissions		Figures unavailable	110			Some		
Inland Revenue		100						
Education Departments of England, Scotland and Ireland			47					
Factory Department of Home Office			18					
Local Government Boards, England, Scotland and Ireland			11					
Board of Trade						Some		
Total in Civil Service				600	2,000			

Source: TNA T162/329 E22833, Introductory Memorandum VIII Relating to the Employment of Women in the Civil Service, Summary of the extent to which women were employed in the Civil Service in 1914, pp.4–5. *Telegraphists, telephonists, Post Office counter work, etc.

Table 1.2 Significant grades open to women in the GPO in 1914 and the numbers employed therein

Significant grades open to women in the GPO in 1914	Observations and available data (for January 1914)
Woman clerk – lower and higher clerical grades	4,000 employed; roughly comparable to first and second division male clerks. Women made up 41.6% of clerical classes.
Girl clerk (part of writing assistant grade from 1915)	246 employed; roughly comparable to boy clerk grade.
Female assistant clerk (combined with girl clerk grade to form writing assistant grade in 1915)	22 employed. Women-only grade.
Women sorters (known as sorting assistants from 1915)*	937 employed. Women-only grade.
Typists/shorthand typists	293. Virtually women only by 1914.
Female telegraphist (Central Telegraph Office, London)	974 employed. 36% of total telegraphists.
Female counter clerk and telegraphist (Post Office counter work and telegraphy in London)	1,077 employed. 59% of grade.
Female sorting clerk and telegraphist (same duties as above but based in provinces)	5,388 employed. 24% of grade.
Telephonist	11,600. Almost entirely women (though grade is distinctive from "night telephonists" grade, which was a men's grade).
Postwoman (NB in rural areas only)	Some established; most unestablished.
Girl probationer/learner (training grade for telephony and telegraphy)	1,021 employed
Postmistress/sub-postmistress** (usually in smaller post offices)	At least 25
Charwoman	574 (established and unestablished)
Matron	Employed in London offices employing large numbers of junior officers

Source: Figures and percentage calculations for women clerks, SC&Ts and telephonists from *Report of the War Cabinet Committee on Women in Industry* (1919), Appendix, Evidence of G. E. P. Murray, p.157. Figures for telegraphists, counter clerks and telegraphists from *Report of the War Cabinet Committee on Women in Industry*, Appendix, Evidence of P&TCA. Other figures from POST 59/147, GPO Establishment Book, 1914 except figure for charwomen from *Hansard*, HC Deb 29 June 1920 vol. 131 cc256-7, Government Offices (Charwomen).

* Despite the connotations of their name, women sorters/sorting assistants did not sort mail. Instead, they worked (largely) in London headquarter offices on filing and paperwork duties.

** Sub-postmistresses were not part of the establishment, whereas postmistresses were.

The LCC began the employment of young women relatively late and looked to the Civil Service as a model for its own practices. In 1898 it began employing female typists and by 1914 there were forty employed. Like many of their Civil Service clerical counterparts, they worked in their own separate building and had to pass a competitive examination in order to be considered for a place.[22] Pennybacker argues that the concept of the "new woman" was used as a means to justify employing women cheaply and, as in the Civil Service, on work beneath their capabilities. She does not quite make clear, however, how the idea of the "new woman" was specifically exploited by the LCC.[23] The typing grades constituted the extent of women's participation in the office work of the LCC before the First World War, with the exception of one or two women clerks.[24] However, like the Civil Service and private organisations around the country, women were also employed as domestic and cleaning staff throughout LCC offices and institutions, quite often with no male equivalents, which again points to the compartmentalisation of "women's work". They also, of course, comprised a large percentage of the nurses and teachers employed by the LCC, although the focus of this volume lies elsewhere.[25]

Campaigners and questioning the gendering of clerical work

As Zimmeck and others have pointed out, clerical work had been initially gendered as "men's work" before beginning a process of re-classification as women's work in the very early twentieth century.[26] This was an interesting theoretical problem in the sense that there was no reason for the work to be gendered at all, compared, for example, to heavy industry which was much easier to define as men's work because of the physical strength involved.[27] The demarcations between men's and women's work in the public service so far discussed are examples of the artificial lengths employers went to in order to separate men's and women's work ostensibly for social acceptability reasons, but also as a means of paying women less and devaluing certain work simply because it was women's.[28] This compartmentalisation of work made it, theoretically, difficult for women clerks to claim an ability to do the same work as men. Despite this, there was a concerted campaign for equal pay for women from the early part of the twentieth century, which will be discussed in Chapters 3 and 4. Clearly entwined in this was the question of the types of work women did and so trying to overturn the gendered structures of work was all-important for equal pay. Moreover, such structures clearly imposed limits on women's equal opportunities and the possibilities of breaking through what we have called in more recent years the "glass ceiling".

Although it was often contended that separate grading structures (or "segregation") in the Civil Service guaranteed women some higher positions, such structures guaranteed men many more: more of the work across departments was open to them, the upper echelons of the hierarchy were closed to women completely, and women generally did more of the routine work which required fewer supervisors. In 1914, the highest grade open to women in most departments was that of first class clerk – aside from the handful of "speciality female" positions such as inspectors of women's and children's hospitals. Once women had reached the first class clerk grade, they had nowhere to go in many departments, and those on the second class clerk grade had to wait for vacancies, which mainly came about through retirement, departure for marriage, or other reasons such as ill health. In the meantime, a considerable number did the work of the grade above whilst not having this reflected in their pay.[29]

Women clerks' frustration, in particular, was palpable in the evidence that the Association of Post Office Women Clerks (APOWC) gave to the MacDonnell Commission of 1912–14.[30] A number of these women would shortly join other Civil Service departments and work under similar conditions.[31] Alexander King, GPO secretary, justified segregation to the Commission on several grounds. It was, he said, his personal opinion that women should be segregated from men. The complaints he had anticipated from both women clerks in the London Telephone Service and their parents about women having to work with men had not apparently been forthcoming, though. He also admitted that women were rarely given opportunities to try men's work, but argued that when such opportunities arose, women generally proved disinclined to take on the responsibility and did not carry out the work as efficiently as men. Underlying these points was King's insistence that the only reason women were employed in the GPO at all was because they could be employed more cheaply than men, and he admitted that men's and women's work in the Savings Bank Department had been deliberately further segregated in order to deter claims for equal pay.[32] Whilst women were given the most routine tasks, the work was of the same type and required the same skills – as King admitted when noting the similarity between the entrance exams for men and women clerks.[33] Thus women provided a required workforce and the lengths departments went to to separate women's work from men's reveals how, in itself, the work was rather more interchangeable and departmental heads more concerned with providing artificial demarcations between the two.

"Men's work", "women's work" and the First World War

The First World War and the demand for labour it created meant that women were eventually employed on work previously available only to men in both the LCC and the Civil Service, often in common with numerous other industries in Britain.[34] In addition, in job grades which had previously been open to both sexes in the Civil Service, women were temporarily taken on in larger numbers so the proportions of women to men were significantly skewed. Whereas the Civil Service included 65,000 women on the outbreak of war – the vast majority of these in the telephony, telegraphy and counter work (or "manipulative" grades) of the Post Office – by the end of the war, 170,000 women were employed.[35] Of these, 51,000 women had been taken on in the Post Office to cover "men's work", including 3,500 working as clerks, 19,000 as sorting clerks and telegraphists and 20,000 as postwomen.[36] The war also brought significant change for women already working for the Board of Trade's labour exchanges. Such was the demand for female exchange staff to help place women in, for example, munitions factories, that the formerly temporary posts for these women civil servants were made permanent.[37] In the War Office and the National Health Insurance Commission, among other departments, the number of women clerks increased by hundreds or in some cases thousands.[38] For valid reasons, historians have focused much more on the extended employment of women on higher-grade work in the Civil Service.[39] However, these figures speak for themselves with regard to the vastly increased employment of women at all levels of the Civil Service. Importantly, segregation and same-sex supervision were often abandoned as a result of wartime pressures.[40]

The LCC also employed female temporary assistants by early 1915 and women as clerical staff, having employed more temporary female typists from late 1914.[41] This marked the moment of the expansion of clerical work to women in the LCC. As in the Civil Service, it was agreed in October 1915 that girl messengers would be employed as a war measure whenever conditions of work rendered this possible, though they would work fewer hours than boys and be paid at a similar hourly rate.[42] Women were also employed temporarily as gardeners, stores assistants, ambulance drivers, conductors on LCC tramcars and at the tramcar repair depot on unskilled work, in a manner that paralleled women's work for other local authorities around the country.[43] Again this revealed that the peacetime demarcations of work by gender could ultimately be overturned with relative ease.

As previously, as the department employing such a significant number of women, the actions of the GPO merit some special focus here. There was a real reluctance to change the gendered structures of work initially, and actions along these lines were taken only when it became clear that there was no real alternative and the Postmaster General had to agree to the mass employment of women. In late 1915, some months after the creation of the Women's War Register and agreements to utilise women as workers more widely in other industries,[44] he made the following statement:

> What I feel is, generally, that ... all the work ... that can be properly done by women ought to be done by women, in order that the men may be set free for the Army and Navy and for work which can only be accomplished by men ... A great deal of the Post Office work – I am far from suggesting all of it – can be efficiently done by women, and therefore it seems to me the policy of extending women's work wherever possible, without undue hardship on the men, ought to be pursued.[45]

The Postmaster General's cautiously phrased pronouncements about female efficiency directly contradicted the peacetime views of many in the GPO hierarchy and there was a real resistance amongst some GPO departments to the idea of women substituting for men. Interestingly, a women's employment agency appears to have first raised the question of increasing women's employment in 1914, writing to the Postmaster General and suggesting women be allowed to undertake mail sorting duties in London.[46] GPO officials had a lengthy debate about this, discussing the lack of toilets and rest accommodation, the arduous nature of the work, the mixed-sex workforce not 'be[ing] congenial to a woman of refinement', the overnight and early morning work, and the need for special stools for women to sit on. Women's employment was ruled so out of the question that Sir Robert Bruce, head of the London Postal Service, talked about gaining permission to raise wages for temporary men sorters in order to attract and retain more men. He conceded that in the last resort, each of these difficulties could be surmounted, but argued that the employment of women as sorters in London 'is, perhaps, somewhat remote'.[47] However, it became a lot less remote very quickly. In the pre-Christmas rush in 1914, post offices in larger towns had already been permitted to employ existing female staff as sorters of mail if they volunteered, providing they could be separately accommodated and that no woman worked alone with men. This stipulation was in keeping with peacetime guidelines and was likely rooted in ideas of social propriety. The Postmaster General ruled further that 'women may be employed on sorting work under similar conditions throughout the war where it is clear that only by resort to this arrangement can men be released for military purposes'.[48] By mid-1915, the employment of women sorters was successfully trialled in London sorting offices. The Fawcett Association, which represented male mail sorters in London, protested against this, largely on the grounds that women were undercutting men because they were paid less and were thus worsening their employment conditions.[49] It labelled women's temporary employment 'by far the most serious menace that the war has at present brought to the London sorters'.[50] G.E.P. Murray, the GPO Secretary, gave the Association short shrift, arguing that 'women have performed sorting duties for many years in the smaller Post Offices in the provinces, and are now performing the work in the S[outh] W[estern] D[istrict] O[ffice] with a considerable degree of efficiency'.[51] In putting down the union's argument, his reply highlighted several anomalies. What had happened routinely in rural areas, where supervisors and postmasters had not always had the luxury of selecting their workers by sex due to labour shortages, was a major wartime discussion point in metropolitan areas where larger numbers of staff were involved. This urban–rural discrepancy also effectively allowed the GPO not to pay women substituting for men the male rates of pay because technically women had always done this work. However, the wartime employment of women also appears to have occasioned better working conditions: in some offices women won concessions for all staff such as seating and formalised coffee breaks.[52]

At the same time as women were employed on sorting duties, they were introduced as postwomen in urban areas, after having done the work in rural areas for many years. They were given special sacks apparently more suited to the female physique, though some women refused to use them, feeling that they were not fit for purpose.[53] However, now that this employment was to be widespread during the war, there was much discussion about women's physical strength and the suitability of their physiques for walking and cycling duties. Whilst these concerns mirror "physical strength" arguments in other industries during the war, it is notable that far less concern seems to have been expressed when fewer women had been in the role in the pre-war years.[54] The issue in wartime seems to have been connected to visibility, the sheer numbers of women involved, and the fact that the GPO had to announce that it was substituting women for men. It is also possible that there were concerns about women walking the streets and entering at least the threshold of strangers' properties unchaperoned.[55] The Postmen's Federation executive was alarmed at widespread substitution of postmen by women, along the same lines as the Fawcett Association had been. At a meeting on 31 January 1915 – earlier than a number of the discussions about women's substitution – they expressed understandable anxieties that women were paid less than men and that in offices where postmen also performed sorting duties, men would be given the worst shift patterns as women could not work at night (though this stipulation did not in fact last throughout the war).[56] The Federation 'admitted that the circumstances are extraordinary, and ... we are not justified in objecting to the employment of women qua women, but we have strong ground of protest in cases where we can show that male labour can be obtained, if the Post Office only pays sufficient money'.[57] This position echoed the debate over the employment of temporary sorters and replicated the line of argument initially offered by the GPO about increasing wages for temporary men, as well as longer-term, familiar arguments about women as cheap labour. It also suggests that there was an emerging consensual "pecking order" for the substitution of combatants, particularly for "male" jobs: temporary men first, with higher wages if necessary, then women. This was a "pecking order" also evident in the LCC's expansion of employment to women.[58] The Federation's fears of the consequences of women's temporary employment were revealed in minutes which noted that 'we ought to try and obtain a guarantee that at the end of the War this employment shall cease'.[59]

Alan Clinton has argued that unions' '[h]ostility to the newcomers did not arise from any particular restrictive spirit, or even from opposition to women'. Instead, it 'represented the continuation of a traditional opposition to a cheese-pairing Department who paid people less for doing the same work'.[60] However, some of the letters and reported behaviour from rank and file members complicate this conclusion. For example, the Organising Secretary of the Postmen's Federation stated that '[s]ome very curious reports have been sent to me on the manner in which local Supervising Officers treat the female staff. They are subjected to complete isolation – having to sort by themselves. How can they thus learn the sorting? ... Have we not sisters of our own, or daughters?'[61] Stereotypes about women seem to have abounded amongst men's unions, such as in the example below, published in the Fawcett Association's journal, which parodies women as feminine romantics constantly distracted from their duties. The woman hurriedly dresses herself on the way to work, applies make up at her desk, leaves the man to carry the parcels and is frightened of a small dog. In the afternoon she converses with female colleagues and neglects her duties, and by nightfall she is kissing a sweetheart, perhaps

The six-panel cartoon is captioned:

8.30 A.M. ON DUTY 5.30 A.M. | PREPARATION FIRST DELIVERY

DISPATCH FIRST DELIVERY | FIRST DELIVERY

SECOND DELIVERY | LAST DELIVERY

POSTWOMEN!

Figure 1.1 'Postwomen!' cartoon, *The Postman's Gazette* [The journal of the Fawcett Association], 4 September 1915 (BPMA, POST 115/420)

from the office. The final scene was suggestively captioned 'Last Delivery' (see Figure 1.1).

From 1915, women were also finally permitted to work in the parcel section of returned letter offices, having been barred from doing so since 1873 on account of the fact that they might uncover something distressing or immoral in the undeliverable mail they were opening.[62] This, then, had been protective legislation designed, from officials' point of view, to uphold morality and emotional well-being. Some officials, remembering a far-distant incident with some photographs, expressed a preference for married women to take on the work in wartime on the assumption that they would better be able to handle "untoward" content in returned mail.[63] Others argued that the likelihood of a woman coming across untoward material was 'not appreciable' and H. S. Carey, Joint Second Secretary to the GPO, went so far as to argue that '[w]hatever may be one's private views, I think that in these days when gently-nurtured girls read Juvenal and walk Hospitals, it would be absurd' to prevent any women from doing this work.[64] As Carey's comment suggests, pragmatism won. Women were employed in large numbers in returned letter offices all over the country, notably in the Royal Engineers Postal Section in Regents Park. However, for all Civil Service officials' attempts to, or debates over whether to, protect women (sometimes needlessly) from untoward details, they could not think of everything. During the war, the decision was taken by GPO officials to recruit girls for telegram delivery rather than boys, so as to leave more boys for mail delivery work. Mrs Johnston was fifteen when she was recruited as a telegram messenger. She recalled knowing when a telegram contained news of a son, father or husband being missing or killed in action because she understood the Morse code transmissions as they came out of the telegraph machines. She recalled movingly how she had to read the contents of War Office telegrams to members of the Jewish community in the East End on their religious holidays. She felt strongly that, as a teenager, she had been required to do something that no young person should have to do. Her experiences stand out here from an employment policy point of view because the Civil Service, for numerous reasons, often took on the role of protective and paternalistic employer when developing policy for women's employment to the point where policies were often – as these chapters show – cumbersome, limiting and overly bureaucratic. However, in Mrs Johnston's case, she was dealing with more distressing situations more regularly. Policy to protect women workers could only go so far and predict so much.[65]

Various grades of the Post Office had been opened to women in circumstances previously thought impractical, unworkable or unthinkable. Such considerations were set aside when there was need for labour. The wartime changes meant increased visibility of women as GPO workers – previously, their work at post office counters had been visible, and their work on telephone exchanges had made them audible. Now they were wearing GPO uniforms (or at least armbands and hats) and were cycling or walking in the streets and carrying bags of mail as men had done.[66] With by far the largest number of employees the GPO had the best-developed set of workplace cultures and printed literature. As such, there was much contemporary comment about these changes, both within the Post Office and outside.[67] Women's adoption of men's jobs elicited comments in the supposedly neutral staff magazine, *St Martin's-Le-Grand*. In the April 1916 edition the cartoon 'My colleague in peace and war' depicted apparent differences between permanent (peacetime) male clerks and wartime temporary female clerks (see Figure 1.2).

Figure 1.2 'My colleague in peace and war', *St Martin's-Le-Grand*, April 1916, p.198 (BPMA, POST 92/1145)

In contrast to the man's respectable professionalism and his intense concentration, the woman is depicted as particularly feminine, youthful, neatly coiffured, and slightly sexualised, looking directly at the viewer whilst appearing to have done no work. A large bouquet of flowers takes up room on her desk. Similarly, when temporary postwomen were first employed as a war measure, another *St Martin's-Le-Grand* cartoon depicted a woman wearing a GPO hat with a feather and a bow attached to it, entitled 'Suggested adaptation of the uniform to suit the present emergency' (see Figure 1.3). This time, the uniform rendered the woman almost androgynous and the hat and placement of the feather, interestingly, seemed to hint at military dress.

The fact that both of these existed in the official staff magazine indicates both the dominance of male staff and of course the fact that such reactions to the women staff were considered both normal and socially acceptable. Depictions of postwomen in the staff magazine could also be reverential and patriotic, perhaps reflecting both the importance of

Figure 1.3 'Suggested adaptation of postmen's uniform to meet the present emergency', *St Martin's-Le-Grand*, October 1915 (BPMA, POST 92/1144)

mail delivery in wartime for public morale and the increasing public gratitude to women working to support the war effort. The frontispiece of the 1917 volume of *St Martin's-Le-Grand* was a watercolour painting of a woman in a GPO uniform delivering mail. She stands in classic portrait pose, with letters in her hand as if in mid-delivery, and against a timeless background. The title of the painting was 'Britain's army of workers: the latest recruit' (Figure 1.4).

As was the case with other employers and industries, it was publicly acknowledged, perhaps for political reasons, how well women temporarily employed in the public service performed during the war.[68] The war proved that segregation and reserving certain posts to men only could be abandoned without ill-effect in both the LCC and the Civil Service. As Penny Summerfield has noted, war can provide an opportunity for aspects of women's lives to change, but this change does not always occur.[69] The question remains, then, as to how far things did change after 1918 and for what reasons.

Britain's Army of Workers: The Latest Recruit.

Figure 1.4 'Britain's Army of Workers: The Latest Recruit', volume frontispiece, *St Martin's-Le-Grand*, 1917 (BPMA, POST 92/1146)

Post-war reconstruction and women's work

It has been argued on several occasions that the government simply sacked all temporary women from the Civil Service at the end of the First World War,[70] but this pronouncement is a little too simplistic. Temporary women, and indeed temporary men, were given the opportunity to compete for permanent posts in the service, but there was, as Zimmeck has shown, much confusion about the process. Ex-servicemen were given priority and the timing of women's exams almost certainly disadvantaged them: they were held after a considerable delay, and the exams for the lowest ranks were held first, meaning that women had to decide whether to opt for an early exam with a chance of earlier employment or to hold out for a later exam and hope that they were successful.[71]

Moreover, there was a mêlée of legislation and competing issues around women's employment. The Restoration of Pre-War Practices Act mandated that men in the forces had to be re-employed in their previous jobs if they so wished. Furthermore, the Postmaster General, amongst others, had made a promise to his male staff that they would be able to return to their former positions. Government legislation that on first glance appeared to promise much to women in the years immediately after the war and following the partial enfranchisement of women actually ended up being deceptive. When the Labour Party proposed the Women's Emancipation Bill in 1919 – intended as a "catch-all" piece of legislation to allow women the same political rights as men – this included equal opportunity in the Civil Service. However, this was swiftly replaced by the government's Sex Disqualification Removal Bill and later Act, which was meant to be a more toned-down version of Labour's Bill, offering fewer rights.[72] Proviso (a) of this, staunchly advocated by the government, famously allowed the government to make exceptions to women's rights to hold posts in the Civil Service.[73] This was backed up by part of the 5 August 1921 parliamentary regulations governing women's admission and status in the Civil Service: although in theory these provided women with equality of entry and status to men, one proviso also effectively gave room to the Civil Service Commissioners to appoint whomever best fitted the requirements of the service.[74] Thus, the Civil Service as an institution retained considerable power and freedom over whom it employed.

The 1921 resolutions – empty though they were in many cases as we will also see in later chapters – were the culmination of post-war reconstruction debates about women in the Civil Service. Discussions about the future staffing of the Civil Service began well before the war ended, with Millicent Fawcett asking in 1915 if the government intended to do anything about the recommendations concerning women in the Royal Commission's report of 1914.[75] In the two years between the Sex Disqualification Removal Act (1919) and the parliamentary regulations, there were fierce debates at an institutional level about how women should be employed in the service. A key issue was whether to continue with horizontal segregation in clerical work or to proceed to a system of aggregation where there would be no distinction between men's and women's work in the clerical grade. Aggregation was more likely to make equal pay – until now a distinctly theoretical question – much more of a real possibility and would, in theory, not restrict promotion opportunities to one sex over another, particularly as it was hoped that aggregation would be naturally accompanied by a promotion list that did not distinguish staff on the grounds of sex. Work at higher grades was now theoretically open to women (the realities of which are discussed in Chapter 2) and so how work was organised beneath these grades had a real bearing on women's opportunities to progress.

An examination of the various government-sponsored committees on the Civil Service is important as it enables us to get a sense of official mindsets. The majority of the War Cabinet Committee on Women in Industry (1919), though more famous for its position on equal pay, argued that the service should become aggregated – at least at the clerical level. It complicated this somewhat by arguing that the government should retain control of the proportions of women to be employed on any particular blocks of work, which undermined the very principle of aggregation.[76] Murray, Secretary of the GPO, told committee members that

> [t]he appointing to the service of men and women indiscriminately by one examination and with the same rates of pay would be very extravagant. If greater numbers of women were successful at the examinations (but it is thought that fewer than now would be successful), more women than men would have to be employed to do the same work. A better type of women [sic] might compete, but for the work on which women are employed at present the standard is quite adequate. The existing organisation of separate examinations for men and women is more efficient.[77]

By Murray's admission, women faced a double-edged sword. If they were successful in the examination, there would still, apparently, have to be more of them employed to do the same work as men despite the fact that they had passed the same qualifying examination. At the same time, the service did not want or need women to perform better as they needed a workforce specifically for routine work. The Civil Service Alliance, a group of staff representative bodies, argued for aggregation and warned against the employment of women 'in a particular job because they are cheap … [because] … the community will, in the long run, suffer'.[78] The majority report eventually advocated a 'closer approximation of equality in pay' alongside 'greater equality of opportunity'. Specifically, the report advocated the abolition of 'special grades for women clerks' and of separate entrance exams, but argued that 'Government Departments should, like private employers, have within their discretion the proportion of women to be employed in any branch or grade'.[79] This was a notable declaration of support which at the same time fell short of a ringing endorsement of women's rights and abilities to be public servants. The LCC also submitted a short report to the War Cabinet Committee. James Bird, the Clerk of the Council, was cautiously optimistic that women would be employed on a wider range of work than they were before the war, but indicated that this would likely be of a routine nature.[80]

The Committee on the Recruitment of the Civil Service after the War was convened in 1918 by the Commissioners of the Treasury. It was chaired by Herbert Gladstone and was composed entirely of male senior civil servants. Though the findings of this committee were not binding, the fact that the report comprised the views of heads of departments had a profound impact on the eventual Reorganisation Report produced by the Civil Service Whitley Council in 1920.[81] The Gladstone report revealed officials' concern that the country was paying too much for its clerical work and suggested several ways to rectify this – not least giving women the bulk of the routine work.[82] The deliberations of committee members reveal many of the reasons why segregation in the clerical grades was firmly re-established in some departments. These various discourses were not new and would prove to be long-standing throughout the interwar period.

As the earliest employer of women in the Civil Service, the GPO was particularly immovable on the issue of moving away from segregation. During the proceedings, Murray wrote questioning whether it was 'necessary' to include women in the junior clerical class, as 'the examination, age limit, and scale of salary are all different [from men's]'. Adding women to the class would, he feared, 'certainly stimulate the agitation for Equal Conditions [?generally]; it suggests and implies that they can be employed indiscriminately with men'. Murray clearly wanted to argue that they could not be. His words revealed awareness that women's claims for equality of opportunity were connected with the desire for equal pay. He argued for segregation of the sexes as the best method of organisation but notably he did 'doubt if you can force this principle on any Dep[artment]s who want to mix them'. The later parts of the letter are less legible but Murray appears to advocate 'keep[ing] the women clerks separate from the men and improv[ing] their scale. In fact, I would differentiate as much as possible instead of camouflaging the distinctions under the guise of a common class'.[83] Similarly, Sir Henry Davies, Controller of the Post Office Savings Bank, advocated segregation but for different reasons. He argued that the system had hitherto produced a 'very efficient force' of women who had impressed all of the departments to which they had transferred or been lent as a wartime measure. He argued that whilst women and men had worked side by side successfully when required to, thus far, women had been men's assistants rather than their equals 'and it is doubtful whether men (of the present generation at any rate) would take kindly to … being supervised by women'. The perceived difficulties of women supervising men would remain an obstacle throughout the interwar years and beyond as many male civil servants and more distanced observers grappled with the social and cultural implications of women holding positions of authority over men. Davies identified a further potential problem with abandoning segregation: it would likely take the present generation of women longer to reach higher posts because currently men had occupied the majority of the intervening positions in the hierarchy and were thus due for promotion first.[84] However, the counter-argument that would be offered by many women's supporters throughout the interwar years, as we will see throughout this chapter and the next, was that aggregation would bring greater equality in the longer-term, even if in the short-term the men were in line for the higher posts first.

Other departments – where the employment of women on clerical work was much newer and in some cases had come about directly as a result of the war – were more open to aggregation and continuing and even expanding the employment of women. Although complaints such as women's slightly higher sick leave and apparent lesser efficiency compared to men's were made, this was often counter-balanced in departmental evidence by the fact that women employed in wartime had not received adequate training so their work was not necessarily representative of what they could offer in peacetime.[85]

The Gladstone Committee report accepted the general principle espoused by the 1912–14 Royal Commission that 'the end in view should be, not to provide employment for women as such, but to secure for the state the advantages of the services of women wherever those services will best promote its interests'. In an affirmation of the pre-war status quo, the Committee believed that 'it would be unsafe to introduce women forthwith, as interchangeable with men'.[86] Though it is true that the Treasury officials and others did see some lower-level male employees as similarly expendable, it is also true that no such blanket comments about male employment were made. That the Gladstone Committee did not demur from the Royal Commission's statement is significant for women's employment in the Civil Service throughout the interwar period.

The Committee chose to give priority to ex-servicemen (including those who had not previously been civil servants), arguing that '[t]he sacrifices of active service are so great as to justify the priority we have recommended and we cannot regard the claim of women as being on the same level'. As the Women's Advisory Committee to the Ministry of Reconstruction pointed out, women were effectively being punished because they were barred from fighting, but the Gladstone Committee did not admit this point.[87] The Committee favoured segregation for large departments and advocated separate recruitment because it 'has the advantage of preserving a definite line of promotion to women [and] an larger proportion of superior posts': was this last point, then, a veiled warning that segregation would guarantee some higher posts for women whereas aggregation might result in a system which ultimately favoured men? Segregation's detractors, though, argued the obvious point that compartmentalising women's work – even if it did guarantee some higher posts – was doing nothing to advance the equality cause. It also seemed 'possible [to the Committee] that eventually a great part of the routine clerical work will be transferred to women'.[88] This was, then, a definite message that the intention was to keep women on routine work, which was the agenda a considerable number of women civil servants feared.

One of the features of the post-war reconstruction of the Civil Service was the institution of Whitleyism, a system of employer–employee negotiation machinery.[89] The Whitley Committee on the Reorganisation of the Civil Service, which reported in 1920 and formed the basis for re-grading throughout the service, had both an official side and a staff side, as would all future Whitley Committees. The official side was composed of high-ranking civil servants who were also of course answerable to heads of departments and ultimately the Treasury. By virtue of this fact and the fact that the Gladstone Committee had reported first, a number of the points outlined in the Gladstone report would feature heavily in the official side's dialogue with the rest of the committee. The final reorganisation report created three main classes for the bulk of Civil Service employment: the administrative grade, for graduate entrants; the executive grade, for entrants with higher schooling levels aged eighteen to nineteen; and the clerical grade for entry between the ages of sixteen and seventeen.[90] The committee was careful to demand neither segregation nor aggregation, but leaned in favour of the latter as it laid down a bold 'experiment'. Significantly, paragraph nine of the report argued that 'in recruitment, status, pay, and general conditions of service there should be no differentiation between the sexes' and that 'within the parallel classes of the Civil Service women should be given a status and authority identical with that accorded to men'.[91] This positive-sounding pronouncement was, of course, the product of negotiations between staff members and officials but the exact arrangements in each department were delegated to local Whitley Committees. Each of the paragraph nine recommendations really needed or even implied aggregation rather than segregation though: the persistence of segregation would mean that women had few opportunities to progress, or to prove themselves capable of other work graded at a similar level. The boldness of the Committee's vision thus contrasted with continued segregation in certain departments and the power the Treasury retained to curb women's employment. This compounded women's frustrations in the interwar years. Separate promotion lists also remained – and were advocated by the Whitley report – which also made aggregation, equality and interchangeability of staff harder to achieve.[92]

Sustained campaigns for women to be allowed to do a wider range of routine work were more common in the Civil Service than the LCC, though traces of the same processes and discourses were also evident there. In a clear desire to have parallel opportunities with the Civil Service, temporary women assistants petitioned the LCC in mid-1919 with the help of the Association of Women Clerks and Secretaries.[93] The petition requested that they be permitted to compete for minor establishment positions in the Council's permanent employment – equivalent roughly to the new clerical and writing assistant grades in the Civil Service. The Council reported favourably in June 1919, opening the grade to women and allocating them 40 per cent of the current vacancies providing they passed the entrance exam. It was stipulated that half of that 40 per cent would be reserved to female typists already working for the LCC, with the other half available via external competition.[94] This was a significant development in that it allowed LCC women to catch up to some of the opportunities for women in the Civil Service. Although women had previously worked as typists across the LCC, they now had a range of opportunities open to them in the minor establishment and women typists had much more favourable odds of promotion than did their counterparts in the typing and writing assistant grades in the Civil Service. The experience of the war was thus of direct benefit to LCC women in the appropriate grades, who had effectively made their case for being allowed to do a wider range of work than in the pre-war years. When the restructuring of the LCC created the general grade in 1920 and the minor establishment began to be merged into it, it was decided that 30 per cent of clerical vacancies would be reserved to women. The upper limit on the number of women would, it was argued, 'enable definite experience to be gained as to the extent to which women can be usefully employed in both clerical and administrative positions in the Council's service'.[95] The 30 per cent quota lasted until 1928 and, interestingly, was abandoned '[h]aving regard to the large number of men in the grade'.[96] Whether the fact that women were cheaper to employ than men had any influence on this decision is not clear.

The realities of the re-grading scheme

The effect of leaving Civil Service staffing arrangements up to departments in the early 1920s was that there was varied practice across the service and the becoming-infamous paragraph nine remained very much an ideal only. A 1924 sub-committee on common seniority lists – that is, one list from which promotions would be drawn – found in favour of such lists by a small margin but there was much debate.[97] The idea behind having one list to denote seniority appears to have been that it would be harder to overlook women for promotion, accidentally or otherwise. However, if staff sections remained segregated by sex, the common seniority list was moot as the sex of the member of staff to be promoted was predetermined by the section in which there was a vacancy. With departments structured differently and no real drive to give women better opportunities at this level across the board, women's position in the clerical grades and below remained rather static throughout the 1920s. This was compounded by the fact that the Federation of Women Civil Servants (FWCS) and the women's section of the Civil Service Clerical Association (CSCA) – collectively the two organisations which represented the most women in this grade – did not agree on aggregation and common seniority: the former argued passionately for them throughout the interwar years but the latter was less convinced.[98] Thus, there was less associational pressure for change than there might have been. The post-war complexities of absorbing former temporary clerks and ex-servicemen into the permanent grades of the service also inhibited progress in some quarters.[99]

The rest of the 1920s was largely consumed with working out the ramifications of the *Reconstruction Report*, including putting aggregation into practice for those departments that chose it. In the post-war reorganisation in the Ministry of Pensions, women were removed from the higher-grade work and left on the routine work akin to that conducted by women in the Post Office Savings Bank in the years before the war. The National Union of Societies for Equal Citizenship protested against this, arguing that half of the work should be reserved for ex-servicemen and the other half for women who had served the Ministry in the war in such a way as allowed both groups to have the opportunity to move on from routine work.[100]

The Ministry of Labour's sections at Kew, West London, became aggregated, to the surprise of some.[101] Work in labour exchanges, the other half of the Ministry of Labour's functions, was demarcated by gender. Whitley Council members gave work one of five classifications: necessarily men's work; more appropriately men's work; work that could be done by either men or women; more appropriately women's work; and necessarily women's work. Work in men's employment exchanges was classified as necessarily men's and work in women's exchanges as necessarily women's. Work in juvenile exchanges was deemed 'more appropriately' the work of the same sex as the juvenile exchange served.[102] This system tended to place the clerical work of men's employment exchanges – as well as the face-to-face interviewing – in the hands of men, a point which was not fully recognised until the late 1930s.[103] An August 1929 memorandum listed the work that 'must necessarily be largely in the hands of women officers' as placing women in domestic work, recruiting women for overseas, and advising and placing girls from high schools and universities.[104] It was noted that on unemployment insurance work, the employment clerk may have to deal with questions or matters relating to pregnancy and illegitimate children, and that these required 'very tactful handling'.[105] There was a clear social work dimension: in understanding a woman's need for work, the (female) labour exchange official also needed to ascertain and understand her family circumstances, her marital status, and any other problems which might affect the woman's ability to work. It was not explicitly stated anywhere but it seems to have been taken as read that women would be best placed to help other women. This of course continued pre-war traditions of female philanthropy and social work.[106] However, as Chapter 2 discusses, this organisation of work had ramifications for women's progression prospects.

Other memoranda reveal that Ministry of Labour officials were clearly keen to avoid having young, inexperienced – and thus presumed innocent – women serving as employment clerks. Officials appealed for women to be appointed between the ages of eighteen and twenty, in the hope that they would prove stronger recruits for being older than the normal age of Civil Service clerical recruitment.[107] There was also clearly a determination to protect the female public from young and inexperienced women clerks, and to protect young women clerks from what they might encounter when meeting the public.[108] It was pointed out that managers did not want to employ girls under the age of eighteen on work dealing with the female public not only because of the perceived sensitivity of youth, but also because applicants for jobs or benefits would be 'reluctant to deal with such raw material'. There were also fears that young female staff would not be able to cope with the volume of work in large exchanges. Most stark of all was the attempt to protect the youngest women. Managers feared 'bring[ing] such young girls into contacts which will force home the sordid facts of life and may tend to establish a system of false values before they have reached the age when they can see isolated cases in a correct perspective'.[109] Furthermore, as might be expected, when women employment clerks were dealing with juveniles, it was desired that they be 'fairly mature if their services are to be utilised in advisory work'.[110] The fact that Civil Service recruits for the grades in question were taken on at such a young age was in clear conflict with the type of women that the Ministry of Labour had in mind for the work, but this was never changed.

The final GPO re-grading scheme was regarded by the APOWC and FWCS as deeply problematic.[111] With the re-grading of women clerks, not only did segregation remain in the process of assimilating old grades into new, but men's grading was prioritised over women's, giving men a greater proportion of the higher clerical posts and the women whatever remained.[112] At a mass meeting of Savings Bank clerks, Miss Horsford protested that the 'relegation of three-fourths of the First Class Women Clerks to the basic class was a direct breach' of the reorganisation agreement.[113] And, as Zimmeck has noted, '[i]nstead of recognizing [the] alignment of planes, assimilation shifted them, rather like an earthquake: men's classes moved up relatively, while women's moved down'.[114] This made it rather plain that women's work and opportunities were not a priority. Indeed, the annual report of the APOWC for the year ending March 1922 noted that there were 72 higher posts available for 928 women clerks and writing assistants and 34 posts available for 78 men clerks.[115] The CSCA labelled the regrading scheme for the Savings Bank Department 'the worst … yet proposed' and argued that the proportion of higher posts for women – one in seventeen – was 'wholly wrong' when compared to between one in five and one in seven for men.[116] In the same year, it was admitted in the House of Commons that women held 90 per cent of all of the positions in the Money Order Department but none in the higher echelons.[117] Women clerks' sense of injustice was palpable. In a 1921 issue of *Opportunity*, the journal of the FWCS, one woman pointedly rewrote Rudyard Kipling's poem 'If'. The final stanza read:

> You are square pegs, and all the holes are spherical;
> You'll never fit, no matter what you've done.
> There are no posts for you but Lower Clerical;
> To be Executive we want a MAN,
>   My son![118]

The fact that across the Civil Service the writing assistant grade, where the most routine of the clerical work was done, remained as women-only further hampered any pretence at equality. Officials could not escape the charge that women workers were relegated to the most routine work with comparatively little hope of promotion.[119] The CSCA worked incessantly throughout the 1920s to try to get promotion opportunities increased for writing assistants across the service.[120] GPO promotion records show that some women waited twenty years or more for promotion, even though the head of the GPO Establishments Branch told the Royal Commission on the Civil Service in 1930 that 'a really good writing assistant can count on promotion after about seven years' service'.[121] Such a notion was further backed up by Maude Lawrence, Director of Women's Establishments at the Treasury, when she was later asked by a Royal Commissioner about the exclusion of men from the writing assistant grade – given that she had argued elsewhere that the existence of the writing grade gave girls at age sixteen more chances to enter the service.[122] Her answer revealed that men were considered as more deserving of promotion throughout the service – a real, substantive contrast to the expectations towards women. 'Men were not taken for [writing assistant] work', she argued, 'because it turned into a blind alley occupation, and I do not think men continue to do the work so well as the women'.[123] This, then, was the real reason that men were not included in this class. Scudamore's judgement of several decades previously that women were peculiarly capable of routine work died hard. Lawrence's further responses also revealed a skewed view of women's employment in the service. As she saw it, women chose to enter the writing assistant classes – but she did not consider that the reason for this might be that this was numerically where the greatest number of vacancies for women were, and where they therefore stood the greatest chance of earning a position in the service especially if continuing in education was not an option for them. The notion of choice was therefore problematic. Lawrence argued that as women only wanted a temporary career this suited them well. This was one of many instances in which the potency of the marriage bar was not acknowledged: if women wanted to marry, they had no choice but to have a temporary career as the service enforced resignation on marriage. Lawrence also argued that women liked routine work: 'Also, if I may say so, I think that they like the work. I have over and over again asked them: "Do you get rather bored with this kind of thing?" and I have had the answer constantly given to me: "Not at all; I can think about something else"'.[124]

The existence of writing assistants with no equivalent grade for men meant that women clerks in the grade above in segregated departments did more complex work than male clerks and did so without suitable remuneration.[125] The effective undergrading of women's work took a variety of other forms. Just as it had been before the First World War it was alleged – and often proven – that work done by men on the executive grade might be graded as 'higher clerical' for women, for example, because women were paid lower salaries.[126] In the late 1920s, the staff side of the Post Office Departmental Whitley Council's Clerical Committee outlined the case for the undergrading of women's work and, via committee meetings, the official side responded, arguing that there was some foundation for these suggestions.[127]

The practice of a "female underclass" spread to the LCC by the late 1920s. In 1928 the LCC followed Civil Service practice, belatedly, and introduced a writing assistant grade (though it called it the 'lower general grade') by taking the most routine work from the ordinary clerical grade and creating a women-only grade. Officials stressed that this permitted both economy and better work for the general grade whilst also insisting that lower general grade workers could be promoted into the general grade, though it argued that by virtue of the LCC's marriage bar the grade would in any case 'be substantially wasted by resignation on marriage'.[128] Here again one facet of institutional policy was seen to reinforce another.

Women in the Post Office: the manipulative grades after the First World War

As we have seen, it was the GPO that had the greatest volume of work structured outside of the main Civil Service grades. Most female postal workers and thus most women civil servants were part of the Post Office manipulative grades and for these reasons the debates about this type of work are significant. Women's struggles to be promoted within these grades and to positions with more responsibility also paralleled those in the wider Civil Service. Once the war was over, the pre-war gender demarcation of roles was re-established and significant chunks of work remained closed to women for the familiar reasons connected with perceived suitability or anxieties about women having to come into contact with working-class men in the course of their duties. Such restrictions of course affected their promotion prospects. There was some support for the wider employment of women, however. The Postal & Telegraph Clerks' Association, later part of the Union of Post Office Workers (UPW), had posited to the War Cabinet Committee on Women in Industry that women and men on the grades it represented should undertake the same entrance examination and then receive the same pay and working conditions, undertaking work interchangeably except for that affected by the ban on women doing nightwork.[129]

In the 1920s there was noticeable agitation on behalf of women by female executive committee members of the UPW and other women prominent in the union. For example, in the pages of *The Post*, the UPW's journal, Marjory Hope conveyed women's frustration by asking readers to '[i]magine the fettered condition of a man if the position were reversed, with nothing in prospect except the dreary round of the rank-and-file, no incentive to equip himself for higher-grade duties – promises of better things, remaining, year after year, only promises'.[130] In a direct challenge to male-dominated hierarchies, she argued for an enquiry into the number of offices where women did not hold supervisory or higher positions, 'even when they outnumber men on the staff', and an examination of the number of cases in which lesser-qualified men 'automatically step over women officials, for no other reason than that of sex'. She added that few would be able to argue that the ability to supervise belonged to men alone but her calls for an enquiry were not taken up.[131]

In late 1925, Mary Herring wrote an article for *The Post* in which she reported that

> [a] year or so ago I tried to obtain opportunities for women in the Traffic Section of the London Telephone Service, but though the women's claim was urged by the Staff Side of the Post Office Departmental Whitley Council, the prejudiced anti-feminist views of at least one of the Departmental Chiefs won the day, and the women, in spite of the Sex Disqualification (Removal) Act and the principles laid down by the National Whitley Council in 1920, were precluded from a share of these appointments. This, too, in a section so predominantly staffed by women that their non-inclusion is little short of a scandal.[132]

In this instance, the UPW supported Herring's attempts to improve promotion prospects for women and it was resistance within the GPO hierarchy that meant her efforts came to nothing. However, the UPW did not unanimously support improvements to the range of work available to women because of the potential impact on men's jobs.

In 1921, a committee had been formed to discuss UPW policy on a number of issues including equal opportunities for women. In its discussions, the Committee argued that 'the right of women to choose their occupation is as unassailable as that of men' and that the Sex Disqualification Removal Act was – in theory – a recognition of that fact, as was Major Hills' May 1920 resolution in the House of Commons. The Committee therefore recommended that 'women should have an equal chance of service' providing they passed a medical examination. Interestingly, the Committee could not make a recommendation with regard to nightwork. Though it argued that nightwork was 'injurious' to both sexes and 'should be reduced to an absolute minimum', it recognised that preferential treatment would 'not ultimately benefit [women]' and was a means for the Department to refuse equal pay. At the same time it felt constrained by the fact that the International Convention of 1906 and the International Labour Conference of 1919 had both prohibited nightwork for women and it recommended that female UPW members be balloted to gauge their opinions, though no ballot ever seems to have taken place.[133] This was another manifestation of a much larger debate about so-called protective legislation which had emerged in the mid-nineteenth century and would continue well into the twentieth.[134]

Although Post Office officials never intended to create aggregated grades for manipulative work, the attitude of the UPW to its women members was, in practice, far more ambivalent than had been expressed in the 1921 report. As the interwar period went on, relations became increasingly hostile: women's employment was increasing on work done by both men and women[135] and they remained the cheaper employees. The union was male-dominated and, arguably, male members saw less incentive to help women members as an improvement to women's position might threaten or disadvantage theirs, either because their labour would be undercut as women could be employed more cheaply, or because they feared worse hours of duty. As one example, UPW members had some fairly bitter disputes about admitting women onto certain routine duties in the cable room. The arguments hinged on the principle of equality and differing interpretations of this, and also the fact that men and women did not have equal pay. Broadly, the men of the cable room and their supporters argued that, were women employed on the same work without the same pay, the GPO would gradually replace men with women or have a case for lowering men's wages. The women who campaigned to be admitted argued – much like their counterparts on the clerical grade – that their performing the same work as men would provide a platform from which to secure equal pay whilst also having allowed them to prove themselves on new work. One female correspondent likened the attitude of men in the cable room to 'that of a small boy in possession of a large cake refusing his little sister a mere bite!', arguing that 'there is no work in the Cable Room which, in the existing conditions of the employment of women in the Post Office, is not proper to a F[emale] S[orting] C[lerk] and T[elegraphist] possessing the necessary linguistic qualifications'.[136] The arguments on both sides of this debate were comprehensible: the women desperately wanted to try new and more interesting work and the men (with ultimately the support of the union) were well aware that progress on equal pay was highly unlikely. With such a division among members themselves, then, little progress was made.

Providing impetus for change: the Royal Commission on the Civil Service, 1929–31

In October 1929, the government appointed a Royal Commission led by Lord Tomlin to examine numerous aspects of Civil Service staffing, including women's employment.[137] As other chapters discuss, the Commission was significant in suggesting a number of changes for the betterment of women's employment, although in other cases it mirrored the dominant thinking amongst Civil Service officials. Tomlin himself had had a legal career and was a judge.[138] The Commission included Mary Agnes Hamilton and Eveline Lowe, the latter an LCC member, and both were advocates of women's rights.[139] Margaret Wintringham, a former Liberal MP and also an advocate of women in public life, was also a Commission member, as was Barbara Ayrton Gould, a former suffragette, Labour politician and advocate of numerous social causes.[140] These three members were the most supportive of women: Katherine, Duchess of Atholl was another Commission member and remained a staunch anti-feminist.[141] The Commission members otherwise included James Black Baillie, an academic and administrator, Sir Percy Jackson, a high-ranking education administrator, and Frank Goldstone, a trade unionist with a background in the National Union of Teachers.[142]

Although the Commission's report was actually helpful in advancing the course of aggregation and greater opportunities for women, the contributions from various Civil Service departments revealed again the opposition to women's advancement from some quarters of the service. R. R. Scott, Controller of the Establishments Department, argued that:

> Where women are obviously, in my view, better than men is in employments that they have in fact made their own; they have driven men out of the field. Those, I think, for the most part are employments in subordinate situations rather than in the higher situations.[143]

This was said without any hint of awareness of Civil Service practice of relegating women to routine work, whilst also attributing full agency to women and seemingly none whatsoever to the employers who actually made hiring decisions. In an apparent misunderstanding of routine work as well as the education system and women's own sense of ambition, he also argued that excessive salaries for routine work would stop women from wanting to go to university.[144] Curiously, at the same time, he did see both aggregation and common seniority lists as positive, which promised, in time, to lead to the opposite of the ideal he laid out above.

The Royal Commission's report recommended no change to the Ministry of Labour's system for distributing work in labour exchanges.[145] The Commissioners were unimpressed by the existence of segregation in the GPO clerical grades and when questioned about its origins, Murray argued that the decision was 'largely historical' and that '[b]roadly speaking, it results in the superior work being given to the men and the more routine work being given to the women'.[146] Thus, by Murray's own admission, the system of employing women in clerical roles was based on an idea from sixty years previously. Furthermore, dividing the work between men's branches and women's branches did not, of course, require that men got the superior work and women the routine work; that decision was clearly also affected by conceptions of gender and entitlement. When pressed to state the advantages of the system of segregation, Murray could only list tradition in its favour: 'I think that the grounds are really more historical than anything else. It is a system of organisation which has been handed down, and which it has been in nobody's interest to change.' Asked a third time to justify segregation, he noted that controlling officers 'generally speaking' supported it, and that 'there has never been any decided movement on the part of the staff in favour of a change'. Perhaps he had forgotten the APOWC's long-standing campaigns. A commissioner suggested that women and men working separately did not preclude a common seniority list for promotions, but Murray argued that this was difficult as it might create a situation in which women might have to supervise men and vice versa.[147] Notably, elsewhere in discussions with the Commissioners, it was admitted that men did sometimes supervise women – so it was clear that the real problem remained the idea of women having authority over men.[148] The growth of women's presence in the workplace was also seemingly a factor in Murray's mind: he made an unguarded remark during his evidence when asked whether the allocation of the inferior clerical work to women meant that they were seen as the inferior sex. He replied that 'I should doubt it very much, because whether she is an inferior being or not, she is rapidly becoming numerically predominant'. This comment revealed his underlying fears about the greater proportion of women in the workplace. This had been a preoccupation in earlier decades too: Zimmeck and Silverstone, amongst others, have noted how increasing numbers of women workers perturbed male clerks – even if women clerks were doing new work rather than directly replacing male clerks.[149]

After Tomlin's commission: the structure of women's work in the 1930s

In their report, the Royal Commissioners advocated a system of aggregation for the clerical classes of the GPO and other departments which still had segregation. As staff campaigners had before them, the commissioners also recognised that aggregation ought to bring women greater access to the higher posts (the realities of which are explored as part of the next chapter).[150] The desire for aggregation was confirmed by the 1934 Whitley Committee Report on Women's Questions and this was followed by departmental councils convened to discuss the practicalities.[151] One major change was that the Post Office Whitley Committee accepted aggregation for the clerical grades, with the exception of the London Postal Service, where the fact that women would have to come into contact with working-class men presumably remained an issue.[152] This meant that the vast majority of all clerical work in the Civil Service was open interchangeably to men and women. Thus, the Royal Commission spurred, and Whitleyism at its various levels enacted, an important symbolic change for some departments.

Reactions to aggregation among GPO staff were definitely mixed initially. At the CSCA Post Office Savings Bank branch annual meeting in 1937, Mr A. F. Johns stated that aggregation 'could not do otherwise than improve the conditions of the Staff, since the women, who form the largest part of the membership, would in future enjoy the conditions and privileges that the male staff already possess'.[153] However, reports from elsewhere told a different story. In February 1938, the National Association of Women Civil Servants (NAWCS) – formed from an amalgamation of the FWCS and the Civil Service section of the Association of Women Clerks and Secretaries – reported 'a regrettable discrepancy, in many Departments, between aggregation on paper and its application' and singled out the London Telephone Service as particularly problematic and having caused 'considerable disappointment'.[154] In April 1939, the NAWCS reported the formation of a men-only organisation in the Post Office Savings Bank with three objectives: to abolish joint seniority lists, to ensure that posts previously designated as male were restored as such, and to prevent women supervising men.[155] Progress and changing attitudes were in some cases scarce.

Individuals at the Post Office do not necessarily seem to have greeted aggregation happily either, which suggests that alterations to long-standing staffing practices caused greater resistance than changes in newer departments. Letters in *Red Tape*, the magazine of the Civil

Service Clerical Association, mostly from Post Office men, reveal anxieties over the fact that women would now supervise men and the social and gender shifts that such a practice suggested. One man argued that it was 'humiliating to have to work under a spinster' and his objections extended to the fact that '[i]n the past, women have had to concede leadership, and generations of this has produced in our modern women an emotional instability, a concentration upon personal things, a proneness to bringing their feelings into their work, and a lack of breadth of mind and human understanding, that is keenly felt by their subordinates'.[156] As far as the letter writer was concerned, women's lack of leadership experience caused "flaws" which now prevented them from acquiring such experience. A letter from a member of the Post Office District Manager's Committee in Liverpool attacked women's abilities as supervisors, the 'psychological disturbances common to female employees in the later years of service' and men's acquiescence in the promotions of women in the workplace. It argued against women's further 'infiltration', and 'reasonably warned [women] that a persistence in their present attitude will inevitably lead to men becoming imbued with a Hitler-Mussolini complex in their dealings with women'. He ended without an apology, arguing that his feelings must be shared by other men.[157] Unsurprisingly, his letter received a strongly worded retort from a female staff member in his office and Leslie Sweet, the Woman Organiser of the CSCA, dismissed his comments as fear.[158]

More significantly, despite an agreement for aggregation, the writing assistant class was left as a large, women-only class across the whole Civil Service, though it was renamed the clerical assistant class. Thus, the agreement removed some of the manifestations of gendered occupational segregation but left the arguably most blatant one still intact. Although there was some brief discussion about employing boys to do the work, this was rejected.[159] The CSCA, in particular, with its large writing assistant/ clerical assistant membership, debated at its 1938 conference whether the grade should continue to be women-only, having spent much of the interwar period trying to secure improved promotion prospects and pay for writing assistants. A variety of viewpoints was expressed during the debate, ranging from the suitability of women for routine work; the fact that allocating routine duties to women promoted the view that that was all women were fit for; the fact that if men were admitted, it would solidify the existence of the clerical assistant grade even further; and the question of whether adding men into the grade might worsen women's promotion prospects. The staff were clearly acutely aware of the symbolism of the clerical assistant grade. Leslie Sweet explained that the executive committee's position was that 'we consider that routine work is best done by women officers, not because they are women, but because they are subject to the marriage bar', which would act as a means for speeding up promotion prospects for the remaining women.[160] In some ways, this was curious logic: by the late 1930s, the CSCA was not far away from pushing for the removal of the marriage bar, as we will see in Chapter 6, and there was debatable evidence as to whether the marriage bar did actually speed up promotions when such a large group of women were employed as a block in any case. Certainly, this logic came close to validating both the employer's traditional positions on the marriage bar and on women as routine workers. Writing on women's employment in the Civil Service in the 1930s, Dorothy Evans also saw the large block of writing assistants in some departments as problematic, arguing that those seeking promotion were best served by being in a small department or a department with a small number of writing assistants.[161] The CSCA came to no definite conclusion from these deliberations and put the matter on hold.[162] The situation in the LCC paralleled the Civil Service. Starting wages for women in the general grade (formerly the minor establishment) were increased in the mid-1930s from 24s. to 28s. per week as a result of the examinations not attracting enough female entrants. This was another marker of the gendered structures of public service work: the LCC needed a specific number of women in order to carry out the tasks designated for women and was prepared to pay more only when this number was becoming difficult to acquire.[163]

Sets of figures for LCC staff are difficult to come by and were not necessarily compiled regularly for the Council as a whole. However, a set compiled for the Royal Commission on Equal Pay in the mid-1940s gives a useful snapshot as it does not include grades on which women were employed for wartime only. As might be expected, women's work in the LCC in the late 1930s looked very much like women's work in the Civil Service and, indeed, in outside professions in terms of the ways in which it was distributed. Women made up very few of the highest echelon posts and a scarcely bigger proportion of professional and technical posts, except for the traditional female career of teaching. The medical auxiliary grades were fairly even in terms of the sex of the workers employed, but far fewer of the social welfare posts belonged to women than might have been expected given the oft-asserted emphasis on work such as this related to women and children. By contrast, women formed the bulk of the nursing grades and were the majority of staff in most domestic and institutional support grades. Interestingly, they made up only just over 26 per cent of clerical posts – despite the abandonment of quotas a decade or so previously – but obviously all of the typing and shorthand-writing grades.[164] In terms of the types of work women undertook, then, there had been relatively little qualitative change in the interwar period. In 1938, possibly inspired by the changes throughout the decade in the Civil Service, the LCC Staff Association had attempted to find out why certain types of work were set aside for either men or women. The results they received for the typing, clerical assistant and some clerical posts being reserved to women were illuminating: on numerous occasions, the respondents' comments were summarised as 'nature of work' or 'obvious', when there was nothing obvious at all about why this work had to be restricted to women only.[165]

The Royal Commission had 'doubt[ed] whether it [was] possible to introduce aggregation' to the manipulative grades of the GPO, but recommended that this question be further considered.[166] A committee reported on this in 1937, arguing that aggregation in the manipulative classes was not possible given the nature of work, the requirement for nightwork and the need to reserve certain posts to men.[167] Furthermore, some members of the staff side felt that women's employment should be curbed rather than expanded because women, as cheaper employees, were undercutting men: the UPW and the Post Office had already agreed on a proportion of two-thirds women to one-third men to be employed in certain roles as a means of assuring the UPW that men would still be employed.[168] The lack of equal pay clearly impinged, here, on women's employment prospects.

By the end of the interwar period, then, the way work was structured in a number of Civil Service departments had changed. On the official side, this was enacted because it offered greater efficiency as supervision did not have to be duplicated and this also had an impact on the wages bill. However, officials also became convinced that it worked: once installed, there were no complaints about aggregation. Female staff generally viewed aggregation as positive as it allowed them to prove they could do other types of work and would open – it was hoped – new promotion opportunities to them. It was also hoped that aggregation would draw out a more unconscious change in attitudes to women workers if women were actively seen to be doing different types of work in "normal" peacetime conditions. However, it is fair to say that whilst a considerable number of departments adopted aggregation by the end of the interwar years, attitudes to women workers and particularly their equal right to occupy positions in the workplace would take much longer to change. The perceived appropriateness of certain types of work for women and the gendered culture of a particular Civil Service department were real determinants in terms of how much women's work in new roles was accepted.

The First World War had some impact on the expansion of women's work in the Civil Service and particularly in the LCC where clerical positions for women were more plentiful than they had been in the past, although the expansion of this work to women was also granted, of course, because it suited the Council. The upper limit of posts for women's clerical work in the 1920s reveals the Council's overall caution about women's work and that the Council prioritised its own interests and men's work.

At the same time as all of this took place, and more starkly for what it said about views of women workers, the writing assistant/clerical assistant grade remained a women-only grade. Although this mirrored other occupations to a great degree, it also undermined any view of the Civil Service as a more progressive workplace and suggested that women's work was not valued in large part because it was women's. It was made clear on a number of occasions that although all public servants served the public, the public service aimed to have job progression for men – whom they argued, sometimes erroneously, would have longer tenure – but did not regard it as necessary to have the same for women.

What is significant in the Civil Service is that by the late 1930s the majority of staff and officials alike were committed to aggregation and the interchangeability – in theory if not yet in practice – of most posts in the clerical grades. This was a mindset which had not always been present throughout the interwar years. This was revealed both by the 1934 Report on Women's Questions and in the tenacity with which the staff side probed the reasons for the remaining gender segregation in a 1938 review of how well the committee's recommendations were being followed.[169] Although much more had to change for women to achieve equal opportunity, changing the workplace structure to a less gendered one and really questioning why certain types of work were closed to women was an important step forward in shifting mindsets. This meant that, despite other unequal conditions remaining for women, some significant overturning of the horizontal segmentation of the workplace had taken place by the end of the interwar years and this provided a (theoretical) foundation for a less gendered Civil Service with the prospect of accompanying improved opportunities for women in the higher grades. The battle for entry into the higher and elite levels of both the Civil Service and the LCC is the subject of the next chapter.

Notes

1 Zimmeck, 'Strategies and Stratagems'; Zimmeck, 'Jobs for the Girls'; Zimmeck, '"Get Out and Get Under"'; Zimmeck, 'The New Woman in the Machinery of Government'; Zimmeck, 'Marry in Haste'; Meta Zimmeck, '"The Mysteries of the Typewriter": Technology and Gender in the British Civil Service, 1870–1914' in Gertjan de Groot and Marlon Schrover (eds), *Women Workers and Technological Change in Europe in the Nineteenth and Twentieth Centuries* (London: Taylor & Francis, 1995).

2 Pennybacker, *A Vision for London*, pp.43–94; Gloria Clifton, 'Members and Officers of the LCC, 1889–1965' in Andrew Saint (ed.), *Politics and the People of London: The London County Council, 1889–1965* (London and Roncevert: The Hambledon Press, 1989), pp.13–26.

3 See, for example, Harriet Bradley, *Men's Work, Women's Work* (Cambridge: Polity Press, 1989); Rosemary Crompton and Kay Sanderson, *Gendered Jobs and Social Change* (London: Unwin Hyman, 1990); Anne Witz, *Professions and Patriarchy* (London: Routledge, 1992); Alison MacEwen Scott (ed.), *Gender Segregation and Social Change: Men and Women in Changing Labour Markets* (Oxford: Oxford University Press, 1994); M. Savage and A. Witz (eds), *Gender and Bureaucracy* (Oxford: Blackwell, 1994).

4 See Cohn, *Process of Occupational Sex-Typing*; Sarah Jenkins, Miguel Martinez Lucio and Mike Noon, 'Return to Gender: An Analysis of Women's Disadvantage in Postal Work', *Gender, Work and Organisation*, vol. 9, no. 1 (January 2002), pp.81–86; Janet Siltanen, *Locating Gender: Occupational Segregation Wages and Domestic Responsibilities*, (London: UCL Press, 1994). The latter focuses on the 1960s and 1970s.

5 Cohn, *Process of Occupational Sex-Typing*, pp.166–172.

6 Jordan, *The Women's Movement and Women's Employment*; Holcombe, *Victorian Ladies at Work*, pp.163–193; Zimmeck, 'Jobs for the Girls'; Davin, 'City Girls', pp.211–213.

7 Davin, 'City Girls'; Jordan, *The Women's Movement and Women's Employment*; Holcombe, *Victorian Ladies at Work*; Lise Shapiro Sanders, *Consuming Fantasies: Labour, Leisure and the London Shopgirl, 1880–1920* (Columbus: Ohio State University Press, 2006).

8 BPMA, POST 82/197, 'Report by Mr Scudamore to Postmaster General'.

9 BPMA, POST 33/330A, 'Married Women in the Post Office, part 2', File 33.

10 Davin, 'City Girls'; Daunton, *Royal Mail*, p.218; Clinton, *Post Office Workers*, p.55.

11 BPMA, POST 122/10863, Civil Service Clerical Association Official recognition, 'Post Office Reports of the Committees on Women's Questions', Appendix Two. Lord MacDonnell, chairing the Royal Commission on the Civil Service in 1912–14, argued that women clerks were less able to deal with the working classes. See R. K. Kelsall, *Higher Civil Servants in Britain: From 1870 to the Present Day* (London: Routledge and Kegan Paul Ltd, 1955), pp.168–169.

12 For a more detailed discussion of this phenomenon, see Zimmeck, 'Jobs for the Girls'; Zimmeck, 'Marry in Haste'.

13 The same appears to have been true for women employed by the telegraph companies before they were nationalised. See John Durham, *Telegraphs in Victorian London* (Cambridge: The Golden Head Press, 1959), p.14; p.22.

14 Daunton, *Royal Mail*, pp.217–218.

15 See GPO Establishment Books for these years, available at BPMA, POST 59. Although they were not technically civil servants, there is a good discussion of the lives of women cleaners in Parliament in the interwar years in Mari Takayanagi, 'Parliament and Women', c.1900–45 (unpublished PhD thesis, King's College, London, 2012), pp.224–226.

16 Evans, *Women and the Civil Service*, pp.6–7; Martindale, *Women Servants of the State*, pp.48–49.

17 Martindale, *Women Servants of the State*, p.64; POST 115/1149, *Association Notes*, 'A Retrospect', January 1913, p.163.

18 Zimmeck, 'Marry in Haste', pp.80–81.

19 BPMA, POST 30/3411A, Writing Assistants: representations by Association of Women Clerks against forming class.

20 For a discussion of women in private office work, see Rosalie Silverstone, 'Office Work for Women: An Historical Review', *Business History*, vol. 18 (1976), pp.98–110 and R. Guerriero Wilson, 'Women's Work in Offices and the Preservation of Men's "Breadwinning" Jobs in Early Twentieth-Century Glasgow', *Women's History Review*, vol. 10, issue 3 (2001). See also BPMA, POST 115/1149, *Association Notes* [the journal of the Association of Post Office Women Clerks], 'London Telephone Service', July 1911, p.104.

21 Zimmeck, ' "The Mysteries of the Typewriter" '.

22 Clifton, 'Members and Officers of the LCC, 1889–1965', p.17; p.19.

23 Pennybacker, *A Vision for London*, p.71.

24 LMA, LCC Staff Lists, 1913–14.

25 For a discussion of women's employment as LCC teachers see, in particular, Copelman, *London's Women Teachers* and Oram, *Women Teachers*.

26 Zimmeck, 'Marry in Haste', p.84; Silverstone, 'Office Work for Women', p.103; p.107; p.109; Sylvia Walby, *Patriarchy at Work* (Cambridge: Polity Press, 1986), p.147; Jordan, *The Women's Movement and Women's Employment*, p.186.

27 Zimmeck, 'Jobs for the Girls', p.158.

28 Zimmeck, 'Jobs for the Girls'; Zimmeck, 'Marry in Haste', pp.72–85; BPMA, POST 33/729A, Alexander King's evidence to the Royal Commission, paras 31,428 and 31,429.

29 Zimmeck, 'Marry in Haste', pp.74–75. *Association Notes*, 'Branch Reports', July 1911, pp.102–103.

30 Zimmeck, 'Marry in Haste', pp.82–85; Kelsall, *Higher Civil Servants*, pp.168–169.

31 *Association Notes*, 'Transfers', July 1912, p.147; 'News from the Board of Trade', October 1912, pp.160–161; 'A Retrospect', January 1913, p.163.

32 POST 33/729A, 'Royal Commission on Civil Service: Evidence of Secretary to Post Office', evidence of Sir Alexander King, paras 31,246–31,258.

33 POST 33/729A, evidence of Sir Alexander King, para. 31,451.

34 See Thom, *Nice Girls and Rude Girls*, *passim*; Braybon, *Women Workers in the First World War*; Braybon and Summerfield, *Out of the Cage*, pp.34–78; Wojtczak, *Railwaywomen*, pp.43–88.

35 TNA, T162/329 E22833, 'Introductory Memorandum VIII Relating to the Employment of Women in the Civil Service', p.9.

36 *Report of the War Cabinet Committee on Women in Industry* (London: HMSO, 1919), Appendix, p.157. In comparison, 22,000 temporary men were taken on as GPO servants during the war.

37 Evans, *Women and the Civil Service*, p.20.

38 TNA, T1/12265, 50322/18, 'Memoranda: Committee on Recruitment of the Civil Service after the War', evidence from individual departments.

39 Jones, *Women in British Public Life*; Martindale, *Women Servants of the State*, pp.77–82.

40 'Memoranda: Committee on Recruitment of the Civil Service after the War'.

41 *Report of the War Cabinet Committee on Women in Industry*, para. 110; London Metropolitan Archives [hereafter LMA], LCC Minutes, 1 December 1914.

42 See BPMA, POST 47/29, 'Record of Women Employed as Temporary Sorters', 26 July 1915–11 March 1916' and POST 47/51, 'Record of Women Employed as Temporary Sorters, 5 April 1917–10 November 1917'. LCC Minutes, 12 October 1915; *Report of the War Cabinet Committee on Women in Industry*, para. 100.

43 LCC Minutes, 13 July 1915; 23 November 1915; 21 December 1915; 8 February 1916.

44 For the wider context of women's employment, see Thom, *Nice Girls and Rude Girls*; Braybon, *Women and the First World War*; Braybon and Summerfield, *Out of the Cage*, pp.11–132; Boston, *Women Workers and the Trade Unions*, pp.96–131.

45 BPMA, POST 115/420, *The Postman's Gazette*, 27 November 1915, p.539.

46 BPMA, POST 30/3430B, 'London Postal Service: Employment of Temporary Female Force on Sorting Duties during Wartime', File I, letter from Marie Hodge, Secretary of the Information Bureau of the Women's Institute, 3 November 1914. This reference to the Women's Institute should not be confused with the more commonly-known Women's Institute (WI). The organisation for which Marie Hodge worked was a London-based club for women 'engaged in professional, educational, social and philanthropic work' and had been formed in the 1890s. See Elizabeth Crawford, *The Women's Suffrage Movement: A Reference Guide 1866–1928* (Abingdon: Routledge, 2001), p.129.

47 POST 30/3430B, File I, Report of Sir Robert Bruce, Controller, London Postal Service, 23 November 1914.

48 POST 30/3430B, File I, Circular 238824/14, ref.15.

49 POST 30/3430B, File III.

50 Clinton, *Post Office Workers*, pp.210–211. Individual Fawcett Association branches were not happy either. See, for example, POST 115/392, *The Post*, 'S.W.D.O.', 'N.W.D.O.', 4 June 1915, pp.217–218; 'South Eastern', 18 June 1915, p.233. In 'Paddington D.O.', 2 July 1915, pp.258–259, fear was expressed about women becoming labourers and men domestic servants.

51 POST 30/3430B, File III, letter to Fawcett Association, 15 June 1915.

52 Imperial War Museum Sound Archive [hereafter IWMSA], 676, interview with Mrs Thomas, 1975.

53 IWMSA, 3151/1, interview with Mary Madden, 1977.

54 When postwomen were first employed during the war, there were discussions with medical officers regarding how much women could safely carry and whether they should cycle or walk. The fact that these discussions appeared not to reference previous discussions or practice suggests that less care had been taken in the past over the issue. See BPMA, POST 30/3720, especially File I.

55 In the context of female police patrols, Philippa Levine notes a number of similar points. Philippa Levine, '"Walking the Streets in a Way No Decent Woman Should": Women Police in World War I', *Journal of Modern History*, vol. 66, no. 1 (March 1994), pp.62–65; p.68; pp.70–71. See also Braybon and Summerfield, *Out of the Cage*, p.34.

56 POST 30/4050, 'Employment of Women at Night – Miscellaneous Papers', *passim*. For women working as sorters overnight during the war, see IWMSA, 676, interview with Mrs Thomas.

57 Modern Records Centre [hereafter MRC], MSS.148/PF/1/2/15 Postmen's Federation, Minutes of the Quarterly Meeting of the Executive, General Secretary's Report, 31 January 1915.

58 LCC Minutes, 13 July 1915; 23 November 1915; 21 December 1915; 8 February 1916.

59 MRC, MSS.148/PF/1/2/15, General Secretary's Report, 31 January 1915. Interestingly, the Committee agreed that this section of the minutes would not be published in *The Postman's Gazette*, the association's journal. For rank and file concerns about women usurping men in peacetime, see POST 115/421, *Postman's Gazette*, letter from Ceste, 'Postwomen', 19 February 1916, p.88 and the replies from the Walthamstow branch, *Postman's Gazette*, 'No Monopoly', 4 March 1916, p.108.

60 Clinton, *Post Office Workers*, p.240.

61 POST 115/420, *Postman's Gazette*, Organising Secretary's Notes, 13 November 1915, p.536.

62 BPMA, POST 30/3577B, 'Returned Letter Work: Women Employed Upon "Opening" Duties as a War Measure'.

63 POST 30/3577B, letter from Postmaster of Bristol and correspondence from Murray to Sir Bruce and Mr Beaton, 13 December 1915.

64 POST 30/3577B, letter from H. S. Carey to Murray, 9 December 1915; letter from Gates to Murray, 8 December 1915.

65 IWMSA, 8889/3, interview with Eileen Johnston, 1985.

66 For discussion of these issues relating to women workers in the First World War in other industries see Levine, '"Walking the Streets"', p.70; Braybon and Summerfield, *Out of the Cage*, p.34.

67 See, for example, *Daily Mirror*, front page photo montage, 12 January 1917; '21,000 Postwomen – Fine Services Rendered During War – Lack of Strength their Only Drawback', 10 March 1919; *Times*, 'Christmas Postwomen', 24 November 1916.

68 See, for example, POST 92/1147, *St Martin's-Le-Grand*, 'The Post Office and the Honours List', April 1918, pp.101–110 and 'The Post Office and the Honours List',

July 1918, pp.171–173 in which women were praised for their bravery and performance during the war years. Although this was for perhaps less – or different – political reasons, the *London County Council Staff Gazette* noted in 1915 that women's wartime employment was successful: December 1915, p.191.

69 Penny Summerfield, 'My Dress for an Army Uniform', inaugural lecture, University of Lancaster, 1997, p.4.

70 Jones, *Women in British Public Life*, p.150; for a more detailed discussion, see Law, *Suffrage and Power*, pp.78–88.

71 Zimmeck, 'Strategies and Stratagems', pp.915–918.

72 For a discussion of the passage of both Bills through Parliament, see Takayanagi, 'Parliament and Women', pp.38–77.

73 For a thorough discussion of attempts to remove or modify proviso (a), see Takayanagi, 'Parliament and Women', pp.58–64.

74 These are quoted in full in *Report of the Royal Commission on the Civil Service* (London: HMSO, 1931), [hereafter Tomlin Commission, *Report*] para. 387.

75 See TNA, T1/12084, 34595/1917 and particularly 17833, Minute: Employment of Women in the Civil Service: Circular to Departments, 6 July 1916.

76 *Report of the War Cabinet Committee on Women in Industry*, para. 223.

77 *Report of the War Cabinet Committee on Women in Industry*, Appendix, p.158.

78 *Report of the War Cabinet Committee on Women in Industry*, Appendix, p.157.

79 *Report of the War Cabinet Committee on Women in Industry*, Majority Report, p.195.

80 *Report of the War Cabinet Committee on Women in Industry*, Appendix, pp.168–169.

81 Zimmeck, 'Strategies and Stratagems', p.917. For a discussion of the adoption and setting up of the Whitley Council system in the Civil Service, see Henry Parris, *Staff Relations in the Civil Service* (London: George Allen & Unwin, 1973), pp.15–31 and Frieda Stack, 'Civil Service Associations and the Whitley Report of 1917', *Political Quarterly*, vol. 40, no. 3 (1969), pp.283–295. For the wider context of the Whitley system, see Henry Pelling, *A History of British Trade Unionism*, 4th edn (Middlesex: Penguin, 1987), p.150 and Pat Thane, *Foundations of the Welfare State*, 2nd edn (Harlow: Longman, 1996), pp.139–140.

82 *Committee on Recruitment for the Civil Service After the War* [hereafter Gladstone Committee, *Report*] Final Report (HMSO, 1919), pp.4–5; p.11.

83 TNA, T1/12266, 'Committee on the Recruitment of the Civil Service after the War', 50322/1918 (Part II), 'Miscellaneous (Un-numbered)', letter from Sir G. E. P. Murray to Sir T. Heath, dated 13 January [no year] [1918?] [1919?].

84 TNA, T1/12265, 50322/18, 'Pt 1. Committee on Recruitment for the Civil Service after the War'.

85 T1/12265, 50322/18, reports from department heads.

86 Gladstone Committee, *Report*, paras 23–25.

87 Gladstone Committee, *Report*, para. 25.

88 Gladstone Committee, *Report*, para. 45.

89 For more on the development of Whitleyism in the Civil Service, see Parris, *Staff Relations in the Civil Service*, pp.15–53.

90 There was much dissatisfaction with the report amongst several quarters of the Civil Service, not least amongst a number of women. The CSCA noted how the official side

duped staff side representatives, who 'worked desperately hard under the delusion that they were really helping to reorganise the Service'. *Red Tape*, 'Bull Dog', 'The Seats of the Mighty', July 1922, p.255.

91 *Report of the Civil Service National Whitley Council Reorganisation Committee* (HMSO, 1920) [hereafter *Reorganisation Report*], para. 9.

92 *Reorganisation Report*, para. 9.

93 British Library, Association of Women Clerks and Secretaries, *What it is and What it has done* (1927), p.7. The original files relating to this petition do not appear to have survived.

94 LCC Minutes, 3 June 1919.

95 LCC Minutes, 21 December 1920.

96 LCC Minutes, 6 March 1928.

97 *Report of the Committee on Common Seniority Lists for Men and Women* (London: HMSO, 1924).

98 MRC, MSS.415/58, Minutes of Women's Grade Committees, 1921–25, meeting of 17 December 1924.

99 Tomlin Commission, *Report*, para. 155.

100 Parliamentary Archives, letter from the NUSEC to Captain Wedgwood Benn, 9 March 1920.

101 POST 33/2951, File X, undated letter [probably 1928?], letter to Mr Bell from Col. Donald Banks.

102 Martindale, *Women Servants of the State*, p.126; TNA, LAB2/ LAB2/1911/ S&E1312/S/1931, Services and Establishments Department: Memorandum by Miss Whyte concerning proposals for recruiting single women in the Departmental Class and a survey of the position of women within the Ministry of Labour. E. Whyte, memo titled 'Director of Establishments', dated 15 May 1929.

103 LAB2/ LAB2/1911/S&E1312/S/1931.

104 E. Whyte, memo titled 'Director of Establishments', dated 15 May 1929.

105 TNA, Lab2/1911/S&E699/1932, 'Report of Duties of Women Officers in the Departmental Clerical Class Employed in Three Typical Employment Exchanges in the South Eastern Area', p.4.

106 See, for example, Vicinus, *Independent Women*, pp.211–246; Jones, *Women in British Public Life*, p.68.

107 Lab2/1911/S&E699/1932, undated memo by E. Whyte.

108 The former point appears to have been an issue in social work too. Mary Stocks recalls being advised against 'inexperienced teenagers' potentially having to cross-question middle-aged, married women. Mary Stocks, *My Commonplace Book: An Autobiography* (Trowbridge and London: Redwood Press, Ltd, 1970), p.58.

109 'Report of Duties of Women Officers in the Departmental Clerical Class Employed in Three Typical Employment Exchanges in the South Eastern Area', p.5.

110 'Report of Duties of Women Officers in the Departmental Clerical Class Employed in Three Typical Employment Exchanges in the South Eastern Area', p.4.

111 See, for example, POST 115/86, *Opportunity*, 'De-grading' about the re-grading scheme in the Savings Bank Department, October 1921, p.111. See also British Library, Federation of Women Civil Servants, *Women in the Civil Service: Grading – or*

De-Grading? Undated (1921)[?]. The Federation representative, Miss Caldcleugh, refused to sign the assimilation agreement which contributed to the re-grading. POST 115/88, *Opportunity*, D. Smyth, 'Special Article: Origin and History of the FWCS' [second part], March 1925, p.47.

112 Zimmeck, 'Strategies and Stratagems', p.917.

113 *Red Tape*, 'Degrading at the P.O.S.B.', July 1922, p.328.

114 Zimmeck, 'Strategies and Stratagems', p.918.

115 POST 115/86, 'Annual Meeting of the Association of Post Office Women Clerks', Supplement to *Opportunity*, June 1922.

116 *Red Tape*, 'Degrading at the POSB', July 1922, p.328.

117 *Hansard*, Post Office (Women), HC Deb 2 March 1922 vol. 151 c596W.

118 POST 115/86, *Opportunity*, 'A Week's Exemption', March 1921, p.24.

119 *Red Tape*, CSCA Women's Notes, January 1929, p.228.

120 Almost every issue of *Red Tape* contained news of campaigns for writing assistants. Just two examples are *Red Tape*, W.J. Brown, 'Association Notes', June 1921, p.201; *Red Tape*, W.J. Brown, 'Association Notes', February 1923, p.164.

121 POST 115/456, *The Post*, Proceedings of the Royal Commission on the Civil Service [reprinted], 21 December 1929, p.515.

122 Tomlin Commission, Evidence, para. 14,976.

123 Tomlin Commission, Evidence, para. 14,971.

124 Tomlin Commission, Evidence, para. 14,972.

125 For an articulation of this argument in the interwar period, see BPMA, POST 33/2951, File VIII, Post Office Departmental Whitley Council – Clerical Committee (Staff Side), 'Memorandum on the Grading of Women's Work', undated, but detail contained in the document places it at 1927 at least.

126 Women's Library, 6APC, FL228, APOWC: Correspondence: Common Seniority 1925–27; Segregation 1927–29, 'Association of Post Office Women Clerks: Memorandum on Segregation', dated February 1922; BPMA, POST 33/3213A, Women Clerks, Segregation vs Aggregation, File V, Notes of the APOWC's deputation, 10 May 1928, with suggestions for amendments from Sir Henry Bunbury.

127 POST 33/2951, File VIII, Post Office Departmental Whitley Council – Clerical Committee (Staff Side), 'Memorandum on the Grading of Women's Work'.

128 'Introduction of Lower General Grade for Women' as quoted in LMA, GLSA/1/32, LCC Staff Association Executive Committee Minutes, meeting of 19 April 1928. The lack of turnover figures for the LCC makes any assessment of the marriage bar's effect on promotions impossible.

129 *Report of the War Cabinet Committee on Women in Industry*, p.162.

130 POST 115/446, *The Post*, Marjory Hope, 'Re-adjustment', 6 September 1924.

131 POST 115/445, *The Post*, Marjory Hope, 'Women and the Public Service', 28 June 1924, p.634.

132 POST 115/450, *The Post*, Mary Herring, 'Of Interest to Women', 19 December 1925, p.1036.

133 MRC, MSS.148/UCW/2/1/5, Executive Committee Meeting, 19–21 October 1921.

134 For discussions of protective legislation, see Graves, *Labour Women*, pp.138–151; Boston, *Women Workers and the Trade Unions*, pp.30–59.

135 BT Archives, POST 33/1987, Telegraph instrument and counter duties: proportion of men to women, part I.

136 POST 115/441, *The Post*, Letters to the Editor, letter from M. T. Law, 24 June 1922, p.634. See also POST 115/442, *The Post*, Letters to the Editor, letter from M. B. Jamieson, 15 July 1922 and *The Post*, Letters to the Editor, letter from 'Femina Victrix', 9 September 1922, pp.246–247.

137 There is no published secondary overview of this Royal Commission. However, Gladden notes that the Commission was generally ineffectual as it came too soon after the MacDonnell Commission to make fresh recommendations, it was hampered by calls for financial restraint in the height of the economic depression and Civil Service recruitment and staffing had not really returned to normal after the war. Gladden also argues that officials failed to get an objective perspective on staffing matters as the evidence received was always connected with making a case. See E. N. Gladden, *Civil Service or Bureaucracy?* (London: Staples Press Ltd, 1956), p.41; p.42.

138 Lord Millett, 'Tomlin, Thomas James Chesshyre, Baron Tomlin (1867–1935)', *Oxford Dictionary of National Biography* (Oxford University Press, 2004) [www.oxforddnb. com/view/article/36531, accessed 11 August 2014].

139 Janet E. Grenier, 'Hamilton, Mary Agnes (1882–1966)', *Oxford Dictionary of National Biography* (Oxford University Press, 2004), online edn, May 2007 [www.oxforddnb. com/view/article/39455, accessed 16 August 2014]; David Howell, 'Lowe, Eveline Mary (1869–1956)', *Oxford Dictionary of National Biography* (Oxford University Press, 2004), online edn, January 2011 [www.oxforddnb.com/view/article/34609, accessed 16 August 2014].

140 Serena Kelly, 'Gould, Barbara Bodichon Ayrton (1886–1950)', *Oxford Dictionary of National Biography* (Oxford University Press, 2004) [www.oxforddnb.com/view/article/50046, accessed 11 August 2014].

141 Duncan Sutherland, 'Murray, Katharine Marjory Stewart-, duchess of Atholl (1874–1960)', *Oxford Dictionary of National Biography* (Oxford University Press, 2004), online edn, January 2011 [www.oxforddnb.com/view/article/36301, accessed 16 August 2014].

142 Duncan Tanner, 'Goldstone, Sir Frank Walter (1870–1955)', *Oxford Dictionary of National Biography* (Oxford University Press, 2004), online edn, January 2008 [www.oxforddnb.com/view/article/47357, accessed 8 February 2015]; Peter Gosden, 'Jackson, Sir Percy Richard (1869–1941)', *Oxford Dictionary of National Biography* (Oxford University Press, 2004) [www.oxforddnb.com/view/article/63811, accessed 8 February 2015].

143 Tomlin Commission, Evidence, para. 881. See also para. 944.

144 Tomlin Commission, Evidence, paras 927–928.

145 Tomlin Commission, *Report*, paras 390; 413.

146 POST 33/729A, Evidence of Sir G. E. P. Murray to the Tomlin Commission, para. 4269.

147 POST 33/729A, Evidence of Sir G. E. P. Murray to the Tomlin Commission, paras. 4278–4280.

148 POST 33/729A, Evidence of Sir G. E. P. Murray and Mr E. Raven, paras 4405–4411; paras 4579–4581.

149 Zimmeck, 'Marry in Haste', p.84; Silverstone, 'Office Work for Women', p.103; p.107; p.109, Walby, *Patriarchy at Work*, p.147.

150 Tomlin Commission, *Report*, para. 411.

151 *Report of the Committee on Women's Questions* (1934), paras 15–18.

152 POST 115/91, *Opportunity*, copy of the 'Committee on Women's Questions. Report of the Clerical Sub-Committee. Post Office Departmental Whitley Council, Committee on Women's Questions, Clerical Sub-Committee. General Agreement on Aggregation', introductory point no. 2, March 1936, p.38. A similar point was made to the Tomlin Commission: POST 33/729A, Post Office statement on the employment of women to the Royal Commission, para. 67.

153 *Red Tape*, 'POSB's Big Gathering', April 1937, p.482.

154 POST 115/92, *Opportunity*, 'The Outlook: Aggregation', February 1938, pp.19–20.

155 POST 115/93, *Opportunity*, 'The Outlook: Efforts to Cultivate an Unfair Field', April 1939, p.52.

156 *Red Tape*, Letters to the Editor, 'Aggregation', B. G. Watson, April 1937, pp.603–604.

157 *Red Tape*, Letters to the Editor, 'Aggregation', C. Haycocks, May 1937, p.664.

158 *Red Tape*, Letters to the Editor, 'Aggregation', from Miss A. E. Holden, July 1937, p.920. Haycocks replied in the next issue. L. M. Sweet, ' "Fair Field and No Favour". A Defence of Aggregation', August 1937, p.940.

159 POST 115/92, *Opportunity*, 'Clerical Assistant Campaign. Must Routine Work Always Be Done By Women?' [report of a debate hosted by the NAWCS and chaired by Vera Brittain], December 1938, p.188; *Red Tape*, Vivien Batchelor, 'Shall they Join the Ladies? Boys and the C.A. Grade', September 1938, p.943; Letters to the Editor, Len W. King, 'Boys Should Not Be C.A.s', October 1938, p.58; Letters to the Editor, Pearl Swain, 'Why Shouldn't Boys Be C.A.s?', November 1938, p.128.

160 *Red Tape*, Annual Conference Report, 'Opening of CA Grade to Boys', June 1938, pp.697–704. The CSCA executive made the same argument to the Tomlin Commission. However, the executive committee also argued for the line between writing assistant and clerical assistant work to be redrawn to give writing assistants a greater share of the more interesting duties. MRC, MSS.297/3/1/4, CSCA, *Statement of Case presented by the CSCA to the Royal Commission on the Civil Service, 1929*, pp.94–95.

161 Evans, *Women and the Civil Service*, p.86.

162 *Red Tape*, Annual Conference Report, 'Opening of CA Grade to Boys', June 1938, pp.697–704.

163 LMA, GLSA/1/35, London County Council Staff Association, Annual Report for 1934–1935.

164 LMA, LCC/CL/ESTAB/1/6, Evidence to the Royal Commission on Equal Pay, 1944, 'Fields of Employment of Women in Relation to Service of the London County Council as a whole'.

165 GLSA/1/37, LCC Staff association executive committee, minutes of 18 July 1938.

166 Tomlin Commission, *Report*, para. 412.

167 BPMA, POST 65/42, Whitley Council Committee on women's questions: report of the sub-committee on manipulative and supervising grades, regarding aggregation of all grades (1937).

168 BT Archives, POST 33/1987, Telegraph instrument and counter duties: proportion of men to women, part I.

169 *Report of the Committee on Women's Questions.* TNA, T162/494/7 Establishment. Women: Report of Committee on Women's Questions; Joint Committee to review application of minutes of meetings.; TNA, T162/450/8, Report of Committee (F.) on Women's Questions. Appointment of Joint Committee to review application of.

2

Trying to get equal opportunities: women in the higher grades of the LCC and the Civil Service in the first half of the twentieth century

Chairman: You contemplate a Lady Secretary to the Post Office?
Miss Cale: Yes, certainly; and a lady Postmaster General eventually.
(Laughter)
Chairman: That really is your claim?
Miss Cale: Yes, that is our ambition.[1]

These were the words of Miss M. Cale to the Holt Select Committee on the Post Office in 1913, which was set up to examine the wages and conditions of Post Office employees. Given the vast numbers of women employed in the Post Office it is not surprising that the drive for women's greater opportunities in the Civil Service, encapsulated in this quotation, originated from the women in this department. The APOWC and its parent organisation the FWCS insistently pushed for the inclusion of women in the higher grades of the service and, along with the more measured Council of Women Civil Servants (CWCS; formed in 1920), the organisations continued to pressure departments whom they felt were not providing suitable opportunities for women throughout the interwar years. In the LCC, the Staff Association took some interest in campaigning for women's advancement higher into the service, although this was less vocal and tended to react to changes or debates in the Civil Service.

The attempt to extend opportunities to women in the higher grades – that is the executive and administrative grades of the Civil Service and the major establishment of the LCC – would in more recent decades have been framed as an "equal opportunities" quest. The issue was inextricably linked to aggregation and creating the interchangeability of posts for two reasons. First, one way into the higher grades was through promotion, but if sections of work remained closed to women at the routine level then they could not, in most cases, be promoted into the posts above those. More widely, aggregation offered a means to remove the association between gender and certain types of posts, with common seniority lists meaning that the next individual in line for promotion would be promoted into the post. As we have seen, aggregation took time – in some departments in particular – and outside this, the issues of continued gender stereotyping, assumptions about women and routine work and the preference for male candidates remained prevalent. Thus, women wishing to join the executive and administrative grades of the Civil Service largely had to wait for Civil Service structures to be re-built to allow this. They also had to confront cultural barriers to women doing certain types of work and the preconceived notion of all women as temporary workers just biding their time until marriage. Although it did not have a formal segregation versus aggregation debate, the LCC posed a number of similar challenges for women. This chapter therefore stands as a case study of the challenges of introducing equal opportunities and, more significantly, the ways in which equal opportunities could be denied or resisted. Although it would be difficult to call either the Civil Service or the LCC pioneering – given that a number of elite professions had begun admitting women to training and professional practice earlier – the breadth and nature of work in both of the institutions meant that many ongoing debates about the suitability of women for particular work were inevitably impinged upon and both organisations were part of the interwar patchwork of potential new opportunities and heated debates about women in employment. Martindale, Zimmeck, Jones and Chapman have all offered reasons to, rightly, question the extent of progress and changed perceptions of women in the Civil Service.[2] However, there has not previously been an attempt to comprehensively examine the degree of equal opportunity in the interwar Civil Service and LCC and the reasons why, and means by which, women's opportunities were curbed.

Women and higher-grade work in the LCC and the Civil Service before 1918

To say that women were scarce in the higher grades of both the LCC and the Civil Service in the very early twentieth century would be an understatement. Women were employed on inspecting work that was thought proper to women – for example in the LCC for shops, employment bureaux and in spaces where public health and education legislation had specific reference to women and young children.[3] The first woman to be employed on such work – and in fact in the entire Council – was Isabel

Grinton Smith in 1894, who was paid two-thirds of the male salary for her post.[4] Much of this higher-grade work mirrored the types of work done by middle-class women volunteers in the late nineteenth century as well as that being conducted by newly professionalised female social workers.[5] Several thousand women teachers were of course employed by the LCC from 1904 and it also employed a considerable number of doctors in its Public Health department, thus providing opportunities for qualified women.

In the Civil Service before the war, there were some notable women in the higher grades, many of whom have come to the attention of historians previously.[6] Much like the LCC, the service employed women factory inspectors, who were employed specifically to inspect the work of bodies such as the Poor Law Commissioners or factories where women were employed in large numbers. Many of these women were, as Helen Jones notes, ad-hoc appointments, established outside of the usual grading and promotion structures as the work was deemed specialist and feminine.[7] When labour exchanges were established in 1910 this provided some work for female university graduates,[8] the longer-term effects of which will be explored in this chapter. Other women employed in higher-grade roles were often supervisors or superintendents of women on the routine work, though such roles remained scarce.[9] This was the extent of women's higher-grade work. There was no access to administrative grade examinations, the highest echelon of the Civil Service, and the MacDonnell Royal Commission of 1912–14 argued that this should continue, principally because it was not the job of the Civil Service to go out of its way to provide new job opportunities for women.[10]

During the First World War, there was some employment of women on higher-grade work in the Civil Service, though clearly to a far lesser extent than in the clerical and typing grades. Like much women's work outside of the accepted norm, this was very much couched in terms of being "for the duration". Much like the expansion of lower-grade and semi-skilled "men's work" to women in the wartime Post Office, it was agreed to only when other options diminished.[11] However, as Martindale has detailed, eventually the Civil Service began to make use of women in higher grades of the service, particularly in departments where there was less of an established tradition of women's employment on routine work only. These included the Board of Agriculture, the Admiralty, the War Office and the Foreign Office where women university graduates were employed. Other departments such as Customs and Excise and the Home Office made use of women at higher levels than hitherto.[12] In 1916, Ministry of Labour clerks approached a senior male official about doing something other than routine work and received an encouraging response.[13] In many cases, segregation was also abandoned, often on the grounds of practicality because same-sex supervision and allocation of work was more time-consuming to organise.[14] The LCC also employed women on its higher-graded work during the war, but reported making less use of them for such work than did the Civil Service.[15] Nonetheless, this was an important step forward in terms of women having a presence on a variety of the Council's work.

The post-war entry of women into the higher grades of the LCC and the Civil Service

Whilst it would be simplistic to argue that the war signalled a turning point in officials' attitudes to women in the higher grades, the temporary recruitment of women for work of greater responsibility did at least provide an unintentional experiment. The reconstruction of the post-war years thus coincided with longer-standing pressure for women to be given the opportunity to do something other than routine work, which had been a key part of the APOWC's and later the FWCS's manifesto.[16] As a whole, the interwar years were paradoxical for women in professional and public life. Whereas the war had brought temporary but significant change to gender roles and the types of work women could do, the interwar years brought both new opportunities in a number of professions whilst, at the same time, ideas about women's roles remained often consistent with pre-war years. As the interwar period continued, the challenges faced by LCC and Civil Service women echoed many of the battles faced by women in the early years of their entering various professions. Work by Carol Dyhouse, Kaarin Michaelsen and others discusses the struggles women faced to be accepted in new roles.[17] Louise A. Jackson has shown, for example, how police forces dealt with the introduction of women in policing in the early- to mid-twentieth century, preserving specifically designated sections of female police who undertook specialist "female" work but also, particularly in rural areas, did more general policing work too.[18] This was segregation and aggregation in action side-by-side in one organisation.

When it announced in late 1919 that women would henceforth be eligible to join the major establishment – roughly equivalent to the administrative grade of the Civil Service[19] – at the level of second class clerks, the LCC argued that women who had done such work during the First World War had 'proved their suitability'.[20] However, the story of their admission was more complex than this. Again, the Council would have been aware of the current Civil Service debates about the position of women, particularly the argument that though women's employment should be extended, it should not be freely extended.[21] In Establishment Committee stage at the LCC, the Clerk of the Council advocated keeping the major establishment as men only; it was agreed, after a motion by Charles G. Ammon, that women should be admitted to a maximum of 10 per cent of the vacancies.[22] It is not possible to uncover the reasons for Ammon's suggestion, though it may be that the quota allowed the LCC to show a small measure of progressiveness and experimentation whilst at the same time ensuring that women would have no more than a foot in the door. Here too was another connection between the LCC and the Civil Service: Ammon was a former postal employee and now worked as paid member of the UPW staff whilst also serving as LCC member for North Camberwell.[23]

Whereas the LCC made its decision about the appointment of a small number of women to higher-grade work with relative ease – though it evidently did so with one eye on Civil Service proceedings – the Civil Service itself was affected by overlapping and sometimes competing factors in the post-war years. There was a diversity of opinion within the post-war committees about women and positions of greater responsibility. In 1919, the Gladstone Committee concluded, with telling language, that after looking at the available evidence of women's wartime employment, it would be 'unsafe' to employ women interchangeably with men.[24] This was one of several committees which examined evidence – though some of it was closer to opinion or stereotype[25] – of women's temporary employment on higher-grade Civil Service work during the conflict. As several other bodies pointed out, this was not drawing evidence from a level playing field as women were minimally trained as last-minute replacements and could therefore not be expected to be as proficient as full-time, permanent male colleagues. However, the Gladstone Committee did suggest the employment of women on a 'liberal scale' for administrative grade work deemed particularly appropriate to women, which in practice meant work relating to children and to other women.[26] Only Frances Durham, the highest-ranked woman in the Ministry of Labour, emerged as a real champion of the female staff, arguing that '[t]he woman in the higher grades in addition to doing her work is continually establishing her right to do it: a most fatiguing struggle!'[27]

By contrast, Haldane's Machinery of Government committee (1918) – which was much-criticised by the Gladstonians – took a notably positive attitude to women in the higher echelons of the Civil Service. It stated in no uncertain terms that the extension of opportunities to women in the Civil Service was a necessary part of government work in the future and, contrary to the MacDonnell Commission a few years earlier, argued 'it is no longer expedient in the public interest to exclude women on the ground of sex from situations usually entered by the Class I examination, or from other situations usually entered by competition'. It maintained that there were certain administrative grade posts 'eminently more suitable for women' but that otherwise, sex of the candidate should be no criterion when appointing individuals.[28] However, later committees and negotiations overrode the optimism of the Haldane Committee. Furthermore, as discussed in the previous chapter, the 1919 Sex Disqualification Removal Act contained a proviso which allowed the government to make its own rules about women's rights to hold posts in the Civil Service. Of the legislation's passage through Parliament, Ray Strachey later observed, '[t]he Civil Service machine seemed absolutely determined not to allow women to come into any but the routine and subordinate grades, and their spokesmen fought with the adroitness of long practice against the threatened interference with their preserves'.[29] Proviso (a) thus meant that there was no guarantee that women's opportunities in the service would advance any further.

As we have seen, the Civil Service Whitley Committee's Reorganisation Report, finally issued in 1920, was in theory the foundation document for women's position in the interwar Civil Service. It opened the executive and administrative grade examinations to women, though it would be several years before any examinations took place because of the post-war need to recalibrate staffing levels. Written with a nod to the more positive spirit of the Sex Disqualification Removal Act, the report spoke of 'breaking new ground', and of doing so 'by common consent', vowing that 'opportunities afforded to women of proving their fitness to discharge the higher administrative duties of the Civil Service shall be full and liberal'. It also warned in passing of the 'novel and complex problems involved in the employment of women, side by side with men' and of the service's 'strictly limited experience' of higher-grade women's employment hitherto.[30] However, although it argued that women should be given equal status with men, the committee's lack of immediate commitment to either aggregation or a combined seniority list hampered this, particularly from the point of view of promotions. It meant that it was already difficult to level the playing field and really make any significant early change to women's long-term prospects, even if in the short-term the need to meet ex-servicemen's requirements and to assimilate now redundant grades had to take precedence. The proviso of the Sex

Disqualification Removal Act and the 1921 legal clarification of the act, to be discussed in Chapter 6, both provided loopholes for the Treasury. Therefore, even amongst assertions that this was a new world of women's work in the public service, women's opportunities appeared to be being publicly extended with one hand and then somewhat rescinded with the other in practice.

As part of the post-war settlement there were also woman establishment officer posts created in each department that employed women in significant numbers with the intention that such officers would represent women's concerns and handle queries relating to their appointment and promotion. However, these appointments were largely ceremonial and in the nature of publicity stunts: most woman establishment officers had no real power and most also appear to have toed the department line or been sidelined by their departments altogether.[31] Maude Lawrence, the Treasury's own Woman Establishment Officer, who theoretically represented all women in the Civil Service, had been appointed chief woman inspector in the Board of Education in 1905. It was social connections that allowed her to get there, and then she was promoted to the position of Woman Establishment Officer as she was perceived as the right sort of female influence in the service – that is, not overly concerned with advancing women's cause.[32] In themselves, then, these responses were indicative of institutional attitudes to women in the Civil Service. In the GPO the woman establishment officer was a quasi-administrative appointment but one which appears to have existed outside of the normal grading structure so as to not, in itself, create a precedent. By the 1930s, the post had been quietly dropped.[33]

New opportunities for women in practice

The complexity of the various post-war pronouncements – via official reports, in Parliament, via legislation and via legal interpretation – reveals that there was both a genuine willingness and pressure to include women more widely in the Civil Service and also that there was a considerable amount of unease and resistance to this. Women *were* admitted to the executive and administrative grades but not with unanimous support and there remained numerous factors which would combine to impede their progress. Such attitudes were much the same with regard to the inclusion of women in department-specific, professional, technical or scientific roles which occurred alongside the admission of women to the service-wide executive and administrative grades. Professional qualifications, rather than the Civil Service exam, determined entry to the professional, technical and scientific work and there was more flexibility over entrants' age as a range of external professional experience was highly valued. As the interwar years progressed, for example, women had opportunities in inspectorates in departments such as the Ministry of Agriculture, the Board of Control and the Board of Inland Revenue and to undertake practice as scientific researchers or doctors in various departments.[34] The opening of this type of work to women was predicated – as elsewhere in the service – on assumptions about work thought proper to women, but also with some regard to women's general progression and advancement in the equivalent career outside the service. The attitudes towards women's appointments to these specialist grades also varied somewhat by department, revealing the significance alternately of individual views or workplace culture as a defining factor in women's participation or even entry into these types of work.[35]

In 1925, the administrative grade examinations were restarted, after a one-off exam in 1923 for women who had temporarily been employed during the war on the grade. Three women were appointed to the service from this exam.[36] Between 1919 and 1925 there were very few women in the higher ranks as they really could only get there via promotion and this was of course highly dependent on the department concerned. One of the women who sat the 1925 exam was Alix Kilroy (later Meynell) who, along with fellow entrants Mary Smieton and Enid Russell, would become one of the foremost female civil servants of her generation. Kilroy joined the Board of Trade, Smieton the Public Record Office, swiftly followed by the Ministry of Labour, and Russell the Ministry of Health.[37] The press lauded the women entrants and their historic new jobs as 'female firsts' in the narrative given to women's progression that Adrian Bingham has identified.[38] What the press did not report was the fact that Kilroy's sister, who sat the examination at the same time, received a slightly lower mark but was never appointed to the service, even though further appointments were made that year. Officials, realising that there was a woman next on the list, did not announce the vacancy, thereby allowing them to move to the next man on the list.[39] By 1928, there were women in the administrative ranks of the Board of Trade, the Board of Education, the Ministry of Health, the Public Record Office and at the Treasury. A total of six women were appointed from the examinations between 1925 and 1929.[40] The examinations for the executive grade resumed in 1928, with 55 women out of a total new staff of 132 being appointed.[41] They joined the 35 women already in the grade across the service compared to 2,230 men.[42]

Out of all of the questions affecting women's employment in the Civil Service, the small numbers of women in grades above the clerical was the one most probed by the Royal Commission on the Civil Service at the end of the 1920s. The persistence of the GPO with segregation meant that there were, officially, no women on the executive and administrative grades because it graded all women as higher clerical, despite some of them manifestly doing executive or administrative-type work. The issue with this in particular – in addition to the unfairness of grading women's work lower because it was done by women – was that the GPO employed by far the greatest number of women in the service and yet its figures for women's advancement were worse than nearly all other departments.[43] Women comprised an equivalent of only 3 per cent of its higher grades because, as a result of segregation, it only admitted women to positions which were specifically designated as women's. The post of Female Superintendent, the highest a woman could hold, was equivalent to the men's post of Assistant Controller (or so GPO officials argued) – except of course the pay for women was lower, women had no designated promotion avenue after Superintendent because it was outside the grading hierarchy and the woman's post was seen as less important.[44]

The GPO's interpretation of including women on higher-grade work effectively meant putting women only in those positions which they felt really had to be held by women. As a result officials were able to strictly preserve segregation and the data for senior women spoke for itself. In other departments there were varying levels of aggregation and segregation, resulting in quite varying proportions of women in the higher grades. Sixteen per cent of the higher-grade posts in the Board of Education were held by women, but most of these were reserved to women.[45] This was an example of the fact that whilst more work was nominated as appropriate for women, more women on the higher grades did not necessarily mean more equalised opportunities for women. Again, it would ultimately be difficult for the proportions of women to increase beyond this point if most of the women in the executive or administrative grades were there in the first place because of the ear-marked positions. Women clearly also remained the junior partners. As Helen Jones has shown, in the 1920s women inspectors at the Board could not participate in policy discussions to the same extent as male inspectors and their role was ultimately more junior. In a parallel with women in labour exchanges, female inspectors could inspect girls' schools and be on the team which inspected a mixed school, but it was male inspectors who had ultimate authority and decision-making power. Although women were given almost carte blanche in nursery inspection, this was, Jones argues, more because of the lesser regard in which nurseries were held, rather than the fact that women were actually granted appropriate authority.[46]

Twenty per cent of posts in the higher grades of the Ministry of Health were held by women and only nine of these were designated as women's positions.[47] Reorganisation had brought about the combination of two women's inspectorate grades and an augmentation of their duties to cover work normally done by general inspectors, so this was accompanied by a rise in salary. This was an instance of a drastic exception being made to the normal age of Civil Service recruitment as it was argued that the best of the new female inspectors would be women who had worked in nursing for many years.[48] In this case, many more of the women on the higher grades were occupying gender-neutral posts, supporting many feminists' contention that given time and a suitable amount of consideration, aggregation could have positive results for women.[49]

The CWCS, a cross-service association for higher-grade women, produced a table for the Royal Commission on women in the executive, administrative and aligned technical grades which makes devastating reading. They noted that across the whole service there were 846 women in such posts compared to more than 4,575 men. The latter figure was a conservative estimate because the method of compilation did not include the male-only executive and administrative posts in the GPO. Of the 846 women, 277 of them were in posts that were segregated or at least designated as special women's posts. The case expressed quantitatively in this way was compelling: whilst there might be reason to designate a small number of posts for men only because of the very particular duties involved (travelling on ships with all-male crews and no female accommodation, for example), justifying such huge disparities between the overall numbers of men and women engaged on higher-grade work was much more difficult.[50]

Much discussion of women's suitability for roles took place during the Royal Commission on the Civil Service from 1929 to 1931. This included some discussion of jobs in the defence ministries and in the Foreign and Commonwealth Office, but much more for positions in the 'Home' Civil Service. Although many of the equivalent jobs in outside employment were categorised by gender it is notable that some of the Commissioners worked hard to probe why certain roles were closed to women in the Civil Service.[51] This forced departmental officials to offer very specific reasons for the demarcations of jobs as male-only. In both the LCC and the Civil Service there were a considerable number of roles from which women were barred on the grounds that the work was not ladylike enough, or would require supervision of men, or in which there was no participation by women in the equivalent work outside.[52] His Majesty's Inspectorate of Taxes, for example, could not employ many women assistant tax inspectors, it felt, because too much of the work would involve travelling to areas deemed unsuitable for lone women, although women were theoretically as eligible to hold such posts as men.[53] In the GPO's statement, the compounding effect of closing certain posts to women was also revealed, as a number of the posts closed to women were *de facto* closed to them because the posts directly beneath the post in question were also closed.[54] Such cases included Postmaster Surveyors, Head Postmasters, District Managers and Contract Managers for the Telephone system. For other posts, the fact that women would have to supervise men, and sometimes tradesmen, precluded their eligibility. However, there were documented instances of women supervising men so this stricture did not apply across the board.[55] Posts which included travel were also closed to women, as were those of telephone contract officers as the duties 'consist mainly in visiting subscribers and potential subscribers at their houses or business premises'. The posts of Surveyor and Assistant Surveyor were closed to women in part because they involved travel and the investigation branch was also closed to women because it involved investigation of criminal offences against the Post Office and thus '[t]he work is not regarded as suitable for women'. For some technical roles, it was noted that women did not have the required qualifications.[56] Women were able to serve as postmistresses in the smaller towns but not the larger ones. No explicit reason for this was given, though it clearly related to perceptions of women's capabilities, the amount of authority it was deemed acceptable for women to exercise and the preference for men to carry out such a role.[57] In the Treasury's submission to the Royal Commission, it was evident that early twentieth-century concepts of the gendering of careers meant that they perceived some posts as never being opened to women: '[t]he spectacle of men inspectors of such subjects as cookery or domestic science would be as equally undesirable as the spectacle of women inspectors of heavy artillery or the coastguard service', it argued. 'It is not so much that men could not attain proficiency in subjects falling within the first category or that women could not attain competence in subjects falling within the second category as the expression of a robust common sense which recognises that in many respects particular functions rightly and conveniently fall to particular sexes.'[58]

In its statement to the Royal Commission, the CWCS had been both encouraging and hesitant about the gendered structure of work in labour exchanges – as discussed in Chapter 1 – and the promotion opportunities it afforded women. The statement expressed more optimism about women's prospects there than in many other areas of the Civil Service but noted that '[t]here is a tendency … to limit unduly the experience of women to work relating to women only and consequently to create some apparent justification for regarding as a preserve for men the bulk of the controlling posts'.[59] The practice of having women to staff female exchanges and consequently not allowing them to manage mixed-sex exchanges contrasted with the way in which the LCC handled the issue of social acceptability and the perceived need to protect female staff. Council officials expressed considerable fears about women working in proximity to distressing situations and the fact that they might not be able to cope, to the extent that a decision appears to have been taken to not employ female welfare officers in the social welfare department to deal with any cases, no matter whether they primarily involved women or not. The official position was that 'girls in their teens and young women might be embarrassed if required to take notice … of cases involving immorality or other irregularities'.[60] However, this was not then used as a barrier to women's involvement in more senior positions in the welfare department. Instead they were involved – at more of a distance – with cases involving female and infant welfare. It followed that such women would be older – having taken time to reach a senior position – and thus perhaps perceived as better able to deal with 'embarrassing' situations. By the outbreak of the Second World War the Council had relented and women were employed as welfare officers and assistant welfare officers. Therefore, rather than being cut off from higher positions throughout the interwar years because they could not be welfare clerks, women's skills were put to use further up the promotional ladder.[61]

Having picked up on the same point as that made by the CWCS, members of the Royal Commission questioned Ministry of Labour officials about why mixed exchanges were always managed by men. Horace Wilson, Permanent Secretary of the Ministry of Labour, responded that 'in most cases at any rate the men's work bulks much more largely than the women's work. If you take the men's side of the exchange, it is very much more important, and has many more complexities than the women's side. That I should expect to be the main sort of principle involved'.[62] There was thus a suggestion here that women were less capable of 'important' and 'complex' work or that such work was by rights men's and not women's. When questioned whether women not managing mixed exchanges was as relevant in areas such as Lancashire, where there were strong traditions of female employment, Wilson gave a rather different response, arguing that there was a:

> general question whether the outside world is yet ready to have its governmental affairs discussed by a woman. As you know, even in

Lancashire, most of the employers are men, and all the trade union officials are men, and while later on that may all be altered, it has not been altered yet. From the point of view of a piece of State machinery which is in very close contact with the outside world, and particularly with the local authorities and education authorities, who in turn are all officered by men, I think there would be practical difficulties in expecting a woman manager at the exchange to be able to do all that is required of a manager. That avoids altogether the question of whether a woman or a particular woman could do the work.[63]

Here, he revealed concerns regarding whether women could interact with local officials and trade unionists and like many of his Civil Service contemporaries, Wilson appears to have needed proof that a woman could do a particular job whilst it was always automatically assumed that men could. Notably, the Association of Officers in the Ministry of Labour also expressed some reservations about women running mixed exchanges in coal-mining areas, but far fewer concerns overall.[64] When Commissioners suggested to Horace Wilson that the Ministry of Labour might create 'a precedent' by allowing women to manage mixed exchanges, he asked:

How far can you go or at what pace can you go? The over-riding consideration to my mind is that you cannot go much faster than the outside world is ready for you to go. If presently the outside prejudice disappears, then, of course, it would be much easier to consider how far you could go, and how far capacity was equal, and how far you could go in utilising that capacity.[65]

Wilson's response was typical of Civil Service rhetoric, both in terms of ideas about equality and in terms of seeing a division, but also an inter-relationship, between the Civil Service and the outside world. As with equal pay, there was an underlying question regarding whether the Civil Service should follow other employers or be the exemplar. Women's organisations and progressive politicians alike often argued the latter. For Wilson, questions regarding how much power and responsibility women could be given were governed by wider social and political considerations and it was the job of the Civil Service to follow rather than to lead. The added twist to Wilson's rhetoric at this point, however, was that the Minister of Labour was currently a woman: Margaret Bondfield. However, despite Wilson's misgivings, some modest progress was made in the following years: seven women were in charge of mixed exchanges by the late 1930s and several others were recognised as deputy managers of mixed exchanges.[66]

Maude Lawrence, Director of Women's Establishments at the Treasury, made a similar point to Wilson when referring to the chief inspectorship of the Board of Education: the outside world was not yet ready.[67] In these and further instances officials spoke in terms of it not yet being the right time to give women greater opportunities, as though they could foresee what such a time might look like. However, Lawrence also conceded that she would like to see greater experimentation with women's work in the higher echelons of the service and that she thought heads of department would be willing to try. This point seemed to contradict some of her other assertions which defended current practice, whilst also having a rather optimistic view of certain male officials in the service.[68]

Of course, we can only speculate how well or otherwise the outside world would have greeted these types of changes. Whilst British society had largely accepted changes to women's roles in wartime, it is notable that the Treasury appeared to think that society continued to have largely conservative and traditional views of women's roles. The Treasury may not have been entirely wrong about society's acceptance of women in positions of authority but it is worth noting that barriers in professions were slowly being broken in the interwar years and if women had been more widely admitted to Civil Service positions of responsibility it is conceivable that this might have been accepted within half a generation or so. At the same time, how far were statements to the Royal Commission about "society's views" smokescreens to hide the Treasury's own desire to keep the status quo, or to mask prejudice against women? Royal Commission evidence sessions largely consisted of Civil Service officials justifying their current policies so it is sometimes more complex to disentangle genuine reason from expedient justification. Even so, evidence of bodies like the London and National Society for Women's Service (LNSWS) also highlighted the lack of commitment the Treasury had made to making more opportunities available to women, accusing it of doing the minimum and leaving the rest for a later generation.[69]

In preparatory notes for their written submission to the Royal Commission in 1929, the Treasury sought to justify why there was a far greater number of women in the routine grades of the Civil Service than other grades. In a paragraph which essentially suggested women were at fault for not being more committed and which ignored all of the other ways in which women's employment in the Civil Service was circumscribed, Treasury officials declared:

> The cause is undoubtedly to be found in the difference of attitude towards a career. In the Civil Service, as the marriage statistics show,

the average career of a woman is comparatively short. This makes them in many cases unwilling to spend time and money in fitting themselves for superior occupations, with the result that they tend to seek positions where they can earn a reasonably satisfactory wage as soon as possible. There can be no doubt that work is often looked upon as a temporary career which occupies the period between school and marriage and is best filled in by quickly learnt repetitive work. So long as this attitude is prevalent there will be found a disparity between men and women in the twin fields of enterprise and ambition.[70]

Had they seen it, the condescension in this pronouncement would have made the blood of the women in the CWCS and FWCS boil, particularly as the Treasury missed out the crucial fact that the Civil Service compelled women to leave when they married. As will be seen in later chapters, Treasury officials had a remarkable blind spot – wilful or not – regarding the implications of their own rulings about married women and paid work. Whilst it is fair to say that a number of women did view work as a stop-gap between school and marriage, the education system also presumed this for all but the elite and wider society also repeatedly suggested this to them, encouraged and underlined by the existence of the marriage bar in public employment and similar expectations in private employment. This was also clearly a circular situation: if the bulk of the work that women were considered suitable for was in the clerical grades, this was where most women would end up.

The Commission discussed the numbers of women in the executive and administrative grades and the progress made. Although the administrative grade had technically been open to women for nine years, there had only been examinations for the previous five years. Progress thus looked bleak, especially in combination with some departments' reluctance to employ women either through prejudice or assumptions about suitability of posts for women, as well as the numbers of long-serving men awaiting promotion effectively blocking opportunities for women. As the LNSWS argued, the public might genuinely have believed that women civil servants had equal opportunities with men, based on the legislation and publicity of the early 1920s, but this had not actually materialised.[71] There were a number of discussions during the Commission's evidence-gathering sessions which addressed why women had not made inroads more quickly on the administrative grade especially. Maude Lawrence argued that there had simply not been enough time and that longer-serving men had prior claims on many administrative posts. She was then asked about a process of – effectively – affirmative action to bring more women into the higher grades of the service. She argued against this is in the strongest terms, stating that the public service would be harmed by ill-feeling created if women came into the higher grades above the heads of existing male staff who were well-qualified.[72] Some women's organisations had made the argument that the public service needed to be staffed by a group more representative of the society it served, although otherwise this precise rhetoric remained largely ahead of its time.[73]

As explored in Chapter 1, the major recommendation made by the Royal Commission in 1931 was that aggregation should be adopted throughout all departments. The negative effects of segregation on women's opportunities had become particularly apparent during the questioning of Murray, the GPO Secretary, about why there were no women at all in the executive and administrative grades.[74] Murray admitted that there was little difference between the higher clerical and the executive grades, but that the latter was closed to women as 'a matter of administrative convenience' and that women's presence would complicate the promotion structures: 'supposing we got one or two women assigned to the executive class, it might give rise to a difficulty of organisation to put them in a class consisting of 200 men.'[75] The fear of this was such that in 1928, the GPO had asked for men to fill their two executive vacancies. The Civil Service Commission told them that 'we expect to be able to assign men from the recent competition to fill your two Executive vacancies' but warned that in future no such promises could be made, given that the executive grade was open to both sexes and no department could insist on members of the grade being from one sex only.[76] In front of the Royal Commissioners, Murray conceded that now that examinations for the administrative grade were open to men and women alike, it was entirely feasible that a woman might be admitted to the administrative grade in the GPO. He noted that 'there would be no separate avenue of promotion; she would simply form part of the administrative class on the same footing as men',[77] revealing that women's opportunities were hitherto lacking compared to men's but also that the common recruitment of men and women and their random assignment after the examination would finally force the GPO to move over to aggregation. Thus, the Royal Commission's recommendation of aggregation – as well as examination practices from the late 1920s – had important repercussions, particularly as these were endorsed by the Whitley Committee Report on Women's Questions in 1934. In turn, departments then had, as per a requirement of the Report on Women's Questions, to publicly state which posts were being reserved to one sex or another and why, in the hope that this would lead to both further clarity and, more particularly, scrutiny of unnecessary reservations.[78]

In 1935, the LCC's quota for women in the major establishment was abandoned. From 1925 – when women could now regularly take part in the Civil Service administrative exams – the LCC Staff Association had begun pressuring for women to be considered for roles in the highest sections of the major establishment – and, more specifically, to be allowed to compete for roles without the 10 per cent quota being in operation.[79] The change was approved by the LCC in 1930,[80] but it took a further five years for it to be put into operation because, like the Civil Service in the 1920s, there were other related staffing questions which had to be settled and the decision was taken to resolve these before allowing women into the grade without a limit.[81] Therefore, by the mid-1930s both the Civil Service and the LCC were operating employment structures where women could theoretically be employed interchangeably with men for a considerable number of posts.

The reality of this was somewhat different, however. In the LCC just as in the Civil Service, there was more open support for women's expanded employment and some real resistance. The LCC staff association undertook a survey in 1938 as preparation for a campaign to open all work to men and women interchangeably. Campaigners wanted reasons to be publicly stated for the reservation of work to one sex, much like the 1934 Whitley Committee's recommendations for the Civil Service. By this time, the majority of staff association sub-committees approved of the employment of women on the same terms of men, though there were some notable anomalies such as the Education Officer's department which retained a relatively high degree of gender segregation, which the staff sub-committee favoured. The institutions run by the Public Assistance department also remained largely segregated, though it is notable that all clerical work was designated as women's only on account of the 'nature of the work'. What was interesting about the returns received for the staff association's survey was that many officials could see that work had been closed to women or (less frequently) to men for arbitrary reasons. Others recognised that just because posts had only ever been held by men it did not necessarily mean that women could never be appointed, thus distinguishing between precedent and agreed practice. The Chief Engineer's office, conversely, declared that engineering would not appeal to women and the surveying section of the Valuation, Housing and Estates department made the slightly surly but obvious remark that for women to be admitted they would have to undergo training as surveyors. It was fully admitted that in the central office sections of council administration there was '[a]lways an unofficial boycott of women as far as central office staff are concerned'.[82] Thus, attitudes were shifting amongst staff – and perhaps among the departments of which they were part, but there was still some way to go and a variety of reasons were, in practice, keeping women out of posts.

In the late 1930s the Civil Service staff representatives involved in the 1934 Committee on Women's Questions asked for, and were granted, an opportunity to review the work which remained closed to either sex – which often in practice meant closure to women. Privately, Civil Service officials admitted that there were '[d]epartments who have not been over-progressive on women's questions and whose policy we have on occasion had some difficulty in defending to the Staff Side'.[83] Complete minutes do not appear to have survived and it is notable that the staff side of the committee chose not to question departmental agreements – such as the GPO's continued gendering of sets of posts – so there were a number of instances where the gendering of work was not questioned further. The Ministry of Labour's designation of some posts as 'more appropriately' men's or women's work was questioned, as was the reason for the closure of the non-manual grades in the Royal Mint to women. More emphasis was also given to questioning individual posts, in particular departments and posts in the defence ministries which remained closed to women.[84] There were some victories: women auditors could now be sent on overnight visits once they had gained more experience – which was likely a coded way of saying that it was more desirable to send older ("spinster") women to do this work. Clerical positions in the Royal Mint were opened to women in 1938 but death coding work and work connected with criminal cases in the Home Office remained closed to women, despite the fact that women were expected to serve – theoretically at least – on juries.[85]

How much progress? Numbers of candidates and women staff in the Civil Service and LCC higher grades, 1925–39

The goal of equal opportunity was not something that could, realistically, have been settled in the interwar years: there had not been enough time since the opening of the higher grades to women and, just as significantly, the labour market was still seen as highly gendered and women's place in society remained often specific and circumscribed. But to what extent were women applying for and promoted or recruited to higher posts in both organisations by the late 1930s?

With generally long staff tenures and only fourteen years of administrative grade examinations and eleven years of executive grade examinations in the Civil Service, numbers of women remained relatively small, particularly in the administrative grade. In the GPO, the legacy of the long-term insistence on segregation was that there were still only two women on administrative grade work (compared with 57 men) and 93 on executive grade work (compared with 1,339 men) in 1936.[86]

Whilst data on promotion decision-making in both organisations is scarce, and broader attitudes to women in the workplace would have played a big part in these outcomes, the fact that men had been employed on executive and administrative work for longer meant that they had the seniority and often the name recognition to be promoted. In the Civil Service it was said that the chief criterion for promotion was merit and not seniority, though 'merit' was never actually defined at the higher levels of work, in contrast to the 'efficiency bar' imposed on some routine workers. In practice it is hard to see that promotion was not determined by 'seniority' and the accompanying 'seniority lists', first and foremost.

In its submission to the Royal Commission on Equal Pay in 1945, the LCC was asked, amongst other things, about women's chances for promotion and the way in which female employees were perceived. In response to a question on whether men and women would be promoted in equal numbers if any "marriage wastage" were discounted, the LCC's representatives reported that though promotion was based on merit, in effect there might be 'a certain amount of prejudice' against women which meant that it was more likely to be the exceptional women who earned promotions. The clear implication echoes that found in other discussions of women trying to advance in careers: they had to be considerably better than the men with whom they were competing.[87] However, the memorandum also dispelled the notion that women might be less concerned with promotion on account of expecting to spend less time in the service, which was a distinct contrast to prevailing Civil Service attitudes.[88]

The LCC's practice of limiting 10 per cent of vacancies to women had had a significant effect on the levels of women's employment in the grades affected, as it was also a means of determining internal promotion as well as new appointments. In 1945 the Royal Commission asked the Council to provide retrospective data on the women actually appointed to major establishment positions in the early 1930s and to estimate how many would have been employed if the 10 per cent maximum had not been in place. Noting that there had been no examinations in 1929 and 1930, the Council supplied the following data (see Table 2.1) for internal examinations.

Although the Council sent it with the caveat that much more research would be needed to determine exactly how women's appointments had been affected by the 10 per cent limit,[89] it was obvious that men

Table 2.1 Candidates and appointments for LCC major establishment vacancies by gender, including estimate of appointments if 10 per cent limit on women had not been in place

Date of exam	No. of male candidates	No. of female candidates	No. of men reaching pass standard	No. of women reaching pass standard	No. of men appointed	No. of women appointed	Estimate of appointments with no restriction on women – men	Estimate of appointments with no restriction on women – women
Internal 1931	154	40	56	24	47	6	38	15
Internal 1932	101	39	34	21	34	6	26	14
Internal 1934	66	26	31	16	31	5	21	15

Source: LMA, LCC, CL/Estab/1/6, Evidence to the Royal Commission on Equal Pay, letter to Miss Cooke from Wilma Hart, 16 February 1946 [bold emphasis added].

benefitted and women lost out: in every case, more women could have been appointed but the 10 per cent ruling held them back. Furthermore, the number of women's appointments was also affected by a ruling that only 20 per cent of appointments for the major establishment could come from the external examination, meaning in effect that women could only be appointed to 2 per cent of these vacancies.[90] Most starkly, in both 1932 and 1934, all men who reached the pass standard were appointed. However, though far fewer women than men were appointed compared to the numbers sitting the examination, it seems that the quota might have been gradually relaxed from 1930, even though the Council had stated it would not be able to do so until 1935.[91] Women were given over 11 per cent of the appointments in 1931, nearly 14 per cent in 1932 and 15 per cent in 1934. Still, the impact of the limit for women was clear and, unlike the Civil Service, where more covert forms of discrimination could be used, the goalposts for women candidates would have been clearer from the beginning of the application process. Was it better to know that there was a prescribed limit than to try one's luck with the Civil Service process?

Data for women's appointments to the major establishment after 1935, when the 10 per cent restriction was lifted, is difficult to read conclusively, as Table 2.2 shows. Figures show that for the years 1935 and after, not many more than 10 per cent of the appointments were given to women and, in 1937, the proportion was notably less. Interestingly, this was the year when there was a large number of candidates as the requirement for internal candidates to have been LCC staff members for five years was removed. In addition to the appointments above, a total of seventeen men were admitted through the Civil Service exam in the period compared to one woman.[92] The obvious exception to the general pattern is 1935, when women who had previously taken the exam under the quota system and not succeeded in getting a position were allowed to take the examination for a second time.[93] Thus, there was a large influx of women into the grade, suggesting also that many women aspired to do this type of work. However, in the years after that, the highest percentage of total appointments given to women was 14.6 per cent in 1939 (though it is also unclear whether conscription affected the proportion of male candidates). Women were therefore not doing appreciably better: removing the upper limit on the numbers of women in the grade was of course not enough.

With this in mind it is worth contemplating the numbers of women candidates presenting themselves for the exams, and then where in the examination and appointment process women were failing to progress.

Table 2.2 Female candidates and appointments to the LCC, 1935–39

Year	Total staff admitted through open competition	Women admitted through open competition	Women's appointments as percentage of total	Total staff admitted through internal exam	Women admitted through internal exam	Women's appointments as percentage of total	Combined total of staff appointed	Total women appointed	No. of women appointed as percentage of total appointments
1935	25	7	28%	31	14	45%	56	21	37.5
1936	29	5	17%	37	4	11%	66	9	13.6
1937	21	3	14%	45	2	4.50%	66	5	7.6
1938	18	2	11%	43	6	14%	61	8	13.1
1939	19	5	26%	70	8	11%	89	13	14.6
Totals	**112**	**22**	**20%**	**226**	**34**	**15%**	**338**	**56**	**16.6**

Source: Adapted from LMA, LCC/ESTAB/1/8, 'Female staff: Positions in Council's service open to women', Women in Senior Positions.

The LCC's method of data compilation for results of individual examinations varied over time, but some conclusions can be drawn from this. No identifying details of unsuccessful candidates were published so it is impossible to ascertain women's participation and success rates. However, from 1936, the LCC offered a more detailed breakdown of success in the examination and interview stages. Although there is no gender breakdown for the total number of candidates, we know that in 1936 sixty candidates passed the examination, including seventeen women. Of these seventeen, six declined an interview and of the remaining eleven interviewed, five women were appointed. These women joined twenty-four men in the grade. When withdrawals from the interview process are taken into account, this means that men had over a 62 per cent chance of being appointed after interview, whereas for women this figure was 45 per cent. In 1937, twenty-two women passed the examination, alongside forty-two men. Twenty-one appointments were made after the interview stage, including three women. LCC records note that some of the successful candidates withdrew themselves from the interview process, so conclusions are tentative at best. However, in contrast to 1936, women had at least a 13.6 per cent chance of gaining an appointment whereas men had at least a 45 per cent chance of being appointed after interview. The proportions are similar for 1938 and 1939 so although this is a relatively small run of data it is suggestive of the fact that women were proportionately less likely to be appointed than men.[94]

It also seems to have been the interview stage in which they fared the worst. It may be that women had received less training – formally or informally in their education – to help them tackle the interview process and they thus fared worse than men. It is also worth noting the possibilities for more subjective marking of interviews compared to the examinations, which were marked by candidate number only. However, if internal candidates were already known to the interviewers, this could potentially have worked for or against them. We also do not know anything about the composition of the interview panels and the impact that this might have had either, although Gibbon and Bell state that the general grade interview panel was composed of three members after 1935, so we could safely assume that the major establishment interview panel was similar.[95] Marks were awarded for the interview and added to the examination total. In 1937, the highest examination mark was awarded to Gwendoline B. Nicholls, but – the possibility that she withdrew from the process aside – she evidently did not perform well enough in the interview to be offered an appointment.[96] What remains striking in the LCC, then, is the consistency in the proportions of women appointed before and after the removal of the maximum limit. Without surviving data regarding numbers of female entrants, however, it is difficult to offer further insights on this.

In a revelatory document from around 1941, in which the Council appeared to search its soul as to why there had not been more women in the major establishment, it was noted that the 10 per cent rule operated in a 'strange method' in the internal examinations. All nine men were chosen from the examination list by name before the one woman was selected, meaning that the woman could potentially be appointed weeks or months after the men and thus was lower on the seniority list than all of the men appointed from the same examination.[97] This aspect of the process was clearly discriminatory. When promotion opportunities thereafter were often so few and far between, this could make a significant difference in terms of the composition of higher grades and the opportunities for advancement.

In the Civil Service, it was estimated that in the years just before the outbreak of the Second World War, 18–20 per cent of vacancies in the executive grade and about 7 per cent of vacancies in the administrative grade went to women, as compared to 40 per cent of clerical vacancies.[98] The administrative grade therefore included proportionally fewer women compared to the LCC. In his study of the higher grades of the Civil Service, Kelsall argued that after the employment of women on administrative work in the Civil Service during the First World War, 'the barriers that had been temporarily and partially removed could not, in post-1918 Britain, be reimposed'.[99] This statement, at face value, is correct but of course questions remain about the extent of change, complicated as it was by numerous factors already explored here. Only 35 women were appointed to 490 administrative posts available through open competition between 1925 and 1939,[100] though a number more came through promotion. For example, by 1929 approximately twelve women were promoted into the grade.[101] Kelsall argued that by the end of the interwar years women candidates were more or less as successful in the examination as men as a proportion of their numbers.[102] Using Table 2.3, this is true for 1928 and 1930, and some of the later 1930s (with the notable exception of 1939), but the record in the early 1930s was dismal, so whilst it is possible to be cautiously optimistic, the sample size and the variance within it is not sufficient to declare women as likely as men to be appointed as a proportion of their numbers.

The underlying issue in this period was women's propensity to apply for the positions in the first place. In an age when women comprised just under 22 per cent of university students this necessarily

Table 2.3 Success rates in the Civil Service administrative grade examination

Year	No. of men attended	No. of women attended	Total	Successful men	Men's success rate as proportion of men candidates	Successful women	Women's success rate as proportion of women candidates	Total appointments
1925	80	27	107	19	23.8	3	11.1	22
1926	106	12	118	22	20.8	1	8.3	23
1927	107	14	121	9	8.4	–	0	9
1928	111	11	122	16	14.4	2	18.2	18
1929	109	10	119	23	21.1	1	10	24
1930	110	9	119	24	21.8	2	22.2	26
1931	146	15	161	18	12.3	–	0	18
1932	152	6	158	19	12.5	–	0	19
1933	108	6	114	29	26.9	–	0	29
1934	150	13	163	36	24	1	7.7	37
1935	162	4	166	41	25.3	1	25	42
1936	235	18	253	50	21.3	6	33.3	56
1937	263	29	292	43	16.3	8	27.6	51
1938	289	44	333	53	18.3	8	18.2	61
1939	305	50	355	53	17.4	2	4	55
Totals	2,433	268	2,701	455	18.7	35	13.1	490

Source: Adapted from *Royal Commission on Equal Pay*, Minutes of Evidence taken before the Royal Commission on Equal Pay, (London: HMSO, 1945), 'First Memorandum of Evidence submitted by HM Treasury: Remuneration of Women in the Crown Service', Analysis of candidature for some of the main home civil service competitions: administrative class, p.11.

made the pool of women applicants for posts in the administrative division of the Civil Service rather small (and this also would have applied for the LCC's examinations too).[103] However as Table 2.3 shows, women often made up rather less than 22 per cent of candidates for the examination. Kelsall has advanced a number of convincing reasons for this. These included the marriage bar and lack of equal pay, the often year-long delay between university graduation and the examinations when other limited career opportunities for women might emerge in the meantime, the ingrained prejudice of certain departments against women, and the time it took for administrative grade appointments to become known as a serious career option for women.[104] We might add, for example, that when administrative grade examinations opened to women in 1925, it would then likely have taken time to become recommended by university appointment boards and recognised by women graduates as a potential career. This can be seen in the data below in terms of the wavering female candidature for the examinations. (The high figure for 1925 can be accounted for by the fact that a wider age cohort of candidates was permitted to sit because the first examination for the grade had been so delayed after the war.) However, in the late 1930s, *The Times* and other outlets providing girls' career advice were routinely advertising the existence of high-ranking opportunities in the Civil Service for women, though not all were uniformly positive about this.[105] This is, at least, indicative of the fact that the option of a career in the administrative grades of the Civil Service was finally becoming a widely recognised option for women. The increasing number of women candidates does bear this out, although with the increase in female candidates also came an increase in male candidates so the overall effect was more limited.

Interestingly, the Civil Service Commissioners, whilst pointing out that the sample size was small, noted that successful women candidates in the administrative examination in the years 1925–29 were considerably less likely to have achieved a first class degree than the successful men. This, they held, was an indication of the lower calibre of women candidates, though this conclusion was rightly questioned by the Royal Commissioners because the women had passed the entrance examination regardless of their degree classification. However, the Civil Service Commissioners, after a little deliberation, argued that women were not appreciably less impressive than men in the *viva voce* stage of the examination, though the comment 'We have not had any great fliers amongst the women; but we have had several very nice women' says more than the original speaker probably realised about conceptions of gender.[106]

Table 2.4 Success rates in the Civil Service executive grade examination

Year	Men attended	Women attended	Total	Successful men	Successful men as percentage of male candidates	Successful women	Successful women as percentage of female candidates	Total number appointed
1928	285	315	600	77	27	55	17.5	132
1930	440	326	766	63	14.3	28	8.6	91
1931	590	324	914	41	6.9	12	3.7	53
1932	675	302	977	48	7.1	4	1.3	52
1933	928	300	1,228	100	10.8	24	8	124
1934	859	321	1,180	115	13.4	16	5	131
1935	1,026	333	1,359	129	12.6	19	5.7	148
1936	1,114	365	1,479	177	15.9	43	11.8	220
1937	1,239	415	1,654	183	14.8	39	9.4	222
1938	1,693	551	2,244	249	14.7	52	9.4	301
1939	2,170	572	2,742	374	17.2	55	9.6	429

Source: Adapted from *Evidence to the Royal Commission on Equal Pay*, [1944–46] 'First Memorandum of Evidence submitted by HM Treasury: Remuneration of Women in the Crown Services', p.11.

The data on women's candidacy for the executive class examination – of which there was no equivalent examination in the LCC – reveal greater problems in terms of women's participation and success rates, which is perhaps surprising given that this did not require a university degree. As Table 2.4 shows, there continued to be more male candidates in every year except the first that the examination was open to women and in every year, the men were also more successful than women. Again, this may indicate that men were better prepared, and more aware of, the executive grade of the Civil Service as a possible career opportunity or that men were more likely to have an education to the age of eighteen.

Conclusion

The differing approaches of the Civil Service and the LCC in endeavouring to handle the subject of higher-grade opportunities for women reveal much about official mindsets about women and highlight the varying constraints in trying to enact significant change. However much women's organisations in the Civil Service would have wished otherwise, there was not going to be anything close to equality achieved in such a short time after decades of male dominance in the upper spheres of the Civil Service, and the same was true for the LCC. In the Civil Service the relative lack of female candidates was problematic, as was the fact that – as is discussed further in Chapter 6 – exemptions to the marriage bar were not actually created in practice until the mid-1930s, meaning women were continually forced to choose between marriage and a career and knew this at the point of application or had perhaps left the service before promotion became a serious prospect. Women's success in some years of the administrative grade examinations was promising, but they still joined grades that had been occupied for decades by men and often had to be pioneers in their own departments in terms of breaking down assumptions about gender and trying to convince superiors of their merits for internal promotion. This was going to be a long-term project: during evidence sessions for the Royal Commission on Equal Pay (1944–46), a Civil Service official was asked how he would feel about an administrative grade comprising 20–25 per cent women – which still, of course, was nowhere near equality. He argued:

> I think one would want to sit back and see whether we were not getting a type of Civil Service so different from the present that we ought to consider whether it was right to allow that process to go on … [W]hatever progressive views the Treasury may have, public opinion

has not reached the stage of accepting women in all positions ... As we have to provide an administrative class which will serve all purposes we should have to take into account that kind of consideration.[107]

Again, the official side-stepped the question, deferring to what he thought public opinion was and wrapping his own answer in that, but it is clear that he was not keen on the idea of an increased female presence in the highest echelons of the service.

By 1950, still less than 7 per cent of the administrative class of the Civil Service was female, although it has been suggested that women candidates were now more plentiful but were less successful at the examination.[108] By the 1970s, women's distribution throughout the Civil Service was still pyramid-shaped.[109] From the early 1980s, several studies bemoaned the lack of women in higher-grade posts and the relative lack of opportunities afforded to women in the service and sought explanations as to why this was.[110] However, despite the fact that problems remained and other solutions had to be found elsewhere, the changes in the interwar years were still important, particularly those enacted in the post-Tomlin years. In the Civil Service, segregation was never going to be compatible with equal opportunities as it was, in its very conceptualisation, anathema to disregarding the gender of the worker. Aggregation, of course, needed time: both time for enough women to filter through into executive and administrative grades after realising the examinations were open to them, and time to convince those with decision-making powers of their abilities. Social propriety also dictated – or appeared to dictate – that certain roles needed to be closed to women. Aggregation remained, however, the key to the longer-term promise of equal opportunity. This in many ways was the lesson of the interwar years in terms of equal opportunities in the Civil Service and the LCC: a new platform for organising work and trying to move beyond the gender of the worker was set. The campaigning of the FWCS and CWCS and the increasingly important Whitley Council in the years immediately after the First World War meant that some changes were made in the 1920s. The contention of the Tomlin Commission of 1931 that some roles were being kept unnecessarily closed to women and that aggregation should be adopted also forced some further change. The LCC, although guaranteeing a maximum of 10 per cent of its higher-grade vacancies to women from 1919 – and thus perhaps providing more higher-grade opportunities for women in the 1920s than the Civil Service did in practice – began to move towards facilitating the idea of equal opportunity by the mid-1930s, although again, significant change was slow to come.

Zimmeck has argued for the Civil Service as a whole that 'in the interwar period male civil servants' organisational damage-limitation programme was effective: senior women made few real gains and, it might be argued, their position was appreciably less advantageous than it had been before 1914'.[111] However, it is hard to see this as the case: although numerically there might not have been many women in the higher grades of the service, the eventual adoption of aggregation had laid the ground for a theoretical application of equal opportunity. This was ultimately preferable to segregation, with its inescapable gendering and pigeon-holing of women's work. It is possible to be both pessimistic and optimistic about the changes in the interwar years. In many ways, it was clear in 1939 that there still needed to be a number of shifts in organisational and societal thinking about women workers before real equality could be achieved. As we will see in later chapters, prevalent attitudes remained that women could not – for social and economic reasons – receive equal pay (in the Civil Service if not the LCC), and also that they were rarely serious about careers and would leave as soon as possible in order to get married. These attitudes worked in tandem with the gendering of roles to limit women's progress. On the one hand, then, if, looking back, we expect miracles and dramatic change, the interwar years are disappointing. If we recognise that the fight would be long and that there would be resistance and objections to women in higher positions even when they were theoretically opened after the First World War, then it is clear that some progress was made in the interwar years. It would take several more decades of agitation and another women's movement to bring about something closer to equal opportunity as we think of it today.

Notes

1 BPMA, POST 30/3889C, 'Writing Assistants: Service Conditions', Association of Post Office Women Clerks, Minutes of Evidence given before The Select Committee on Post Office Servants, 1913 (Holt Committee), p.5. As things turned out, there might well have been a 'Lady Postmaster General' before a 'Lady Secretary' given that women were able to become MPs from 1918, but there was never a female Secretary (or later, Director-General) to the GPO.

2 Martindale, *Women Servants of the State*; Zimmeck, 'New Woman' and 'Strategies and Stratagems'; Jones, *Women in British Public Life*, pp.130–160; Richard A. Chapman, *The Civil Service Commission, 1855–1991: A Bureau Biography* (London: Routledge, 2004), p.216; p.220.

3 *Report of the War Cabinet Committee on Women in Industry*, para. 30; LMA, LCC Staff List, 1913–14.

4 Clifton, 'Members and Officers of the LCC', pp.18–19.

5 Celia Davies, 'The Health Visitor as Mother's Friend: A Woman's Place in Public Health, 1900–1914', *Journal of the Social History of Medicine*, vol.1., no.1, (1988), pp.39–59; Jones, *Women in British Public Life*, pp.62–72; Jane Lewis, *Women and Social Action in Late Victorian and Edwardian Britain* (Cheltenham: Edward Elgar, 1991).

6 In particular, see Jones, *Women in British Public Life*, p.16; p.23; p.65; pp.151–158. In addition see Helen Jones, 'Martindale, Hilda (1875–1952)', *Oxford Dictionary of National Biography* (Oxford University Press, 2004) [www.oxforddnb.com/view/article/34912, accessed 28 July 2014]; Mark Pottle, 'Durham, Frances Hermia (1873–1948)', *Oxford Dictionary of National Biography* (Oxford University Press, 2004) [www.oxforddnb.com/view/article/62141, accessed 28 July 2014]; Meta Zimmeck, 'Anderson, Dame Adelaide Mary (1863–1936)', rev. *Oxford Dictionary of National Biography* (Oxford University Press, 2004) [www.oxforddnb.com/view/article/37113, accessed 28 July 2014].

7 Jones, *Women in British Public Life*, p.11; Ruth Livesey, 'The Politics of Work: Feminism, Professionalization and Women Inspectors of Factories and Workshops', *Women's History Review*, vol. 13, no. 2 (2004), pp.233–262.

8 Jones, *Women in British Public Life*, p.11.

9 See, for example, the interesting case of Maria Constance Smith. Meta Zimmeck, 'Smith, Maria Constance (1853–1930)', *Oxford Dictionary of National Biography* (Oxford University Press, 2004), online edn, January 2008 [www.oxforddnb.com/view/article/48846, accessed 24 July 2013].

10 As quoted in Tomlin Commission, *Report*, para. 382.

11 Jones, *Women in British Public Life*, p.15.

12 Martindale, *Women Servants of the State*, pp.77–81.

13 Evans, *Women and the Civil Service*, pp.20–21.

14 TNA, T1/12265, 'Memoranda: Committee on Recruitment of the Civil Service after the War', evidence from Board of Revenue, Ministry of Pensions and National Health Insurance Commission.

15 *Report of the War Cabinet Committee on Women in Industry*, para. 110.

16 POST 115/1149, *Association Notes*, October 1911, p.106.

17 Jones, *Women in British Public Life*; Dyhouse, *No Distinction of Sex?*; Carol Dyhouse, 'Women Students and the London Medical Schools, 1914–1939: The Anatomy of a Masculine Culture', *Gender and History*, vol. 10, issue 1 (1998), pp.110–132; Kaarin Michaelsen, ' "Union is Strength": The Medical Women's Federation and the Politics of Professionalism, 1917–30' in Krista Cowman and Louise Jackson (eds), *Women and Work Culture: Britain c.1850–1950* (Aldershot: Ashgate, 2005); Anne Logan, 'In Search of Equal Citizenship: The Campaign for Women Magistrates in England and Wales, 1910–1939', *Women's History Review*, vol. 16, no. 4 (September 2007), pp.501–518; McCarthy, 'Petticoat Diplomacy'; Carroll Pursell, ' "Am I a Lady or an Engineer?" The Origins of the Women's Engineering Society in Britain, 1918–1940', *Technology and Culture*, vol. 34, no. 1 (January 1993), pp.78–97.

18 Jackson, *Women Police*.

19 Tomlin Commission, Evidence, para. 1159.

20 LMA, LCC minutes, 29 July 1919.

21 Gladstone Committee, *Report*, paras 38–40.

22 LMA, LCC CL/ESTAB/1/8, Female Staff: Positions in Council's Service Open to Women, 'History and Present Position of Women in the Major Establishment' [1941?]; LMA, LCC Establishment Committee Minutes, 10 July 1919.

23 Alan Clinton, 'Ammon, Charles George (1873–1960)', *Oxford Dictionary of National Biography* (Oxford University Press, 2004) [www.oxforddnb.com/view/article/47321, accessed 11 December 2012].

24 Gladstone Committee, *Report*, para. 25.

25 TNA, T1/12265. Sometimes 'evidence' was impressionistic on the one hand and then more considered within a single document. See, for example, the evidence of the War Office and the Ministry of Pensions in this file.

26 Gladstone Committee, *Report*, paras 41–42.

27 T1/12265, file 33, Evidence of Miss F. H. Durham.

28 *Ministry of Reconstruction: Machinery of Government Committee Report* [hereafter 'Haldane Report'] (London: HMSO, 1918), paras 38–40; paras 43–45. Importantly, one member wrote a reservation about these passages of the report, arguing that 'They appear to be based on an assumption which I believe to be fallacious – namely that (for all purposes relevant to the present question) women and men can be employed indiscriminately without loss of efficiency and without increase of cost. Enquiries are being conducted by other Committees into the whole question of the employment of women in the service of Government; and until the results of these enquiries are known any definite conclusions must be premature' (p.80).

29 Ray Strachey, *The Cause* [1928] (London: Virago, 1979), p.376.

30 *Reorganisation Report*, para. 8.

31 For the GPO's reluctance to appoint a woman establishment officer, see BPMA, POST 33/624B, 'Woman Establishment Officer in Post Office: First Appointment', c.1922.

32 Jane Martin, *Women and the Politics of Schooling* (London: Cassell, 1999), p.144. Zimmeck, 'Strategies and Stratagems', p.922.

33 POST 59/169–171, GPO Establishment Books, 1937–1939.

34 Council of Women Civil Servants (Higher Grades), *Higher Appointments Open to Women in the Civil Service*, 3rd edn (P. S. King and Son, Ltd, 1935), pp.8–18.

35 Tomlin Commission, Evidence, paras 15,650–15,750; 15,765; 15,818–15,973; 16,690–16,860; 17,661.

36 Kelsall, *Higher Civil Servants*, p.175.

37 Alix Meynell, *Public Servant, Private Woman* (London: Victor Gollancz, 1988), p.80. Geoffrey Cockerill, 'Smieton, Dame Mary Guillan (1902–2005)', *Oxford Dictionary of National Biography* (Oxford University Press, January 2009), online edn, September 2010 [www.oxforddnb.com/view/article/65554, accessed 21 October 2013].

38 Adrian Bingham, *Gender, Modernity, and the Popular Press in Inter-War Britain* (Oxford: Oxford University Press, 2004), pp.65–66. See *Manchester Guardian*, 'Woman's Appointment to High Civil Service Office', 15 December 1926.

39 Meynell, *Public Servant, Private Woman*, p.87.

40 Tomlin Commission, Evidence, part I, 11–15 November 1929, 'Tables Handed in by the Civil Service Commissioners', Table 1.

41 *Evidence to the Royal Commission on Equal Pay* [1944–1946] 'First Memorandum of Evidence Submitted by HM Treasury: Remuneration of Women in the Crown Services', p.11.

42 Tomlin Commission, Evidence, London and National Society for Women's Service, para. 28.

43 TNA, T162/71/11, Establishment. Seniority: Common Seniority Lists for men and women in the Civil Service; Report of Treasury Committee, 1924 figures.

44 BPMA, Post 33/3213A, File A, statement to Royal Commission, p.1.

45 Percentages calculated from British Library, Council of Women Civil Servants, 'Statement to the Royal Commission on the Civil Service', Appendix C.

46 Jones, *Women in British Public Life*, pp.60–61.

47 Percentages calculated from Council of Women Civil Servants, 'Statement to the Royal Commission on the Civil Service', Appendix C.

48 TNA, T162/323, ESTABLISHMENT. Health Ministry: Inspectorate: Ministry of Health: (1) General Inspectorate (2) Women Inspectorate, Women Inspectors (Poor Law) and Maternity and Child Welfare Inspectors, paras 22–23.

49 For a discussion of how aggregation was worked out, see Council of Women Civil Servants (Higher Grades), *Statement Prepared for the Royal Commission*, para. 177.

50 Council of Women Civil Servants (Higher Grades), *Statement Prepared for the Royal Commission*, Appendix A.

51 Tomlin Commission, Evidence, paras 14,808; 14,820; 15818; 15898, amongst others.

52 For the LCC, see LMA, GLSA//1/37, Minutes of the LCC Staff Association Executive Committee, meeting of 18 July 1938.

53 Tomlin Commission, Evidence, para. 17,914.

54 Officials at the GPO appear to have worked hard to ensure that the statement did not, in their words, 'look so bad'. POST 33/3213A, File B, draft memo.

55 POST 33/729A, Evidence of Murray and Raven, para. 4579; *Report of the War Cabinet Committee on Women in Industry*, Appendix, Evidence of the Federation of Post Office Supervisors etc, p.159.

56 POST 33/3213A, File B, 'Posts de jure reserved to men'.

57 POST 33/729A, Evidence of Murray and Raven, para. 4654.

58 TNA, T162/50, Women in the Civil Service: supplementary memorandum for the Royal Commission, Notes, p.1.

59 Council of Women Civil Servants (Higher Grades), *Statement Prepared for the Royal Commission*, para. 83.

60 LCC/CL/ESTAB/1/6 Royal Commission on Equal Pay (1944), Evidence, 'Memo dated 21 November 1944 from the E C Bligh of the Social Welfare Department, Employment of Women in the Social Welfare Department'.

61 CL/ESTAB/1/6 'Memo dated 21 November 1944 from the E C Bligh of the Social Welfare Department, Employment of Women in the Social Welfare Department'.

62 Tomlin Commission, Evidence, para. 12,518.

63 Tomlin Commission, Evidence, para, 12,519.

64 *Civil Service Argus*, extracts from evidence to the Royal Commission on the Civil Service, March 1931, p.55.

65 Tomlin Commission, Evidence, para. 12,522.

66 Martindale, *Women Servants of the State*, p.127.

67 Tomlin Commission, Evidence, paras 14,934; 14,936.

68 Tomlin Commission, Evidence, paras 14,808–14,824; 14,944–14,947; 15,004.

69 *Royal Commission on the Civil Service*, written evidence of the London & National Society for Women's Service, paras 29–33. In her 1928 book, Vera Brittain also lamented the slow progress in introducing women to the higher ranks of the Civil Service. See Vera Brittain, *Women's Work in Modern England* (London: Noel Douglas, 1928), pp.117–118.

70 TNA, T162/50, Women in the Civil Service: Supplementary Notes for Royal Commission, Notes, p.5.

71 *Royal Commission on the Civil Service*, written evidence of the London & National Society for Women's Service, para. 4. For examples of the type of press coverage the LNSWS may have been referring to, see *Daily Mirror*, 'Woman's Future in the Civil Service. Better Opportunities for the Girl Clerk', 30 July 1919, p.7; *Manchester Guardian*, 'Woman's Appointment to High Civil Service Office', 15 December 1926; *Daily Mirror*, 'Women the "Personality" Sex? They Stand Best Chance in Civil Service Tests', 7 October 1933.

72 Tomlin Commission, Evidence, paras 14,810–14811. Brimelow called for affirmative action as late as 1980, seeing it as the only way to improve the representation of women at those echelons of the service. E. Brimelow, 'Women in the Civil Service', *Public Administration*, vol. LIX (1981), pp.332–333.

73 Written evidence of the London & National Society for Women's Service, para. 7. For an example of this in the late 1970s/early 1980s, see Brimelow, 'Women in the Civil Service', p.325, who actually questioned some of this rhetoric but nonetheless acknowledged that it existed.

74 The LNSWS pointed out in its written evidence that the GPO 'appear[ed] to have made no alteration whatever' in the way that it employed women. Written evidence of the London & National Society for Women's Service, para. 10.

75 POST 33/3213A, evidence of Murray to Tomlin Commission, paras 3941; 4536.

76 POST 33/2951, file VII, Letter from Weeks of the Civil Service Commission to Weightman at the GPO, 18 December 1928.

77 Evidence of Murray to Tomlin Commission, para. 4256.

78 *Report on Women's Question*, paras 3–4. See also T162/762/11, Treasury Circular E.OC.149, 11 March 1935.

79 LCC Staff Association Gazette, March 1925, p.75; April 1925, p.97.

80 LMA, LCC MIN/12730, Minutes of the Joint Committee of Members and Staff, 7 March 1930.

81 *London Town*, May 1930, pp.138–139; LMA, LCC Minutes, 12 March 1935.

82 LMA, GLSA/1/37, Minutes of the LCC Staff Association Executive Committee, 18 July 1938.

83 TNA, T162/450/8, Report of Committee (F.) on Women's Questions. Appointment of Joint Committee to review application of, memorandum of Miss E. M. Whyte, 28 June 1937.

84 T275/266, Committee on Women's Questions, 'Note for the Women's Questions Review Committee' [1939], 'Memo by the Civil Service National Whitley Council Staff Side, 17th April 1939: The Exclusion of Women from the Administrative Class of the Defence Departments'.

85 TNA, T162/494, 3754/012/02, Minutes of first meeting of Review Committee, 1938. For a full discussion of the complexities surrounding women and jury service in this period, see Anne Logan, ' "Building a New and Better Order"? Women and Jury Service in England and Wales, 1920–1970', *Women's History Review*, vol. 22, no. 5 (2013), pp.701–716.

86 POST 59/168, GPO Establishment Book, 1936; Hilda Martindale, Director of Women's Establishments at the Treasury from 1934, reports that the GPO was one of several departments before 1937 where women's opportunities were not what they should have been. Hilda Martindale, *From One Generation to Another, 1839–1944: A Book of Memoirs* (London: George Allen & Unwin, Ltd, 1944), p.196.

87 LCC/CL/ESTAB/1/6, Evidence of Sir Eric Salmon, para. 730.

88 MRC, MSS.148/UCW/3/7/2, Union of Post Office Workers, N.W.C. Equal Pay (1935 Campaign) – Committee Minutes, 'Civil Service National Whitley Council Staff Side, Royal Commission on Equal Pay, 16.3.45, Notes of Evidence given to the Royal Commission on Equal Pay by the London County Council'.

89 LCC/CL/ESTAB/1/6, Letter to Wilma Harte, Assistant Secretary to the Royal Commission from Miss Cooke of the LCC, 4 March 1946.

90 LCC/CL/ESTAB/1/8, 'Why, if women have proved well fitted for administrative jobs in the LCC service, have so few succeeded in attaining to the higher positions?' [1944].

91 *London Town*, Letters to the Editor, May 1930, pp.138–139.

92 LCC/CL/ESTAB/1/8, 'Female staff: Positions in Council's service open to women', Women in Senior Positions. As Richard A. Chapman notes, the Civil Service acted as a 'recruitment agency' for the LCC in this respect, charging a fee for the details of each of the candidates it passed on. Richard A. Chapman, *Leadership in the British Civil Service* (London and Sydney: Croom Helm, 1984), p.92.

93 LMA, LCC/CL/ESTAB/1/6 Royal Commission on Equal Pay (1944), Evidence. Evidence submitted to Royal Commission, 16 March 1945.

94 LMA, 18.3 LCC Staff Examination Papers, 1930–1941.

95 Gibbon and Bell, *History of the London County Council*, p.206.

96 LMA, 18.3 LCC, Staff Examination Papers, 1930–1941.

97 LCC/CL/ESTAB/1/8, 'Why, if women have proved well fitted for administrative jobs in the LCC service, have so few succeeded in attaining to the higher positions?' [1944].

98 *Royal Commission on Equal Pay*, Minutes of Evidence taken before the Royal Commission on Equal Pay [hereafter *Royal Commission on Equal Pay*, Evidence] (London: HMSO, 1945), para. 1550.

99 Kelsall, *Higher Civil Servants*, p.170.

100 Kelsall, *Higher Civil Servants*, p.171.

101 Promotions calculated from Treasury figures in conjunction with examination data. See TNA, T 162/50/23, 'Women in the Civil Service: Supplementary Memorandum for the Royal Commission', 'Employment of Women' table. The figure in the text is approximate because it is not clear whether these were twelve women appointed to twelve separate posts or whether some were appointed and subsequently left for marriage, meaning that replacements had to be employed.

102 Kelsall, *Higher Civil Servants*, p.171.

103 Figures for 1937/1938 and percentage calculated from Carol Dyhouse, *Students: A Gendered History* (Oxford: Routledge, 2006), p.4.

104 Kelsall, *Higher Civil Servants*, pp.171–174.

105 TNA T162/329, 'Introductory Memorandum VIII Relating to the Employment of Women in the Civil Service', Appendix IV, p.43. See also *The Times*, 'Careers for Girls – XII Patent Agents and Examiners at the Patent Office', 15 March 1939 and 'Careers for Girls: XVII: The Civil Service – I', 8 May 1939. The Civil Service at all levels was also promoted in, for example, the Letts School Girls' Diary in the late 1930s where matter-of-fact information was provided about joining the service. I am grateful to Alison Twells for sharing the latter source with me.

106 Tomlin Commission, Evidence, paras 1070; 1076; 1411.

107 *Royal Commission on Equal Pay*, Evidence, para. 1551.

108 Kelsall, *Higher Civil Servants*, p.176.

109 E. M. Kemp-Jones, *The Employment of Women in the Civil Service*, Civil Service Department Management Studies 3 (HMSO: Edinburgh, 1971), Appendix B.

110 See, for example, Brimelow, 'Women in the Civil Service'; Barbara Bagilhole, *Women, Work and Equal Opportunity: Underachievement in the Civil Service* (Aldershot: Ashgate, 1994).

111 Zimmeck, 'New Woman', p.200.

3

'Endless arguments about sex and salaries'[1]: the First World War, reconstruction and the campaigns for equal pay, 1914–24

When war broke out in 1914, campaigns for equal pay had already become prominent in certain parts of the Civil Service, notably among women in the clerical grades and amongst some professional women. The APOWC had declared an equal pay policy in 1908 and carried it to sister associations throughout the Civil Service under the umbrella of the FWCS. As most female employees in the LCC before the war were typists or domestic staff and there were only a handful of women spread across multiple departments who did the same work as men, the pre-war equal pay campaigns tended to be confined to the large number of women teachers employed by the LCC.[2] In the wider climate of the First World War and women taking on "men's jobs" in numerous fields of employment, the lack of vocal, sustained equal pay campaigning in the LCC is, however, striking. In the Civil Service on the other hand, permanent women civil servants continued to press their claims for equal pay, and temporary women civil servants doing men's work for the duration of the war also asked for equal pay. The rhetoric and the experiences of peacetime and then wartime equal pay campaigns continued into the interwar years. Although there were ebbs and flows in the debate, as the next three chapters explore, the issue never disappeared from discourse about the public service.

In employment in general, equal pay for women had been slowly emerging as a discourse from the 1890s across a range of industries and only grew stronger during the First World War because of the employment of women on work conventionally done by men.[3] It will be contended here that the First World War, though it in theory provided an occasion for equalising women's pay with men's, did not have a significant, positive effect on equal pay across the public service as a whole. However, throughout this whole period, there was an extra layer to these debates for those women in the public service who did the same work as men: they were being paid from public funds and the work came with relative prestige. The familiar debate about the state as model employer was highly relevant here and numerous different organisations levelled criticism in its direction for paying female employees less than men. In 1914, for example, Edith Morley, writing for the Fabian Women's Group, argued that

> So far as the position of its women workers is concerned, the State is very far from being the model employer it sometimes professes to be. When one considers the very wide disparity existing between the salaries for similar work of women and of men, one realises to what an enormous extent the Exchequer, and, consequently, the taxpayer, has benefited by the economies practised at the expense of the women Civil Servants ever since their introduction in the early seventies. There is not a shadow of doubt that economy was the motive for their employment, but even economy would not have justified the continued increase in their numbers, had they not exhibited what has been called by a high official, 'remarkable efficiency,' and also the very desirable qualities of docility, patience, and conscientiousness.[4]

This argument reached the heart of many of the early twentieth-century concerns about women's work. Women were being employed in such large numbers transparently because they were cheaper[5] but at the same time, they were manifestly good workers – otherwise another solution for cheap workers would have been found.

Despite the prevalence of debates about equal pay in public – and in some private – employment in this period, historians have yet to reflect on the breadth and depth of the rhetoric. This chapter presents an opportunity to do this. The context of equal pay debates in public employment necessarily has relevance for other sectors of employment which remain under-researched. Campaigns for equal pay in teaching have been explored in the most depth, and indeed the work of Alison Oram in particular provides important context.[6] Historians of the Civil Service, though offering a number of insights on related issues, have not provided detailed accounts or analysis of equal pay campaigns, either as a whole or in individual departments.[7] Keith Grint's article, 'Women and equality: the acquisition of equal pay in the Post Office 1870–1961', is the only piece of research to directly address equal pay issues in the Civil Service in the early twentieth century. However, he rather optimistically asserts that 'by 1920 equal pay had been achieved in particular grades for specific age groups, and this remarkable achievement was extended to almost all women in major grades by 1961' without offering detailed analysis of the relevant records and wider historical context of the war and interwar years.[8] He fails to notice, for example, that the equal pay for young workers was part of a structure of pay which legitimised the idea of the male breadwinner: as we will see, men received higher increments and higher wages than women as they went into their twenties, on the assumption that they would marry and have children to support, and this therefore severely undermined any victory for youths' pay. Harold Smith's work on interwar feminism provides some analysis of the parliamentary campaigns for equal pay and the London and National Society for Women's Service's involvement in these. However, the main focus of his argument was to demonstrate the presence and continuance of British feminism in the period rather than to consider equal pay per se.[9] As we have seen in earlier chapters, there is no substantial historiography of the LCC as an employer and Gloria Clifton's work only briefly touches on issues of gendered pay leading up to the LCC's relatively sudden decision to grant equal pay after the Second World War.[10] This study thus addresses many of the outstanding questions, whilst also providing a significant case study of the nature and evolution of British equal pay campaigns in the interwar years. As the public service represented one of a handful of industries where women and men did the same work, it accounted for much of the interwar discussion of equal pay and the interwar campaigns were formative in generating the experience and momentum for the post-Second World War struggles. This chapter addresses the First World War and the period of reconstruction until 1924, whilst Chapter 4 examines the more intensive campaigns in the years that followed and Chapter 5 discusses the eventual passage of equal pay for women civil servants and LCC staff on most grades.

The Civil Service, the LCC and equal pay campaigns before the First World War

As the first department to employ women, and the department which employed the most women, many of the earliest calls for equal pay in the Civil Service came from the Post Office, especially as many women did work of a similar nature, if not exactly the same type, as men. Though Alan Clinton has claimed the Postal and Telegraph Clerks' Association (P&TCA) as the first GPO organisation to adopt equal pay as a campaign policy in 1910, the APOWC adopted an equal pay stance in 1908.[11] It reasoned as follows:

> When we tell a Committee of the House of Commons, mostly business men, that we have to a large extent been doing the work of male clerks who go forward to a maximum of £250, and that therefore we ask for

only £150, they naturally think we have not the courage of our convictions. But in future we trust the Association Committee will not have to tie itself to such weak arguments. We want to say instead: 'If we do the same work as, or work equal in value to, that of a male clerk, we claim the same pay'.[12]

Significantly, the issue of Post Office women's pay was brought up in 1910 during a debate about equalising the franchise, the most prominent women's issue of the day. Edward Goulding, a Conservative MP, remarked that:

In the Post Office you have male and female sorters. No matter how ingenious you may be, you cannot make much difference in the work of sorting letters. What is the treatment meted out by the Government to the men and women who do this work? The male sorters … start at a weekly wage of 20s., going up to 60s. a week, and the female sorters start at 14s. a week, with a maximum of 30s. a week. The treatment of the clerks, male and female, in the Post Office, is exactly the same … There is no distinction in the work they do, yet what happens? The male clerk starts at a minimum of £70 a year, with a possible maximum of £250 a year, while the female clerk starts with a minimum of £65 a year, and goes to a maximum of £110 a year. Does anyone for one moment contend that if women in the past had had votes … female employés in either one class or the other would have been left in the disparaging position in which they are to-day?[13]

In the same year as this debate, the Civil Service (Women) Bill was introduced into the House of Commons by Sir Charles McClaren with the aim of giving women equal entry conditions and pay with men. Philip Snowden introduced the bill a second time but it failed to get beyond the second reading.[14] Around the same time, a group of Post Office women clerks in the Savings Bank Department (SBD) applied for equal pay with men because they were doing the same work. In response, SBD officials pointedly moved the women to different work so there was no longer a basis for their claim, but this also revealed that the demarcation between men's and women's work was artificial.[15] By contrast, however, there was soon emerging evidence that some Civil Service departments were coming around to the idea of equal pay, or were at least not seeing the justifications for sex-differentiated pay. Mona Wilson, when appointed as a National Health Insurance Commissioner, was paid at the same rate as her male colleagues, and stands as one of several examples of differentiations not being made for women in professional posts.[16] Furthermore, as Miss Cale of the FWCS remarked, when giving evidence to the Holt Committee on Post Office Servants in 1913, women clerks in the unemployment insurance service and labour exchanges at the Board of Trade were also paid the same as their male counterparts, seemingly anomalously in the service as a whole.[17]

However, when asked by the Holt Committee whether female Post Office servants doing the same amount of work, and work of equal value, as men should receive equal pay, Alexander King, Secretary of the Post Office, disagreed. This was one of the first public denials of women's right for equal pay amongst Civil Service officials and it was symptomatic of the type of reasoning that would be offered. He argued 'I do not think so. It would be too expensive'. He clarified this further: 'Even assuming that she does the same amount of work, the expenses connected with the female staff are greater than with the male staff. There is more sick leave; you cannot put them on overtime in times of pressure and the accommodation has to be special and pro-vided at great expense.'[18] Sick leave and the reported extra costs were used throughout the interwar years as justifications for women's lower pay. Though he had admitted that women did the same work as men, King also suggested that if women clerks' work were transferred to men, it would be given to assistant clerks rather than clerks, presumably in order to justify the lower pay. When questioned by another member of the Committee, King argued that women clerks ought to be paid rela-tive to women in outside employment, but was not able to deny that the GPO profited from the fact that women were paid at a lower rate.[19] The relativity with outside employment was one of the recurring themes in official discourse refusing equal pay throughout the interwar years. At varying times, officials oscillated between comparing women's work to men's on the same grade and comparing it to women's work in out-side employment. Therefore the point of comparison moved to suit the circumstances.

Equal pay was one of a wide range of issues discussed by the 1912–14 MacDonnell Royal Commission on the Civil Service. King was asked specifically to comment on the issue as his was the department with the greatest experience of women's employment. In his evidence, he once again stressed that women's greater sick leave was not a specific reason for their lesser pay, but that it would prevent them from being paid the same rates as men. This was typical of Civil Service rhetoric: on the one hand, a specific issue was not the reason women did not receive equal treatment, but in a hypothetical situation, it could be. To continue covering all even-tualities, King also felt that women's sick leave was unlikely to decrease if they were paid the same as men, though he of course could not have had any evidence for this.[20]

The MacDonnell Commissioners were divided over equal pay. The Majority Report recommended ambiguously that 'so far as the character and conditions of the work performed by women … approximate to identity' with men's, their pay 'should be approximate to equality with that of men'. The Majority had, however, received evidence which apparently indicated that women were less efficient – the first of many public instances of alleged female inefficiency in this period. These alleged differences were deemed to warrant the continuance of higher salaries for men, but it was argued that differences in men's and women's salaries not based on disparities in efficiency should be removed. The problem, of course, would be definitively defining which disparities were based on efficiency and which were not, and this alone gave Treasury officials ample leeway. To make matters more complicated, there was a split among the Majority signatories into a majority and a minority. The minority argued that women should be paid less than men when the two were 'in similar situations' on account of evidence from outside employment where men earned more than women and men's productivity was higher than women's, though no thought appears to have been given to the fact that men's better pay might have assisted their greater productivity. Finally, it was argued that '[t]o make the rates for men and women equal, in disregard of economic considerations, would ultimately have the effect of impeding or precluding the employment of women in the Public Service. It would be found less costly in the long run to employ men'.[21] In this scenario, women were there by grace of their cheaper salaries: their chief value to the state as employees was their relative inexpensiveness. This was neither the first nor last projection of the consequences of introducing equal pay. In the years to come, commentators would argue both ways – that equal pay would lead to the sole employment of men, or that it would create the sole employment of women. Either way, such hypothetical ideas were scaremongering, and identified as such by Miss Cale of the APOWC.[22]

The main Minority Report of the MacDonnell Commission contained similar vague rhetoric regarding men's and women's pay. It stated that 'we think that the answer to the riddle will best be found by leaving it to the play of circumstance rather than by attempting to define a dogma with precision'. However, the signatories again relied on evidence suggesting that women's output was lower than men's and that, as work was paid on a time basis, women should be paid less, which was, they suggested, 'not necessarily a violation of equal remuneration for men and women'. Significantly, the signatories seemed to concede that making judgements about the work of a grade on which large numbers were employed was difficult: '[w]hat acceptance of the principle comes to seems really to be this, that for single situations, where the quality and quantity of the work can be measured with accuracy, the salary should be the same for a woman as for a man; but that for situations grouped in large classes the salaries, when women are employed in them, should be somewhat lower than if the staff were male. Understood in this sense we accept the principle [of equal pay].'[23] Effectively, in cases involving small numbers where unequal pay would be obviously unfair, equal remuneration was permitted; where the numbers of women were larger, women were assumed to be less efficient until they could prove otherwise. It was this type of logic which allowed women like Mona Wilson and many Civil Service doctors, with British Medical Association (BMA) pressure, to be paid the same as men.[24] The conclusions of the MacDonnell Commission were never acted upon because of the outbreak of war, but in fact many in government, Parliament and the upper levels of the Civil Service shared the Commission's lacklustre commitment to equal pay, and many others still remained definitively opposed. In the LCC, assistant medical staff were paid equally regardless of sex – mirroring most Civil Service practice and BMA directives – as were assistant education inspectors. Interestingly in each case their superiors were paid along gendered lines.[25] In addition, when Philippa Fawcett was appointed as principal assistant in the Education department in 1905 she was paid the same as her male colleagues.[26] Equal pay did exist, then, in mostly very isolated cases but there were, as a whole, far fewer instances of women doing the same work as men compared to the Civil Service. The LCC staff association was also very new and not particularly politicised[27] meaning that campaigning was far less likely.

The First World War and equal pay

There was much debate about women's wages during the war, especially for those who were replacing men who had volunteered or were later conscripted. The Defence of the Realm Act allowed for replacement labour to be paid 'the rate for the job' so as to guarantee wages for men returning from the front, but it was rarely expressed officially as 'equal pay'.[28] However, the definition of 'replacement labour' often became caught up with the practices of substitution and dilution and the distinction between the two complicated this, as Deborah Thom has shown.[29] In practice, few women in the First World War received equal pay for doing men's work.[30] Most prominently, women transport workers outside of the LCC went on strike for equal war bonus with the men they were replacing. There were also prominent campaigns amongst women munitions workers, employed to do much-publicised and dangerous work, for equal pay.[31] Equal pay issues remained profoundly frustrating for female public servants employed both permanently and temporarily, and the attitudes of the public service hierarchy revealed fears of the implications of granting equal pay for even temporary work.

Representatives of the 3,000 or so women clerks employed permanently across the Civil Service continued their longer-term campaign for equal pay, and were repeatedly denied this on the grounds of the effect that this would have on the general policy of equal pay for the service as a whole.[32] For women in temporary posts, the story was a similar one of frustration: ultimately the Civil Service would not concede the principle of equal pay to temporary women in case it set a precedent which could be used by its permanent staff. As explained in Chapter 1, the employment of women on mail delivery duties was evidently not classed as new in the First World War: postwomen had been employed in the provinces before the war to meet labour shortages. The Postmen's Federation (PF) argued for equal pay for postmen and temporary postwomen because of the wartime emergency, citing the equal rates paid to women transport and munitions workers in support of their argument. In reply, the GPO simply stated that it could not consider the claim for equality. The PF was also denied recourse through the Civil Service Conciliation and Arbitration Board (CAB), which argued that equal pay was outside its remit and that it had always been Civil Service principle to 'pay a lower wage to women than to men' – although as earlier examples in this chapter show, this was not strictly true. This encapsulated the tone for the rest of the war. In the case of postwomen, not only did their lesser physical strength apparently undermine equal pay arguments, the supposition that all temporary postwomen were single and that all postmen were married with families was used to suggest that equal pay would constitute an unfair distribution of wages. This was not a new argument but would become all too familiar in the interwar years. The GPO went even further, suggesting that if single women had the men's wage to themselves, not only would they have a higher standard of living, a higher class women might be attracted to the work which would 'only result in discontent and friction' between the men and women.[33] The result of the claim for London mail delivery staff was 47s. or 45s. for postmen, depending on the division in which they served, and a flat rate of 37s. for temporary postwomen.[34] This constituted a significant difference between men's and women's rates and no recognition of the principle that women were substituting for men during the national emergency. Liftwomen in government offices also campaigned for equal pay with men in 1918 and threatened to strike if their demand was not met. Their demand was taken to the CAB by the National Federation of Women Workers and, as previously, the board ruled that equal pay was a matter of employment policy and could not be conceded.[35]

The wartime culture surrounding equal pay was markedly different in the LCC. The LCC Staff Association campaigned only on urgent issues during the war and clearly did not consider equal pay as significant enough.[36] It also recorded an agreement in March 1915, on the Clerk of the Council's suggestion, that officers who took on higher duties for the period of the war should not be paid extra for them.[37] This "goodwill agreement" presumably covered permanent women staff taking on duties formerly done by men and by implication temporary women as well. The LCC Staff Association was certainly less political than its equivalents in the Civil Service who would not have entertained making such an agreement, even if their campaigns for equal pay were fruitless. Thus, the majority of women taking on men's work temporarily in the LCC were paid less than men: there was an agreed range of rates for temporary women assistants, related to age and experience, which had to be amended as it became clear that the wages were not sufficient enough to attract women.[38] Young employees under the age of 21 tended, like their Civil Service counterparts, to be paid the same rates regardless of sex.[39] The exception to this general practice appears to have been women undertaking roles in transportation as drivers or conductors: in November 1915, women tram car conductors were paid for their work at the male rate, pro rata, and when women ambulance drivers were hired in February 1916, they were paid the male rate of 38s. per week with a bonus of £5 for each complete six-month period worked. This was also a distinctive form of temporary work in the sense that all male ambulance drivers were ordinarily employed temporarily.[40] In contrast, at the same time as women conductors were given equal pay, female mechanics were given their own scale of pay for unskilled work.[41]

Gender distinctions remained for rates of war bonus in both the LCC and the Civil Service – as Deborah Thom has noted for other types of women's war work – and this highlighted several facets of the equal pay debate.[42] By definition, war bonus was paid to employees to help them meet new costs created by wartime inflation, and these new expenses were clearly not differentiated by gender. However, the Treasury and the CAB insisted on maintaining a distinction between men and women for the Civil Service war bonus. The FWCS labelled this publicly as 'slovenly and muddle-headed thinking', their criticism of the Treasury and CAB plain.[43] Such distinction would continue in peacetime with the cost of living bonus and was encapsulated in the assumption that women employees never had dependents.[44] The LCC's war bonus scheme was even more differentiated. In the first iteration, men over 21 regardless of marital status received the highest amount, which was also paid to younger men if they were married. For single men under 21 and all women, a smaller amount was paid. By July 1915, the scheme was updated and nuanced for men only, with an additional grant according to marital status and the number of dependents paid on top of the existing war bonus derived from the original criteria.[45] In a number of ways this mirrored discourses about the state providing increased economic support for dependents, which was gaining currency throughout the war through the government's separation allowance scheme and the creation of the Family Endowment Committee in 1917.[46] However, the LCC's scheme, like so many others, failed to recognise that women might have dependents themselves regardless of their marital status. Women's bonus remained at the lowest rate throughout the war, regardless of age, marital status or existence of dependents.[47] For women employed temporarily, as for temporary men, the bonus did not apply at all as their rate of pay was calculated with inflation taken into account. Whilst war bonus for permanent men was attempted with some subtlety in mind, women's was much more crudely designed and clearly upheld the idea of the male breadwinner.

Reconstruction and the equal pay debate

Whilst Harold Smith's assessment that '[i]n the immediate post war years good reason existed to believe that female public employees would prove successful in their effort to obtain equal pay'[48] is perhaps overly optimistic, there were some endorsements of the policy. The majority report of the War Cabinet Committee on Industry[49] argued that manipulative grades in the Civil Service – for example, the telephonists and telegraphists in the GPO, who clearly did the same work as men – should be granted equal pay, with extra allowances paid for employees performing night duty.[50] This was an early solution to the problem of the manipulative grades and the fact that men did nightwork and women did not, but it was not taken forward.[51] By contrast, the Gladstone Committee – clearly not in favour of making any improvements to women's position – warned that, if pay were equalised, there would be no guarantee that women's wages would be raised to men's; instead, men's might be lowered to the level of women's.[52]

When women were allowed to take the minor establishment competitive examinations from 1919 in the LCC, they were awarded five-sixths of the men's scale, which, as we will see, roughly mirrored the distinctions between men's and women's pay in current Civil Service grades. This seems to have been a clear example of Civil Service and LCC employment policymakers looking to one another. The Staff Association protested against the inequality in pay on the grounds that the Council had clearly not employed six women to do the jobs previously carried out by five men, but such representations were to no avail.[53] However, a month later, women were also permitted to compete for second division clerkships in the major establishment of the LCC, sitting the same examination and receiving the same salary as men.[54] Although the *LCC Staff Gazette* described the 1919 decision as a 'landmark' moment,[55] it is interesting that far less fanfare was made than would likely have been had the same policy been passed in the Civil Service. Enthusiasm may well have been tempered by the fact that women were limited to 10 per cent of the vacancies and were thus regarded as an experiment. With the continued differentiation in war bonus, they were also not in practical terms receiving equal pay.[56] In later years, Council officials admitted to reversing some of the implied logic of parts of the 1912–14 MacDonnell Commission's recommendations for the Civil Service with regard to women in more professional and technical roles:

> There had ... been too little experience of their work in this capacity to form any judgment on its relative quality, and the quantitative measure was not in any case possible of application. It was decided therefore to make no differentiation in rate at the outset. Nothing has occurred since to suggest any need for revising this decision, and its analogy has been followed in dealing with women in professional and technical grades not lending themselves to quantitative measure of work.[57]

As such work could not be quantified, women were given the benefit of the doubt initially and no reason was found to change this. Such opinions would have rankled with women civil servants and other female LCC employees who were deemed to not be capable of the same work as men and were not given such benefit of the doubt. In January 1920, 'Minimus' spoke out in a letter to the *LCC Staff Gazette* asking '[f]inally, what of the women members, who are justly indignant that, whilst their rate of pay is only five-sixths of that of their male colleagues, the Council intends to pay men and women in the second class equally. Is this fair to them?'[58] At around the same time the LCC Staff Association adopted an equal pay policy, though – beyond periodic requests to the Council for adoption of equal pay – their campaigning was relatively sedate.

However, the fact that equal pay was granted, albeit to small numbers of women, meant that the battle for equal pay in the LCC was in theory partially won without members of staff really having started the war. The contrast with the Civil Service could not have been starker, particularly in light of the forthcoming changes to Civil Service pay, discussed below, and the continuing fight for equal pay into the interwar years and beyond. Two questions immediately emerge in terms of why women in the highest echelons of the LCC were granted equal pay. Though the LCC's rationale seems honest and might be taken at face value, it is significant that Council members felt confident enough to sanction the principle of equal pay for these grades when they must have known it was being so obstinately resisted in the Civil Service. In turn, it also begs the question of why the same logic quoted above was not applied to other grades in the LCC. Was it a question of numbers and not wanting to open the floodgates, and perhaps feeling they could not diverge too far from Civil Service practice? Was it that women in professional work were often paid at the same rates as men,[59] and many of the administrative positions in the LCC were also akin to professional work? There ended up emerging a hierarchy based on class, though it is not clear that this was ostensibly originally about class.

In contrast to the situation in the administrative grades was the fact that in August of the same year, women teachers in the LCC, following a long, public campaign, were refused equal pay. In early 1918, the London Teachers' Association had asked the LCC to investigate the possibility of equal pay plus dependents' allowances for male and female teachers, in a mirroring of recent wider debates.[60] The rejection of equal pay was in large part, no doubt, because the Burnham Committee had been convened to agree national scales for teaching,[61] but the reactions among the staff, the press and other commentators are significant. The *LCC Staff Association Gazette* reported the official reason given for the decision, by which it appeared to be less than convinced:

> It is interesting to note that the Council has not seen its way to accede to the exceedingly vocal demand of the women teachers for 'equal pay for equal work'. To have agreed to this principle would have had the effect, it is considered, of making teaching wholly a woman's profession, with a probable adverse effect upon the national character.[62]

This was symptomatic of fears that equalisation of pay would mean complete feminisation of a type of work. *The Times*, perhaps not surprisingly, weighed in in support of the LCC's justification for its decision, drawing on the discourse of fears of the feminisation of teaching:

> It is not clear that the work of men and women in education is 'equal'. Much depends on the age of the children and the conditions of work. But, assuming equality, what will be the effect on salaries all round, and what will be the effect of the new standard of salary on the inclination of men to join the teaching service? In our view, equality of pay in the long run means, if not a fall in salaries, a check in the rise which, under the 'unequal' system, now seems likely to continue. Otherwise, by the logic of facts, if not words, the best men will avoid the profession. A national system of education controlled by women would not be good.[63]

Whereas *The Times* feared that 'the best men' would withdraw themselves from a "feminised" profession, the argument could also be made in terms of men being undercut. The Fabian Women's Group argued in 1914 that unequal pay might lead men to be excluded from the profession as women would be cheaper to employ. Thus, '[o]nly when there is equality of pay can there be security that the best candidate will be appointed, irrespective of sex'.[64] The campaign for equal pay for women teachers continued nationwide and intersected at various points with the campaign for equal pay for women in the public service.[65]

The Civil Service and the early battles for equal pay

The introduction of Whitleyism in the Civil Service after the First World War might have given hope to some that equal pay would consequently be more forthcoming, but such hopes were dashed with repeated assertions that the Whitley Council would not be permitted to discuss such a significant matter of policy.[66] The Whitley Committee Report on the Reorganisation of the Civil Service, published in February 1920, decreed for the main grades of the Civil Service that starting pay and increments up to age twenty-two should be the same, whereafter there would be a differentiation.[67] The maxima of women's scales were either three-quarters or four-fifths of those of men, and men would receive larger annual increments. Pay for women on the GPO manipulative grades – including telegraphists, telephonists and post office counter staff – followed the same formula of no differentiation up to a certain age, but there were no guidelines for calculating the differentials between men's and women's pay thereafter and so in practice the gap between men's and women's pay tended to be bigger than for the clerical grades.[68] The equal starting pay is what Grint has seen as the major breakthrough, though it actually proved to be anything but.[69] Whilst the increased rates for women were undoubtedly welcomed, the rationale for its existence was based on gendered assumptions about lifestyle and responsibilities which also ensured that equal pay would not be granted further up the scale.[70] As Oram has noted for the Burnham scheme for teachers, '[o]nce the 4:5 ratio had been established it was difficult to effect any change later' and this would also prove to be the case for women public servants more widely.[71] Moreover, the convergence of Burnham, the LCC's actions for the minor establishment and the Civil Service reconstruction was no accident. Though these three were separate bodies, they were operating in the same culture of attitudes to equal pay. More immediately and prosaically, the discussions of each of the three committees were publicly available and therefore served as a means to inform, inspire or bolster support for particular ways of thinking.

In settling the question of the relative levels of men's and women's pay, these decrees also meant that the previous, idiosyncratic instances of equal pay in the Civil Service had to be gradually undone. This brought with it new complications which had significant implications for promotions. In 1920, for example, the Ministry of Labour discussed the various more senior grades in which women were hitherto paid the same as men and how they would handle the question of seniority henceforth. Some Ministry officials appeared to recognise that differentials in pay coupled with a new grading structure would mean that women were effectively losing twice: not only were they now paid less, they would also be placed on grades less senior to men in part because of their lower pay.[72]

The majority of mixed-sex Civil Service staff associations and unions declared equal pay policies by the early 1920s in response to the reorganisation of the grading structures. All of these unions or associations were majority male membership. Few unions adopted the policies purely because they supported women's equality but rather from a desire to protect men's wages and jobs and they varied in their active commitment to the issue.[73] For example, the Civil Service Clerical Association began representing women (in addition to men) after the reorganisation and it swiftly adopted an equal pay policy. Its tens of thousands of members across the service meant that it was a prominent feature in staff side Whitley Council discussions.[74] Similarly, the UPW was the largest union in the Civil Service and was therefore much more influential than its name might suggest in staff politics in the service. It had the largest number of seats on the central Whitley Council and even though the telephonists, mail delivery, counter staff and telegraphists it represented were not on the central Civil Service grades and therefore even further from earning equal pay, it took a prominent part in all of the debates about women's pay. Its discussions in the early 1920s were also symptomatic of the issues that mixed-sex unions found themselves grappling with. The UPW adopted an equal pay policy when it was formed in 1919 from the amalgamation of several associations.[75] However, the reasoning behind this policy was often more about protecting men's position – ensuring that women did not undercut them and become first choice as employees – than about equality. Rarely did male members – either executive or from the mass membership – appear to accept the justice of the argument that women themselves had a right to earn the same money as men for the same work. Adding to these debates were the complexities of nightwork and the repeated assertion that male employees always had dependents and female employees never did. In the event, the UPW repeatedly compromised in its wage negotiations throughout this period. It often agreed to push for something less than equal pay for women members, sometimes because it was considered "too early" to demand equal pay, and often because the executive feared that a claim for equal pay would delay other aspects of a wage claim.

One of the UPW's earliest wage claims, to secure wages with 1914 spending power, exemplified this problem. A discussion ensued amongst the executive committee over what to do about equal pay. Mary Herring, the most outspokenly feminist of the female UPW executive members, argued that the executive 'ought not to give any indication that they were prepared to accept anything less for work done by women when it was admitted that it was as valuable as that done by men'. Drawing perhaps on the zeitgeist of the post-war women's enfranchisement or the climate of Civil Service reforms Mabel Bray, an executive committee member, stated that if now was not the right time to raise the issue of equal pay, there might never be a right time. Her colleague Mr Middleton drew on the single versus family wage discourse which permeated the interwar period, and questioned the wisdom of asking for equal pay for single women – presumed to be without dependents – whilst men – presumed to always have dependents – supported families. He added that if the union were to make more modest claims for salary improvement they might have a greater chance of success, and the larger the proposed reform, the longer it would take to settle with the GPO and the Treasury. In the end, the debate came down to the difference between pragmatism and principle. Herring expressed her fears that by confining their request to an extra 10s. a week for women 'they were again letting the women down by admitting the principle of inequality of pay. The women would be up in arms against that'. Eventually, a motion to include equal pay was lost by sixteen votes to ten, one of the closer margins in UPW votes of the period, and the claim was submitted without reference to equal pay.[76] In 1923, the issue was removed from the UPW wage claim principally because of the delay it might cause, but minutes reveal that it was the idea of the family wage which was again a stumbling block.[77] Similar attitudes emerged in the UPW executive's discussion of the Reorganisation Report in early 1920. One executive member argued that men should receive a bigger allowance once they married; another argued that single women should be paid at the same rate as men so that they did not become the more attractive employees on financial grounds. The two positions were clearly irreconcilable and such divisions would permeate the interwar period.[78]

Around the same time as the publication of the Reorganisation Report, the House of Commons declared its support for equal pay for women in the Civil Service. The Commons, as we have seen in previous chapters, had a number of MPs who were sympathetic to women's and feminist aims and the immediate post-franchise years saw greater discussion of women's issues in Parliament than was the case before women were granted the right to vote.[79] A resolution, passed on 19 May 1920, called for equal pay for women civil servants. However, the government refused to accept the resolution.[80] A year and a half later, in August 1921, the series of resolutions regarding the Civil Service was passed and the final resolution promised a review of equal pay within three years.[81] This resolution seemed more promising to the FWCS, since the government did not reject it, and it occurred in the context of other resolutions which seemed to confirm the promise of much for women in the Civil Service and are outlined in other chapters.[82] The FWCS noted that 'to press the claim for equal pay at that moment might imperil the whole Resolution and lose for us the opportunity of really valuable gains on other points'.[83] Walter Baker, Assistant General Secretary of the UPW, greeted the resolution with similar optimism, arguing that 'the reaffirmation of the principle, even though its application will be postponed for three years, has made it inconceivable that any future government will dare to recede from that promise'.[84]

This optimism amongst civil servants proved to be misplaced. As the three years after the House of Commons resolution elapsed, it became clear that equal pay was nowhere in sight. In 1923, the Committee on the Pay etc. of Civil Servants, chaired by Alan Garrett Anderson[85] ruled against equal pay for men and women on three grounds. First, it was noted that market forces should be allowed to operate: 'the employer should offer women what is necessary to recruit the type he needs and to keep his service healthy and efficient.'[86] The committee members also argued that women were less valuable to their employers in their younger years because of the "risk" that they might marry, and that as women's capabilities for the same work had not yet been proven, women's pay should remain lower than men's until adequate proof had been ascertained.[87] This was typical of official and government responses to the equal pay throughout the interwar years, especially the hiding behind the idea that proof was needed that women could work as effectively as men before they could be paid equally. Garrett Anderson's second point was also a further instance of Civil Service policies for women having a knock-on effect on each other and working to compound women's circumstances: there was of course a very real "risk" of women leaving for marriage when there was a marriage bar in place across the service. The CSCA labelled this conclusion 'unmitigated nonsense'[88] and, in addition to hosting a protest meeting about the whole report, satirically addressed Garrett Anderson via a re-writing of the nursery rhyme 'Sing a song of sixpence':

> Sing a song of women,
> Equal work and pay.
> What a funny sentiment
> To express to-day!
> 'women sometimes marry,
> Therefore pay them less.'
> Isn't that an argument
> To lighten their distress?[89]

By 1924, when the three-year time period promised by the government for an equal pay review was over, staff associations in the Civil Service and their external supporters turned their attention with renewed vigour to a new phase in the equal pay campaigns. This is explored in the next chapter. Although few women in either the LCC or the Civil Service received equal pay before or during the war, the wider wartime social debates about women's rights to equal pay and the importance of paying the rate for the job had helped to keep the issue in the public eye. As this chapter has explored, the period of post-war reconstruction in both organisations in 1919–20 was seen as a potential opportunity for change in women's public service employment. The substantial change in terms of salaries was a measure of equal pay for women in the LCC; the wider question for the following period was why this measure of equal pay did not translate into broader and stronger campaigns on the issue in the

LCC. Women civil servants, on the other hand, were aware by 1924 that they were just as far from equal pay as they had ever been. However, the broad, recurring arguments for and against equal pay were set and so in this sense the rhetoric of the debate was well-established. As a result of the restructuring, considerable numbers of women public servants now had the same or similar entrance conditions as men, did work of equivalent skill levels, if not exactly the same tasks, and their increased numbers made them both conspicuous and somewhat easier to unionise. These factors left them in a stronger position compared to many other women workers to campaign for equal pay.[90]

Notes

1 *The Times*, 'Sex and Salaries', 16 July 1919, p.13.

2 For a full discussion of this, see Copelman, *London's Women Teachers*, p.229 and Oram, *Women Teachers*, pp.124–129.

3 Boston, *Women Workers and the Trade Unions*, p.41; Millicent G. Fawcett, 'Equal Pay for Equal Work', *The Economic Journal*, vol. 28, no. 109 (March 1918), pp.1–6; F. Y. Edgeworth, 'Equal Pay to Men and Women for Equal Work', *The Economic Journal*, vol. 32, no. 128 (December 1922), pp.431–457; Eleanor Rathbone, 'The Remuneration of Women's Services', *The Economic Journal*, vol. 27, no. 105 (March 1917), pp.55–68; Beatrice Webb, *The Wages of Men and Women: Should They Be Equal?* (London: Fabian Society, 1919).

4 Edith Morley (ed.), *Women Workers in Seven Professions* (London: Fabian Society, 1914), pp.260–261.

5 For a discussion of the pre-1914 employment of women in the Civil Service on the grounds that they were cheaper to employ, see Zimmeck, 'Jobs for the Girls'; Holcombe, *Victorian Ladies at Work*, pp.174–175; Jordan, *The Women's Movement and Women's Employment*, pp.181–182.

6 Oram, *Women Teachers, passim*.

7 Clinton, *Post Office Workers, passim*; Zimmeck, 'Marry in Haste', p.74; Jones, *Women in British Public Life*, p.155; Martindale, *Women Servants of the State*, pp.158–175.

8 Grint, 'Women and Equality', p.88.

9 Harold L. Smith, 'British Feminism and the Equal Pay Issue in the 1930s', *Women's History Review*, vol. 5, no. 1 (1996), pp.97–110.

10 Gloria Clifton, 'Members and Officers of the LCC', p.20.

11 The policy was adopted formally at the committee meeting of 21 May 1908. See history of equal pay campaigns in Women's Library, 6NCS, box FL435, NAWCS [sic] equal pay, 1929 General Election, 'Equal Pay'. Alan Clinton, *Post Office Workers*, p.8.

12 As quoted in BPMA, POST 92/1137, *St Martin's-Le-Grand*, July 1908, p.319.

13 *Hansard*, Parliamentary Franchise (Women) Bill, HC Deb 11 July 1910 vol. 19 c.127.

14 *Hansard*, Bills Presented, HC Deb 14 March 1910, vol. 15 cc37-8; Civil Service (Women) Bill, HC Deb, 3 April 1911, vol. 23, cc.1814-5. See also Women's Library,

6NCS, Box Number FL435, NAWCS Equal Pay Campaign, 1929 General election, booklet produced by Federation of Women Civil Servants entitled 'Equal Pay'.

15 Zimmeck, 'Marry in Haste', p.79. See also Alexander King's evidence to the MacDonnell Commission, POST 33/729A, 'Royal Commission on Civil Service: Evidence of Secretary to Post Office', paras 31,473–31,474

16 Elaine Harrison, 'Wilson, Mona (1872–1954)', *Oxford Dictionary of National Biography* (Oxford University Press, 2004), online edn, January 2008 [www.oxforddnb.com/view/article/70137, accessed 13 December 2011]. See also Tomlin Commission, *Report*, para. 444.

17 BPMA, POST 33/729A, Holt Committee, evidence of Miss Cale, p.17. See also the *Report of the War Cabinet Committee on Women in Industry*, para. 76.

18 Holt Committee, evidence of Alexander King.

19 Holt Committee, evidence of Alexander King, p.29.

20 POST 33/729A, Evidence of Sir Alexander King, paras 31,263; 31,394; 31,453; paras. 31,458–31,461.

21 As quoted in Tomlin Commission, *Report*, para. 444.

22 Holt Committee, evidence of Miss Cale, p.19.

23 As quoted in Tomlin Commission, *Report*, para. 445.

24 For more on the pay of female medical assistants, see Wellcome Library, SA/MWF/D/1, 'Payment of Medical Women under the Post Office, 1919–1930' and *Hansard*, Salary Scales (Medical Officers), HC Deb 27 July 1936 vol. 315 c1097.

25 *Report of the War Cabinet Committee on Women in Industry*, para. 77.

26 Rita McWilliams Tullberg, 'Fawcett, Philippa Garrett (1868–1948)', *Oxford Dictionary of National Biography* (Oxford University Press, 2004) [www.oxforddnb.com/view/article/39169, accessed 1 August 2014].

27 Clifton, 'Members and Officers of the LCC', p.13.

28 Pugh, *Women and the Women's Movement*, p.27.

29 Thom, *Nice Girls and Rude Girls*, pp.43–44; p.54; p.60.

30 Thom, *Nice Girls and Rude Girls*, p.44; p.150. See also Braybon and Summerfield, *Out of the Cage*, p.50.

31 Thom, *Nice Girls and Rude Girls*, pp.43–44.

32 TNA, T1/12223, correspondence from FWCS to Treasury, 17 November 1917 and from GPO to Treasury, 21 January 1918, and T1/12545, correspondence between the Conciliation and Arbitration Board and the Treasury, 9 March 1918 and correspondence between the Conciliation and Arbitration Board and the FWCS, 26 March 1918.

33 BPMA, POST 60/154, 'Arbitration Proceedings re pay of temporary postmen and postwomen', undated document [probably late 1918] 'Reply to the further claim of the Postmen's Federation on behalf of temporary postmen and postwomen'.

34 BPMA, POST 60/38, Civil Service Arbitration Board: Awards and Agreements vol. 1, 1 May 1917 to 1 August 1919, Award No. 46, 31 May 1918, Temporary Postmen and Postwomen (London).

35 *The Times*, 'Liftwomen's Grievances: Official Delay', 12 September 1918, p.3.

36 LMA, GLSA/1/65, LCC Staff Association Annual General Meetings and Reports, 17 July 1919.

37 *London County Council Staff Gazette*, 'Notes of the Month', March 1915, p.31.
38 LMA, LCC Minutes, 16 February 1915; 29 June 1915; 30 July 1918; 12 October 1918.
39 LCC Minutes, 12 July 1915; 13 October 1915.
40 LCC Minutes, 23 November 1915; 8 February 1916.
41 LCC Minutes, 23 November 1915.
42 Thom, *Nice Girls and Rude Girls*, p.44. See also Braybon and Summerfield, *Out of the Cage*, p.50.
43 POST 115/1152, Federation of Women Civil Servants, *Association Notes*, April 1917, p.153.
44 This was refuted on many occasions, as will be discussed in further detail in Chapter 4. For similar discussions involving women teachers, see Oram, *Women Teachers*, pp.64–67.
45 *LCC Staff Association Gazette*, July 1915, p.110; March 1918, p.36.
46 Susan Pedersen, 'Gender, Welfare and Citizenship in Britain during the Great War', *The American Historical Review*, vol. 95, no. 4 (October 1990), pp.983–1006; Colleen Margaret Forrest, 'Familial Poverty, Family Allowances, and the Normative Family Structure in Britain, 1917–1945', *Journal of Family History*, vol. 26, no. 4 (2001), pp.508–528.
47 See cases cited above, as well as, for example, *LCC Staff Gazette*, p.94; p.108.
48 Harold L. Smith, 'Sex vs. Class: British Feminists and the Labour Movement 1919–1929', *The Historian*, 47 (1984), p.31.
49 For more on the political agenda and setting up of the War Cabinet Committee on Women in Industry, see Thom, *Nice Girls and Rude Girls*, p.54; pp.195–196.
50 *Report of the War Cabinet Committee on Women in Industry*, para. 223.
51 This proposed solution was, in fact, remarkably similar to that which was finally put in place – not unproblematically – from 1960 and eventually finalised in the 1970s. See Clinton, *Post Office Workers*, pp.434–435.
52 Gladstone Committee, *Report*, para. 10.
53 LMA, LCC/CL/ESTAB/1/6 Royal Commission on Equal Pay (1944), Evidence from the LCC Staff Association to the Commission. See also LMA, LCC/GLSA/1/28, LCC Staff Association executive committee minutes, Report of the Minor Establishment and Typists Sub-Committee, 21 December 1920.
54 LCC Minutes, 29 July 1919.
55 *LCC Staff Gazette*, January 1920, p.10.
56 LCC Minutes, 16 December 1919, p.1680.
57 LMA, CL/ESTAB/1/6 Royal Commission on Equal Pay, (1944), LCC's statement to Royal Commission: Notes to Appendix B: Factors determining differentiation in rates in grades employed on same duties [undated].
58 *London County Council Staff Gazette*, January 1920, p.11.
59 The British Medical Association, for example, insisted on equal pay and chastised those – such as the Post Office – who refused it to female doctors, as is discussed in Chapter 4. Women MPs were also paid at the same rate as men.
60 LCC Minutes, 19 March 1918. As Dina Copelman notes, the London Teachers' Association had adopted a formal equal pay policy by 1919. See Copelman, *London's Women Teachers*, p.229.

61 Oram, *Women Teachers*, p.3; p.124.

62 *LCC Staff Gazette*, August 1919, p.108.

63 *The Times*, 'Sex and Salaries', 16 July 1919, p.13

64 Morley (ed.), *Women Workers*, p.44.

65 See Oram, *Women Teachers*, esp. pp.124–129; pp.161–166.

66 MRC, MSS.148/UCW/2/1/8, executive committee meeting 16–18 July 1924, report of Mr J. Bowen; executive committee meeting 14–16 October 1924.

67 *Reorganisation Report*, para. 10. The Treasury recognised that the women's organisations would feel that the report did not go far enough on the equal pay question. See TNA, T162/50/18, Establishment. Women: General correspondence, rules, examinations, etc. regarding employment of women in the Civil Service. Draft memorandum to the Chancellor of the Exchequer from M. G. Ramsay, dated November 1920, point 16.

68 Tomlin Commission, *Report*, para. 447; para. 451.

69 Grint, 'Women and Equality'.

70 UPW executive meeting, 8 January 1920; see also *Reorganisation Report*, para. 10.

71 Oram, *Women Teachers*, p.161.

72 TNA, LAB2/1727/ceb677, Central Establishments Branch of the Establishments Department: Correspondence regarding the seniority of men and women clerks in the Ministry of Labour.

73 Boston has made a similar point with regard to the TUC and the trade union movement as a whole. Boston, *Women Workers and the Trade Unions*, p.121.

74 MRC, MSS.415/36/1, meeting of 6 September 1921.

75 The Union of Post Office Workers (UPW) was an amalgamation of the Postmen's Federation, the Fawcett Association and the Postal & Telegraph Clerks Association and was constituted in 1919. For more on this, see Alan Clinton, *Post Office Workers*, p.8. For more on women in the UPW and its predecessors, and on union policy concerning women, see Helen Glew, 'Women's Employment in the General Post Office, 1914–1939' (unpublished PhD thesis, University of London, 2010), chapter 5.

76 MRC, MSS.148/UCW/2/1/1, first executive committee meeting, 3 October 1919.

77 MRC, MSS.148/UCW/2/1/6, executive committee meeting, 17–19 January 1923.

78 MRC, MSS.148/UCW/2/1/2, executive committee meeting, 8 January 1920

79 For a broader discussion of the impact the vote had on the discussion of women's issues, see Pat Thane, 'What Difference did the Vote Make? Women in Public and Private Life in Britain since 1918', *Historical Research*, vol. lxxvi (2003), pp.268–285.

80 *Hansard*, Civil Service (Women, Pay), HC Deb 1 April 1936 vol. 310 cc.2017–2018; Tomlin Commission, *Report*, para. 448.

81 Tomlin Commission, *Report*, para. 449.

82 The resolution about the equal pay review was passed alongside the resolution, discussed in Chapter 1, theoretically granting equal opportunity to men and women in certain grades of the Civil Service.

83 BPMA, POST 115/86, *Opportunity*, 'Federation of Women Civil Servants: Report for Year Ending March 31, 1922', supplement to *Opportunity*, June 1922. As it turned out, these 'really valuable gains' did not immediately bring about that which they

seemed to promise, as is discussed in Chapter 1. See also Johanna Alberti, *Beyond Suffrage: Feminists in War and Peace, 1914–1928* (London and Basingstoke: Macmillan, 1989), p.148.

84 POST 115/440, *The Post*, Walter Baker [Assistant General Secretary], 'General Secretary's Letter', 13 August 1921, p.140.

85 Freda Harcourt, 'Anderson, Sir Alan Garrett (1877–1952)', *Oxford Dictionary of National Biography* (Oxford University Press, 2004), online edn, January 2013 [www.oxforddnb.com/view/article/30404, accessed 4 February 2015].

86 *Report of the Committee on the Pay etc. of Civil Servants* [hereafter Anderson Committee, *Report*], p.36, available in TNA T 162/674/4, 'Equal Pay for Women and Men Employed on Similar Duties in the Civil Service'.

87 Anderson Committee, *Report*, pp.35–36.

88 *Red Tape*, 'Anderson Report Condemned', October 1923, p.9.

89 *Red Tape*, October 1923, p.18.

90 See also Oram, *Women Teachers*, p.4.

4

'As a matter of justice'[1]: the equal pay campaigns from 1924 to 1939

Jack and Jill, the Executive Twins

Twin brother and sister, young Jack and Jill
Set out to climb the Executive hill,
For he was as bright and as keen as she,
And both were clever as clever could be.

Now, hear the tale of this youth and this maid.
They passed the exam for the Training Grade.
They took up their posts on the self-same day,
They did the same work, and got the same pay.

But this was short-lived. The work, it is true,
Developed alike for each of the two;
But not so the pay – alas and alack!
Poor Jill was soon getting far less than Jack.

And when, in due course, they got to their max.,
Jill's money was only three-fourths of Jack's.
And so it remained until both were made
Executive Officers (Higher Grade).

And then, you might think, they'd be paid the same.
But no! When this longed-for promotion came,
The new scale for Jack (this is true – don't scoff!)
Began at the point where Jill's would leave off!

And if they go higher, as well they may,
They'll travel still farther from equal pay,
Though their work, of course, will be equal still.
How lucky for Jack, and how sad for Jill![2]

This poem was written by the NAWCS at the end of the interwar period and is an example of the publicity used in equal pay campaigns. Here, the simplicity of re-writing a nursery rhyme and the 'Jack and Jill' allusions were used to pinpoint the illogicalities of gender-differentiated pay.

As we saw in the previous chapter, the question of equal pay was consistently raised throughout the First World War, though ultimately to no avail for women civil servants. The LCC, in granting equal pay to women in the higher grades in 1919 on the basis that it had no good reason for not doing so, set a precedent in the public service. It is surprising that more use was not made of this by Civil Service campaigners and LCC staff in other grades. By 1924, the three-year time period specified in the August 1921 parliamentary resolutions had elapsed and so the campaigners of the Civil Service began a systematic and ongoing drive to publicise the equal pay cause and to persuade successive governments to see the justice of the claims. From then on, the manner and style of these highly public equal pay debates were set and would remain largely unaltered until the campaigns succeeded. Equal pay discussions in this period are significant for their repetitiveness – despite some morally and psychologically important victories in the 1930s – and the clear entrenchment in some quarters of attitudes against women's equal remuneration. Numerous discourses surrounding women's role in and out of the workplace contributed to an atmosphere of popular and official opposition, and ultimately the fervent opposition of several governments ensured that equal pay remained an unresolved issue in 1939 and for a considerable number of years afterwards.

Equal pay has often been cited as a key feminist issue in the interwar period[3] but there has yet to be a study which comprehensively examines the various dimensions of the public service battle, the most prominent of the equal pay campaigns in this period. It is also important to see the equal pay campaigns in the context of the other elements of women's public service employment. For example, in a history of women and trade unionism, Shelia Lewenhak has argued that by allowing the women-only clerical assistant grade to continue after 1936 (as documented in Chapter 1), the CSCA 'agreed ... to the hiving-off of female staff into a separate, lower-paid, lower grade, instead of trying to maintain the notion of equality in existing lower grades ... Naturally this benefitted the female minority in higher-graded work as well as men'. It constituted, she argues, 'just one more of the differences that arose among women over equal pay'.[4] However, her argument is mistaken on several grounds: the 1936 agreement she refers to was the product of staff side negotiations, not just those by the CSCA, and the majority of those involved in completing them were men rather than women: it is difficult to sustain the argument that this was a deliberate class issue between women, as she implies. It was also not at all clear in 1936 that any women in the Civil Service would be granted equal pay so whilst the point about the unfairness of crowding women into lower paid grades stands, it is somewhat anachronistic to suggest that the grading issue was fundamentally also about equal pay at this point. Therefore, thinking about the ways in which different facets of discrimination against women civil servants worked both independently and together is imperative.

The story of equal pay campaigns in the interwar years is one of continuity rather than any tangible change. Multiple elements of "logic" and rhetoric were used by those with the power to make decisions in attempts to deflate equal pay demands and to ensure that no cumulative change could be effected. Although arguments about government finance were consistently used, arguments with more social cache – such as the presumed normativity of the male breadwinner and the supposition that women were less effective as workers – were also prominent. Out of all sectors of employment, the Civil Service's equal pay campaign was the most prominent in this period. In the LCC, there was somewhat less momentum – in part because higher-grade workers already received equal pay – and also because the Staff Association was less politicised and therefore less active itself at campaigning.

With no other recourse, civil servants appealed to successive governments to take the lead on introducing equal pay. Women in the clerical, executive and administrative grades that spanned most Civil Service departments – and the unions and associations that represented them – led the campaigns as the similarity of their work to men's was such that it was hoped a victory here would then propel equal pay into the other Civil Service grades and indeed more widely beyond the service.[5] Furthermore, as both Oram and Pugh have noted, women teachers (the other large group of women very obviously doing the same work as men and being paid from public funds) and civil servants kept the issue of equal pay on the agenda throughout the interwar years, helped by a number feminist organisations. Both groups of women had a strong case, on which the government, had it so chosen, could have taken action.[6] Thus, although the campaigns by and on behalf of the (usually) middle class women of the clerical grades and above in the Civil Service may have seemed to be class-based, it was widely acknowledged by all concerned that this was the best possible starting point: grades which employed women only, such as typists and writing assistants, would complicate the claim by not having a male equivalent. It was hoped that a successful initial claim for the clerical grades and above would propel favourable change for women's pay further down the hierarchy.

The formation of the 1920s campaigns

Various campaigns for equal pay had gradually gathered momentum in the Civil Service after 1924. Several male MPs continued to be supportive, including Colonel Clifton Brown who wrote to Churchill, then Chancellor, in 1925 to argue that the government could not be seen to be avoiding a definitive statement on the issue of equal pay. Churchill's instructions to his staff drafting his reply were given in his inimitable style: 'refuse, resist and in the last resort, defy'.[7] In the Civil Service, the staff side of the National Whitley Council formed an equal pay campaign committee onto which the FWCS, not normally a part of the national Whitley Council,[8] was co-opted. The committee co-ordinated the efforts of individual Civil Service unions and associations, worked with sympathetic MPs, held debates and rallies and looked for opportunities to publicise the equal pay cause more widely.[9] This committee existed until 1931 when it disbanded over differences of opinion on how to proceed.[10]

In addition to the staff side committee, individual associations continued with their own campaigns. The FWCS continued to press for equal pay by organising debates, guest speakers, public meetings and (peaceful) demonstrations on the issue as a group and in co-operation with other organisations representing middle class women workers. On paper both the CSCA and the UPW had an equal pay policy. However, in its 1926–27 wage claim, the UPW removed a demand for equal pay, as Sarah Boston has also noted, because it was felt that little headway would be made with authorities on the issue.[11] As with earlier wage claims discussed in the previous chapter, this was a difficult choice between principle and practicality: no headway would have been made with equal pay given the government's stance, but keeping it as part of the claim might have outlined the union's seriousness about the issue. Boston argues that the UPW paid the price for not pursuing equal pay more forcefully ten years later when women started replacing men on certain duties.[12] However, whilst it is tempting to think that a 100,000-member strong union such as the UPW might have made headway on equal pay in this period, all campaigns for equal pay existed alongside the immovability of successive interwar governments.

The persistence of the male breadwinner model – and the belief that this always reflected family situations – meant that the issue of equal pay was continually caught up in debates about support for dependents, both within mixed-sex associations and in wider public debates about the suitability or otherwise of equal pay. As such, there was a common assumption that women needed only a wage to support themselves and men always needed a family wage.[13] This meant that rank-and-file members of unions and associations that had a formal equal pay policy were sometimes at odds with the organisation to which they belonged. There was also, at times, a stalemate in debates within unions, much like the UPW's discussions in the early 1920s covered in the previous chapter: on the one hand, men feared their jobs being "undercut" by women being paid less, but at the same time others would not agree to equal pay because they believed men needed to provide for dependents and women never did.

This reasoning that only men provided for family members proved flawed on many occasions. As Alison Oram has noted, 'women teachers were invariably depicted as spinsters and counterposed to the married man teacher in need of a family wage'.[14] Writing in the *Daily Herald* in 1938, Vera Brittain pointed out that the Burnham Committee, which fixed teachers' salaries, had assumed that men's expenses were greater: however, she pointed out, 'I have yet to learn of any commercial company which charges a woman four-fifths of a man's rate for gas, electricity, food, water and transport'.[15] Research by Oram, Guerriero Wilson and Todd, for example, has shown the extent to which women workers contributed to family incomes or supported dependents, which could include siblings, parents or even grandparents.[16] There were countless examples across the Civil Service. In November 1921, Lilian Sayers tumbled to her death down a staircase at Brixton Telephone Exchange. At her inquest, it was noted that she 'was one of the many women who, in these days of abnormal employment, had much to do at home. Her father and mother are well on in years, and she had a delicate sister who is frequently incapacitated from earning anything, and consequently all three were partially dependent upon the earnings of Miss Sayers'.[17] In 1929, Mabel Bray, formerly a UPW executive member and now a member of the FWCS after promotion to clerical roles in the Ministry of Labour and later the Ministry of Pensions, wrote to her local parliamentary candidate on the subject of equal pay. She noted that she was supporting herself and her dependent mother with her wages.[18] An anonymous woman clerk wrote to the General Secretary of the NAWCS in 1933 to detail the financial responsibilities she had to fulfil. Her case was printed in *Opportunity*, the NAWCS journal, with a plea for other women civil servants to come forward, give their names and talk about their own situations. The woman clerk in question had held her position for fifteen years. Thirteen years previously, her father had lost his job and, as a result of his age, had been unable to secure further employment. She had four younger siblings who were still at school and legally too young to leave. As a result, she had had to contribute to the school fees of each child and had taken sole responsibility for the maintenance of her sister who was aged seventeen and unemployed. She revealed how she had been unable to accrue any savings or take a holiday, was spending as little as possible on food and was walking six miles at the start and end of each day in order to save money otherwise spent on railway fares. As she concluded, '[i]t is just about time that the public and others should be made to realise that a large number of women Civil Servants have relatives dependent on them'.[19] Cases such as these undermined the near-sacrosanct position ascribed to the male breadwinner model, but still it persisted, with the assumption that men always had dependents never questioned.

The movement for family allowances was led by Eleanor Rathbone, a feminist, National Union of Societies for Equal Citizenship president and later MP. Emerging before the First World War, the campaign for family allowances – for Rathbone, specifically the endowment of motherhood – rose to prominence by the end of the war.[20] The question of family allowances attracted both support and controversy amongst feminists (some of whom feared this would reinforce gender stereotypes of the woman as chief carer) and the labour movement, including some civil servants, who feared that such allowances would provide employers with a justification to reduce wages.[21] Family allowances combined with equal pay might have seemed the best compromise to solve the dilemma that some trade unionists found themselves in: women paid equally with men would then not undercut men in the workplace as many men so feared they would, women would be paid fairly, and, if dependents' allowances were paid to all who needed them, this would ensure parity. This was the line taken by a number of Civil Service organisations who otherwise were wary of the implications of such allowances. A number of rank-and-file members seem to have taken this position, albeit whilst still believing only men had dependents. M. Lewis of the Glasgow Telephonists wrote to the editor of *The Post*, the UPW's journal, in 1924 asking '[w]hy not pay justly and equally for equal work, while supporting in just proportion a man's manly responsibilities?' In October 1929, another correspondent argued that 'it is imperative that if equal pay for equal work is instituted (as I hope it will be), it shall be accompanied by a system of family allowances payable in respect of children of Civil Servants'.[22]

By comparison to the lengthy and often public debates in Civil Service unions and associations, the activities of the LCC Staff Association in this decade seemed more muted. It is worth considering how different this might have been if LCC female staff had not been effectively divided into two groups: those who had equal pay and those who did not. Furthermore, the presence of the FWCS/NAWCS and the CWCS in the Civil Service meant that women's issues were permanently on the agenda, but there was no equivalent in the LCC. That said, with one eye clearly on the civil servants, the LCC Staff Association raised the issue of equal pay for the minor establishment grades intermittently within the *Staff Gazette*.[23] The Association had had an equal pay policy throughout the decade, though its assertion in 1929 that it would pursue equal pay 'should there be a really big movement in favour of [it]' was rather meek and cautious. The Council was clearly looking to the Civil Service and other bodies, telling the staff side two weeks later that it would not discuss equal pay unless it became a national issue.[24] Thus, there was much hedging of bets and 'waiting and seeing' going on amongst both Council staff and members, as well as a clear implication that the Civil Service should be the leading employer for all other public service employers to emulate. All concerned must have been aware of the concurrent debates in the Civil Service and the appointment of the Royal Commission in autumn 1929.

The Royal Commission, 1929–31

When he took office in 1929 a deputation from the Joint Committee on Women in the Civil Service – an alliance of women's representatives in the Civil Service and their supporters – went to see Prime Minister Ramsay MacDonald, who pledged to implement equal pay for women civil servants.[25] This might have seemed promising but proved, essentially, to be in the same vein as the affirmations of equal pay in Parliament in the 1920s. MacDonald's Labour government appointed the Royal Commission chaired by Lord Tomlin in October 1929. The Royal Commissioners, when they reported in 1931, were divided on the issue of equal pay but its supporters did not go so far as to insist on signing their own minority report. It was apparently disappointing to Tomlin that the Commissioners had not been able to find agreement on the issue.[26] In many ways, as we shall see, the arguments used by Commissioners on both sides of the debate were essentially a continuation and foreshadowing of the arguments that would permeate the interwar years.

In presenting evidence to the Commissioners, the staff side of the National Whitley Council argued for equal pay to be made effective immediately and argued that the cost could be alleviated by allowing existing women civil servants to proceed to the relevant men's maximum via the increments given to men.[27] The CWCS, the FWCS and the Civil Service section of the Association of Women Clerks and Secretaries also gave evidence in support of equal pay. The FWCS argued that the perceptions of women in the Civil Service were affected by their unequal pay and – although they did not use this exact phrase – they based their claim on the idea of the rate for the job. For women in posts with no male equivalent, they argued that women should be paid the rate that a man would demand, and receive, for the job.[28] The CWCS performed less surely at times under the Commissioners' questioning but essentially took the same line, arguing for pay which did not distinguish between men and women and also for recognition of work of equal value by the same pay.[29]

Predictably, the Whitley Council Official Side spoke against equal pay.[30] It argued that the present system caused no administrative difficulties (which was clearly seen as reason enough not to change things) and that, as other employers paid women less than men, they felt that the Civil Service should not do otherwise. Efficiency was another much-discussed term and those who opposed equal pay drew upon the idea and "evidence", which was largely anecdotal, that women were the less efficient sex. For example, Murray, the GPO Secretary, told the Commission that 'it would be undesirable for the Post Office ... to pay higher rates to women than prevailed in outside industry' as he 'did not consider that the output of the average woman is equal to that of the average man'.[31] The Treasury, it will be recalled, had argued in 1917 that efficiency in clerical work was hard to determine – also in order to turn down a claim for equal pay. However, as with Murray, this difficulty was apparently overcome by Sir Warren Fisher, Head of the Civil Service, who told the Tomlin Commissioners in 1930 that 'pay levels were currently justifiable by the fact that men are more efficient than women'.[32] Such pronouncements were the result, then, of essentialising the capabilities of women, assuming that they were always all less efficient than all men, and of concerted attempts to stave off or delay demands for equal conditions. After toeing the Civil Service line about women's value being less than men's, R. R. Scott, Controller of the Establishments Branch at the Treasury, refused to comment on the fact that men were paid on the assumption that they all had dependents. He also argued that equal pay might lead to overqualified women working in the Civil Service, which seemed to be an argument against higher pay full-stop, rather than necessarily against equal pay.[33]

The Commissioners, as we have seen from Chapters 1 and 2, were an important group in terms of the debate they facilitated and some of the changes that the Commission helped to stimulate, though their stalemate in 1931 on this issue mirrored the divisions between staff and officials in the Civil Service. As we have seen, the Commissioners included four women who were advocates of women's issues but also Katharine, Duchess of Atholl, who would later vote against equal pay for women in the Civil Service.[34] Sir Percy Richard Jackson, a high-ranking educational administrator, sat on the Burnham Committee, which decided teachers' salaries, as did Frank Goldstone, a trade unionist and former Labour MP.[35] In the report, the Commissioners argued that equal pay remained too expensive for the nation to fund. They quoted an Exchequer figure of £3 million as an implementation cost, though this was hotly debated at the time and later.[36] Those in favour, however, argued that cost was an irrelevant factor and that as the government had accepted the principle in 1920, the principle had to remain accepted now.[37] Of course acceptance of a principle was not the same thing as a Bill having been passed so, although a moral point, this assertion meant nothing. Significantly, the Commissioners decided to abandon the principle of the Civil Service being regarded as the model employer – even though this idea had been used, to the Treasury's advantage, for considerable years.[38] The Commissioners opposing equal pay felt that there was no reason for the Civil Service to deviate from outside employment practice and that to deviate from the current principles would mean disrupting the 'fair relativity with comparable outside employment'. Women in outside employment had, the commissioners felt, 'not yet secured equality of payment with men' and though instances could be quoted where they had, these did not invalidate the general position as the exceptions often related to the professions. The commissioners noted that '[t]he differences between the remuneration paid to men and women in certain occupations are no doubt partly accounted for by the fact that women outside the service are frequently employed in separate sections and on duties somewhat inferior to those assigned to men'. This was, in effect, a concession that women's employment in the Civil Service was fundamentally different from women's employment elsewhere because of the numbers of women employed alongside men, but the fact that outside employment should not therefore be a point of comparison seems not to have occurred to them. With all of this in mind, 'the conclusion is reached that the treatment of women in the service, in the matter of remuneration is at least abreast of general outside practice' – and "abreast" was clearly judged by these commissioners to be enough. Similarly, it was later observed that the '[s]tate is practically the only employer which has thrown open considerable spheres of employment to men and women alike, without reserving to itself the right to employ men only in those spheres. To base upon this situation a claim for the payment of women at rates above those ruling outside is not justified in common fairness'.[39] Thus, the position was that the state was already ahead of other employers and had therefore done sufficient and so should not be required to treat women doing identical work to men equally.

By contrast, those Tomlin Commissioners who favoured equal pay grounded their argument differently, arguing instead that the government should look to the Civil Service in other countries. They pointed out that government services in parts of the Commonwealth, in Ireland, the United States and in parts of Europe made no distinction between remuneration for men and women. They also pointed out the practice of the LCC in regard to higher-grade employees.[40] They argued that entrance examinations taken by both men and women provided a marker of efficiency and were akin to professional qualifications, thus proving fitness for equal pay. More significantly, they recognised that evidence presented to the Commission of women's inefficiency 'was [no] more than a matter of opinion, and of opinion related rather to the future than to the present'.[41] They also acknowledged the unsatisfactory nature of the assumption that women in the Civil Service did not have dependents:

> After the first few years [women] are subject to a discriminating factor in regard to their pay which is not related to anything but their sex. The man's rate is not in fact varied according to the number of his dependents; were this element admitted, it would be found that the existence of dependents is common to both sexes, and found in widely varying proportions in regard to both sexes.[42]

The Royal Commission process had also highlighted some continuing anomalies in pay across the Civil Service. Evidence from the Board of Education revealed that it paid its female medical officers the same as their male counterparts, as per the stipulations of the BMA, but the GPO had not paid its assistant female medical staff at the same rate as men for the past two decades.[43] There had in fact been a campaign instigated by the GPO's senior medical officer, Dr Minnie Madgshon, before the First World War which encompassed the Medical Women's Federation, the

BMA, the Institution of Professional Civil Servants as well as significant correspondence in publications such as *The Times* and *The Lancet*. The GPO had, in fact, originally paid its assistant women medical officers at the same rate as the assistant men but the policy appeared to have been changed in 1911, despite the Postmaster General's representative stating otherwise in the early 1920s.[44] The GPO stood steadfast in its policy throughout the interwar years: it was sympathetic but unmoved by the fact that women doctors were professionals and as such were paid at the same rates as their male counterparts in outside employment. Furthermore, it argued that other Civil Service departments were not akin to the GPO, implying that to allow assistant women medical officers equal pay with men would mean a policy change on the issue of equal pay as a whole.[45] Women clerks of the GPO had, of course, been long-standing campaigners for equal pay and were numerically significant. The GPO was clearly fearful of opening the floodgates, even though they could have relied on the Board of Education's precedent. Despite exposure by the Royal Commission and a later assertion that Civil Service medical professionals earned equal pay, the anomaly in the GPO remained.[46]

After Tomlin: the activism of the 1930s

Immediately after the Royal Commission, the economic depression prevented any furtherance of equal pay campaigns – and in fact, Civil Service salaries were cut as a response to the financial situation.[47] In the LCC, attention became focused on fixing the disparity in salaries between entrants before and after April 1930 following the absorption of the Poor Law Guardians infrastructure by the Council. This campaign preoccupied the Staff Association for much of the 1930s.[48] When unemployment levels were high and there was general vocal opposition to even the employment of women, the NAWCS 'felt that an intensive campaign for equal pay would be likely … to do more harm than good' and vowed to resume it 'as soon as the omens are reasonably propitious'.[49] The Joint Committee on Women in the Civil Service went only so far as to affirm that it would seek assurances that any parliamentary denials of equal pay were related to the country's financial situation and not as a rebuttal of the principle.[50] None of the post-Tomlin service-wide committees were empowered to discuss equal pay, as this was again declared a matter of government policy. The NAWCS was disappointed by this but optimistically saw it as 'at least preferable to a definitely adverse pronouncement'.[51] The staff side of the Committee on Women's Questions included V. Appleby and Dorothy Evans of the NAWCS (co-opted), A. J. T. Day and Edith Howse of the UPW, and William J. Brown and Leslie M. Sweet of the CSCA, the latter acting as the staff side secretary of the committee. Many of these individuals would soon also form the second Civil Service Equal Pay Committee. When the Committee on Women's Questions issued its report on 23 March 1934, the staff side insisted on including the following:

> [E]qual pay as between men and women employed in the same class or grade is the logical accompaniment of 'a fair field and no favour' and of aggregation. It has been held that the question of equal pay is outside the terms of reference of this Committee but the Staff Side desire to make it clear that the Service Associations, through other channels, will continue to press for equal pay between the sexes which they regard as indispensable to the real achievement of 'a fair field and no favour'.[52]

By late 1934, with the country's finances in a slightly better state, various equal pay campaigns had begun again. The second of the Civil Service Equal Pay Committees was formed by the staff side and the NAWCS used its connections with outside women's groups to raise awareness of the issue.[53] There developed a certain competitiveness verging on bitterness between the staff side committee and the NAWCS over the origination of various of the minor milestones.[54] Such distractions were not helpful – particularly when any victories were often a result of the raised profile of the issue more widely, to which all campaigners had contributed – but such competitiveness was unfortunately symptomatic of the current relationship between the mixed associations and the single-sex NAWCS. Relations between the Joint Committee on Women in the Civil Service and the staff side committee were somewhat better.

The most compelling moments of the equal pay campaign in this decade came in June 1935 and April 1936 via debates in Parliament. Both debates became notorious amongst Civil Service staff for two different reasons: in 1935, because of the claims made by the Financial Secretary to the Treasury; in 1936, because of the dramatic conclusion to the debates. On 7 June 1935 the debate was introduced in the Commons by Conservative MP Colonel Clifton Brown. He had helped to convene a parliamentary committee on the issue of equal pay for women in the Civil Service and also had close contacts in the staff side equal pay committee, who had briefed him and a number of other MPs friendly to the equal pay cause. He also had long-standing connections with the Joint Committee on Women in the Civil Service and the NAWCS.[55] He rooted his speech in the male unemployment of the early 1930s and, by comparison, the steady growth of women's employment owing to the fact that women were paid lower wages. In setting out his argument, he perpetuated the idea that women wanted to marry and have children as soon as possible:

> What women really want is to have their own homes as early as they can. By remaining in industry, by taking the place of men, they are preventing men from marrying, and, therefore, they are preventing themselves from having their own homes and their own families, and doing exactly what their natural instincts tell them. Therefore, even if a few women were put out of industry, a great many more would be enabled to marry and have their own homes, so that what they lost in one direction they would gain in another, and I believe it would result in greater happiness.

This may not have been received particularly well amongst those interwar feminists who wanted careers rather than marriage but Clifton Brown used all of these points to argue that the government should take the lead on equal pay in order to ensure that women, with lower pay, did not become the preferred employees.[56] Clifton Brown's motion was seconded by George Lansbury, the Labour leader, revealing the extent of cross-party support for the issue. Mavis Tate, an emerging advocate of women's issues and a Conservative MP, also spoke in favour, though argued that the basis for Clifton Brown's argument was mistaken and that equal pay was, quite simply, about fair remuneration for work done regardless of the sex of the worker.[57] Major Hills, a Conservative MP and a long time advocate of the improvement of women's position in the Civil Service, asserted that unequal pay 'puts a woman in a wrong position because it puts her in the position of being a sort of inferior man, of being there by grace and favour, of being permitted to be there so long as she will accept smaller pay instead of having all the equality which she requires'. He argued that the cost for the service-wide classes of introducing equal pay was more like £1 million rather than the £3 million quoted in the Tomlin report[58] – though neither of these figures would have been palatable in the economic climate of the 1930s. Duff Cooper, the Financial Secretary to the Treasury, made what would become an infamous set of assertions during the debate.[59] He modified somewhat the discourse about the government as a model employer, arguing that the government should be at the head of the best employers – and it was already at this point, he said, because men and women had the same mode of admission – but that it should not pressure employers by introducing equal pay.[60]

He attempted to complicate the question of "equal work" further by arguing that:

The demand has been summed up in the cry: 'equal pay for equal work'. Very often a slogan is extremely misleading, and the words 'equal pay for equal work' are misleading, because they imply what appears to be an obvious justice, namely, that two people doing exactly the same work should receive exactly the same remuneration whatever their sex. I would suggest that we should get nearer to the truth and we should be able to form a juster conception of the whole problem, because it is a problem, if instead of saying 'equal pay for equal work' we said, 'equal pay for equal value'.[61]

He went on to state why equal value was not obtained from women, citing – as was becoming so commonplace in debates such as these – differences in efficiency, attendance and length of service. "Equal value", in Duff Cooper's sense of the term, was obviously an extremely slippery concept and it would be difficult to identify how and why one task or one person provided more value than another. Overall, though, whether the concept was termed "equal efficiency", "equal work" or "work of equal value", it did not hide the refusal by Duff Cooper and others to countenance the fact that women might be as good as men at a particular job, and serve the state just as well.

Duff Cooper was not the only person to express anxieties about women's sick leave – this went back at least as far as Alexander King in 1913[62] – but he did much to propagate the myth that women's sick leave was much higher than men's. In the debate he argued that the extent of women's sick leave made their work less valuable than men's and quoted figures showing women's sick leave as being 50 per cent higher than men's.[63] A year later it emerged that this 50 per cent had been based on problematic data: whilst women's sick leave was, on average, twelve days per year, and men's eight, the data for men excluded those who had been disabled by the war but that for women had included all women civil servants, including charwomen and attendants whose sick leave was often higher.[64] Thus, the averages were not strictly comparable. As Ellen Wilkinson pointed out, Lord Tomlin himself, when chairing the Royal Commission, had refused to consider sick leave as a criterion for equal pay, arguing that the differences (an average of two days) between men and women were negligible.[65]

Adding to the notoriety of his statement to the Commons, Duff Cooper pointed out that figures had shown that marriage wastage was 'very much higher among women than among men'.[66] Whilst this was technically true – how many men would have resigned when they got married unless compelled? – he, like so many others, failed to acknowledge that women in the Civil Service were compelled by the Service's own regulations to leave when marrying. Furthermore, although women's departure rate for marriage was very obviously higher than men's, women's resignations on marriage in the GPO – where the greatest number of women were employed – were not overly significant in comparison with superannuation and departures for other reasons by both sexes, as Chapter 6 describes. However, the argument persisted. It was only in 1946 that the report of the Royal Commission on Equal Pay finally argued that marriage wastage should not be taken into account in equal pay arguments because of the existence of the marriage bar.[68]

In all, although the 1935 debate allowed the airing of a wide range of issues in Parliament, Duff Cooper's assertions culminated in a resounding 'not now' for the equal pay question. There was much comment on this debate in the press and amongst women's organisations. The National Council of Women sent a resolution to Duff Cooper which 'recorded their pride in the work of women Civil Servants, challenged the truth of Mr Duff Cooper's statements in regard to it and called on the Government to give equal pay to men and women in the common grades'.[69]

The staff side equal pay campaign committee wrote to Duff Cooper to refute many of his arguments, and also made plans for a parliamentary question:

> To ask the financial secretary to the Treasury whether, in view of the fact that it is the avowed policy of H.M. Government to keep abreast of the best employers in the country, he is prepared to follow the example of the organisation most comparable in points of structure and functions to the Civil Service, that is the L.C.C., and to apply equal pay forthwith to those Civil Service staffs whose major functions and status correspond to those of the Major Establishment of the L.C.C.[70]

Had it been asked, this would have been a clever question. Drawing on the 'abreast of the best employers' argument rather than insisting on the government as the model employer, the committee simply asked the government to equal the LCC and, in so doing, reminded them that the precedent had been set elsewhere. It is debatable, though, whether altering the demand to equal pay for the higher grades would have been a desirable move, after a blanket campaign hitherto and with all the class implications that such a line of argument would have had. Nonetheless, the discussion of this argument at this point also highlights that a possible comparison with the LCC had been under-used hitherto.

The LCC staff association kept a close eye on proceedings and conducted its own referendum on the issue in late 1935. Some 2,148 ballot papers were returned, with the vast majority being in favour of equal pay. Tellingly, only 26 of the 550 women who participated in the vote were against equal pay for women, compared to 479 of the nearly 1,600 men who voted.[71] The Association followed this up with its own sub-committee in 1936. The report focused on the problems with the assumption that men were supporting dependents and women never were, and also pointed out that although equal pay seemed costly, it would only be the same as if an intake to the general grade happened to be all-male one year and thus all staff had to be paid the same.[72]

On 1 April 1936, Ellen Wilkinson, Labour MP for Jarrow, who had argued that equal pay was a class not a sex issue,[73] introduced a Private Members' Bill, supported by the staff associations, for equal pay for women in the clerical, executive and administrative grades in the Civil Service and found support from numerous MPs but not from the government. The resolution passed initially, but on 6 April the government turned the issue into a vote of confidence, whereupon, unsurprisingly, the House fell into line with the government.[74] The staff associations were livid, feeling that they had been deprived of their only constitutional recourse: throughout the war and the 1920s, successive governments had forbidden the Civil Service CAB and the National Whitley Council to negotiate on equal pay, stating that it was a government matter. It was now felt that the government's actions in forcing a vote of confidence had been unconstitutional. Representatives from a large number of women's organisations wrote a letter of protest, stating that '[w]e are convinced that the maintenance of two rates of pay for the same work is contrary to the interests of both the men and the women workers and endangers their standard of living, and that a change in this system of remuneration is overdue'.[75] This was interesting wording: the point about feminism and equality was still there but in the post-depression era, where standards of living had become familiar elements of public rhetoric, this emphasis from largely middle-class organisations was significant.

Meanwhile, the Committee on Sex Differentiation in Pay had been convened in March 1935 at the request of the Civil Service staff side, as a sub-committee of the general purposes' committee of the National Whitley Council. It reported at the end of June 1937. From the outset, the official side had refused to discuss equal pay, arguing that it was a government policy issue and outside their powers. As a result the staff side reserved the right to continue to seek equal pay by alternative means and used the committee to focus on 'adjusting anomalies and lessening differentials within the system as it stands at present'.[76] The main outcome of the committee was a ruling which stated that women's salary scales should not be less than 75 per cent of men's for the same grade and that this should constitute a difference of not more than £175 per year.[77] Whilst it was hailed as 'a move towards equal pay for equal work' by some in the UPW, and as immediately improving the circumstances of hundreds of women by the CSCA (which it indeed did), for others it was merely a means to solidify and justify the differences between men's and women's pay.[78] The NAWCS, ever committed to nothing less than fully equal pay, referred to the committee as the 'Committee on Unequal Pay' and co-hosted a public meeting at the end of 1937 with the Women's Freedom League.[79] The meeting made their alliances with key women's organisations and individuals plain. It was chaired by Mrs J. L. Blythe, Mayor of Islington, and speakers included Teresa Billington Greig, suffragette and Women's Freedom League (WFL) organiser, Alderman Gwyn Jones, MP, Rose Simpson, secretary of the Women's Co-Operative Guild, F. A. Underwood, WFL secretary and Nancy Stewart-Parnell of the St Joan's Social and Political Alliance. The Savings Bank branch of the NAWCS co-organised another equal pay meeting in Hammersmith at which, among others, Edith Summerskill, MP, spoke, sharing the platform with the president of the National Union of Women Teachers.[80] The Civil Service Equal Pay Committee also continued its work, though as war loomed closer it was more difficult for them to attract MPs' attention to the cause of equal pay, unless it was linked to an aspect of the war, such as the pay of ARP wardens.[81] As a whole, this activity undermines Harold Smith's assertion that after the 1936 House of Commons incident the equal pay campaigners became inactive. It may have been the case that 'the possibility of achieving equal pay seemed so remote' but the Committee's continued meetings, networking and endeavours do not suggest the sense of defeat he sees in the very late 1930s.[82]

LCC agitation also increased for a time. In February 1937, in direct reference to the Civil Service Whitley debates, the staff side of the LCC's Joint Committee of Members and Staff asked for clarification of the Council's policy of differentiation between male and female salary scales and for a general picture on the issue of equal pay.[83] Several months later the Council decided to advertise the position of female estate clerk with a lower salary scale than that available for men. The LCC staff side initially refused to accept a lower salary scale for women and sent the decision back to the official side, who ultimately came back with a refusal to change their position because it impinged on the issue of equal pay more generally.

The staff side, echoing the stance of so many public service associations before it, decided to regretfully accept the decision without prejudicing their right to continue an equal pay campaign.[84] Deadlock thus avoided, the LCC Staff Association went through a period of soul-searching several months later about whether the staff side's compromise had been appropriate, which suggested that the Association was perhaps looking to begin a more vociferous campaign. The decision provoked a more immediate backlash against the Council in *London Town* columns and letters, particularly against the Council's Labour majority whose party professed to support equal pay. It was pointed out that the LCC was entirely inconsistent in the way in which it treated women on the major compared to the general grades. One letter writer issued a call to arms:

> It is high time the Association found means to convince the Council of the indefensible injustice perpetrated, during all these post-war years, on a large section of its women staff. The Association should devote all its resources to procure for the woman officer on the general grade the equality accorded to women on the major establishment. The removal of this injustice would pave the way to better conditions in every other section of the Council's service. If arbitration is necessary, then by all means let us have it.[85]

However, such rhetoric ultimately did not lead to a substantial campaign at this point. There was some communication between the LCC Staff Association and the Civil Service Equal Pay Campaign Committee but the Staff Association eventually decided not to join a wider campaign or pursue campaigns of their own for fear of disrupting otherwise good relations with the Labour majority on the LCC.[86] Thus, campaigning for equal pay for women was sacrificed to a wider cause.

Although the UPW had worked with the Civil Service Equal Pay Committee in both its 1920s and 1930s iterations, the UPW's female members were not of course in grades that would first be considered for equal pay (even though they were manifestly very often doing the same work as men). However, the UPW's membership was becoming particularly concerned about the lack of equal pay in the late 1930s and the ramifications. The numbers of women employed on particular tasks was increasing – particularly in telegraphy – because they were cheaper to employ.[87] As Sarah Boston has also noted, there was vitriol directed at women postal workers and UPW members at conferences in the late 1930s which was hardly helpful.[88] The union's position was encapsulated by its passing of emergency equal pay resolutions at three successive annual conferences (1935, 1936, 1937) and also passing resolutions to ensure that a suitable number of posts remained available for men.[89] Thus, it ended up pushing for equal pay even when a number of its members believed in the male breadwinner/family wage discourse because the GPO was increasing the numbers of women on certain types of work. Thus the fears of lower paid women being given more work than men were being played out.

Although it is difficult to say categorically that a moral victory of sorts for equal pay was won by the end of the interwar period, it is clear that the continued public airings of facets of the debate played an important role in trying to educate the public and the decision-making elites alike. The sympathies of some of the Royal Commissioners and, in particular, the parliamentary support in 1935 and 1936 is significant. When the issue of equal pay for public servants was picked up again towards the end of the Second World War, the idea that the work women did deserved the same pay as men was largely accepted and the terms of the debate shifted – as the following chapter will discuss in more depth. Wider public opinion on equal pay in the interwar period remains under-researched and such research would highlight the inter-relationship between the public service campaigns and other discussions, opinions or coverage of equal pay.

All the significant unions and associations in the public service – the NAWCS, the CSCA, the UPW and the LCC staff association – had equal pay policies. It was the NAWCS and its predecessors, as the largest women's association in the Civil Service, who most consistently reiterated the desire for equal pay. Sarah Boston, amongst others, has criticised the UPW for not pursuing the issue more forcefully – for example in 1927, when it was dropped from the pay negotiations.[90] Although this, along with semi-regular expressions of a lack of belief in equal pay among individual union members, must have undermined women's faith in the unions' real commitment to equal pay at various points, it is difficult to see what more unions and associations could have done in this period beyond the campaigning they undertook and the alliances they sought. As this chapter and the previous one showed, Civil Service authorities (and therefore also the LCC in this period) were so vehemently against equal pay that it is hard to see that insisting on equal pay would have done any good. As striking was effectively banned for public servants, combinations with other parties and unions were prevented after 1915 for the LCC Staff Association and after the 1927 Trades Dispute Act for the Civil Service, and equal pay was disallowed from arbitration, public servants were left with no real constitutional recourse. Public opinion was also not yet strong enough with regard to equal pay for politicians to have to consider it as a possible vote-winning mechanism.

Although arguments about efficiency were one of the cornerstones of official side evidence to the Tomlin Commission, it became more common as the 1930s wore on for women in the Civil Service to do the same work as men, thus at least shifting the argument somewhat about the comparability of men's and women's work. However, the persistence of segregation in sections of the Post Office – including indefinitely on the manipulative grades – meant that arguments that men and women did not do the same work were able to persist, even if in practice the work was actually very similar but just labelled differently. The cultural assumption also persisted – inside the public service and outside – that all women workers were single and, almost as significantly, that single women did not have to provide for anyone, not even, sometimes, themselves. Though it was customary for married women of the middle classes to give up work on marriage, the marriage bar in the Civil Service and for large sections of the LCC enforced this trend. Thus, the stereotype of the single woman earning pin money only was perceived to be bolstered by the existence of the marriage bar.

The unwavering factor in this period was the obstinacy of successive governments and, thus, the Treasury. In the early 1920s the government's acceptance of the equal pay resolution was, in effect, meaningless. Despite parliamentary victories for the cause in the 1930s, the issue was deemed to be of such significance that it was turned into a spark for a vote of confidence. Clearly, the vote was a tactic only, but it proved effective. At the same time, the fact that such a tactic was needed reveals the growing, underlying strength of support for the issue in Parliament and the traction the issue had gained in the interwar years.

Notes

1 BPMA, POST 115/456, *The Post*, Letters to the Editor, letter from H. Brewer, 19 October 1929, p.318.

2 POST 115/93, *Opportunity*, 'Civil Service Rhymes – IV', March 1939, p.39.

3 Smith, 'British Feminism and the Equal Pay Issue', pp.97–110; Oram, *Women Teachers*, p.4; Graves, *Labour Women*, p.132; Boston, *Women Workers and the Trade Unions*, p.46.

4 Lewenhak, *Women and Trade Unions*, p.229.

5 See, for example, POST 115/451, *The Post*, 'Equal Pay', 26 February 1927, p.188; Tomlin Commission, *Report*, para. 463.

6 Oram, *Women Teachers*, p.4; Pugh, *Women and the Women's Movement*, p.96. For a discussion of the importances of the FWCS/NAWCS see Glew, 'Women in the Post Office', chapter 4 and B.V. Humphries, *Clerical Unions in the Civil Service*, (Oxford: Oxford University Press, 1958), p.154.

7 TNA, T162/674/4, 'Establishment. Salary: General: Equal pay for men and women employed on similar duties in the Civil Service', memorandum from Churchill to his staff, 28 May 1925.

8 The FWCS chose to leave the Civil Service Alliance in 1921 over fears that they would be forced to compromise on their feminist principles. They had a seat on the Whitley Council by virtue of being part of the Alliance but their withdrawal meant the loss of the seat. BPMA, POST 115/86, *Opportunity*, Annual Report of the FWCS, Supplement to *Opportunity*, June 1922, p.v.

9 The activities of the association are best documented in the UPW minutes. See MRC, MSS.148/UCW/2/1 and subsequent minutes of meetings.

10 Correspondence and decision as quoted in MRC, MSS.148/UCW/2/1/14, UPW executive committee meeting 14–16 April 1931.

11 POST 115/449, *The Post*, 'Report of Conference Proceedings', 12 June 1926, pp.431–432. Boston, *Women Workers and the Trade Unions*, pp.168–169.

12 Boston, *Women Workers and the Trade Unions*, pp.168–169. The NAWCS made a similar point: BPMA, POST 115/90, *Opportunity*, 'The Outlook: Each for All and All for Each', June 1934, pp.97–98.

13 This was widely discussed. For an overview of the debates and opposition see Hilary Land, 'The Family Wage', *Feminist Review*, no. 6 (1980), pp.55–77.

14 Oram, *Women Teachers*, p.50; p.59.

15 Vera Brittain, 'Women Still Wait for Equality', *Daily Herald*, 26 March 1938, reprinted in Paul Berry and Alan Bishop (eds), *Testament of a Generation: The Journalism of Vera Brittain and Winifred Holtby* (London: Virago, 1985), pp.144–147.

16 Oram, *Women Teachers*, p.63; Wilson, 'Women's Work in Offices and the Preservation of Men's "Breadwinning" Jobs', p.472; Todd, *Young Women, Work and the Family*, pp.54–84.

17 BPMA, POST 115/441, *The Post*, 'Telephone Secretary's Letter', March 1922, p.269.

18 WL, 6NCS, Box FL435, NAWCS [*sic*]: equal pay, 1929 general election.

19 BPMA, POST 115/90, *Opportunity*, 'Dependent Relatives and the Cost of Living', June 1933, p.95.

20 Susan Pedersen, *Eleanor Rathbone and the Politics of Conscience* (New Haven and London: Yale University Press, 2004), p.152; Pat Thane, *Foundations of the Welfare State*, 2nd edn (Harlow: Longman, 1996), pp.200–203. Rathbone, 'The Remuneration of Women's Services'.

21 Smith, 'Sex vs Class', pp.27–8; Law, *Suffrage and Power*, p.166; *Report of the War Cabinet Committee on Women in Industry*, Appendix, pp.155–156; MRC, MSS.148/UCW/3/7/2, Civil Service Equal Pay Committee, folder no. 5, 'Equal Pay and Family Allowances', 16 July 1935.

22 POST 115/445. *The Post*, letter from M. Lewis of the Glasgow Telephonists, 28 June 1924, p.647. See also *The Post*, 21 June 1924, p.619; POST 115/454, *The Post*, letter from H. Brewer, 19 October 1929, p.318. See also POST 115/445, *The Post*, 'Equal Pay for Equal Work: Is There An Alternative?', 28 June 1924, p.632; POST 115/446, *The Post*, Letters to the Editor, 8 November 1924, p.378; General Secretary's letter, 15 November 1924, p.386; Geo M. Dowling, Letters to the Editor, 'Family Allowances', 6 December 1924, p.456; POST 115/452, *The Post*, 'Equal Pay and Family Allowances', 1 October 1927, p.256.

23 *London County Council Staff Association Gazette*, March 1926, p.79; May 1926, p.133; June 1926, p.174. For a discussion of the importances of the FWCS/NAWCS see Glew, 'Women in the Post Office', chapter 4 and B.V. Humphries, *Clerical Unions in the Civil Service*, (Oxford: Oxford University Press, 1958), p.154.

24 *London Town*, 'Annual General Meeting', January 1929, p.8. LMA, LCC MIN/12730, meetings of 26 November 1929 and 4 December 1929.

25 WL, 6/JCS/A1, Box FL 339, Joint Committee on Women in the Civil Service, meeting of 20 June 1929.

26 Lord Millett, 'Tomlin, Thomas James Chesshyre, Baron Tomlin (1867–1935)', *Oxford Dictionary of National Biography* (Oxford University Press, 2004) [www.oxforddnb. com/view/article/36531, accessed 11 August 2014].

27 Tomlin Commission, Evidence, paras 1741–1750; 1872.

28 Tomlin Commission, Evidence, paras 14261–14,288.

29 Tomlin Commission, Evidence of the Council of Women Civil Servants, para. 14,652; para. 14,657.

30 Tomlin Commission, *Report*, para. 455.

31 POST 33/729A, Evidence of Sir G. E. P. Murray and Mr E. Raven, paras 3688–3691.

32 BPMA, POST 115/458, *The Post*, Report of Evidence given to the Royal Commission, evidence of Sir Warren Fisher, 27 December 1930, p.580.

33 Tomlin Commission, Evidence, paras. 866, 884–887, 927–928, 962.

34 *Hansard*, Civil Service (Women, Pay) HC Deb 1 April 1936 vol. 310 cc.2017-96.

35 Duncan Tanner, 'Goldstone, Sir Frank Walter (1870–1955)', *Oxford Dictionary of National Biography* (Oxford University Press, 2004), online edn, January 2008 [www.oxforddnb.com/view/article/47357, accessed 8 February 2015]; Peter Gosden, 'Jackson, Sir Percy Richard (1869–1941)', *Oxford Dictionary of National Biography* (Oxford University Press, 2004) [www.oxforddnb.com/view/article/63811, accessed 8 February 2015].

36 Tomlin Commission Report, para. 358; *Hansard*, Salaries and Wages (Sex Equality), HC Deb 7 June 1935, vol. 302, c.2230.

37 Tomlin Commission, *Report*, para. 471.

38 Gladden, *Civil Service or Bureaucracy?*, p.52.

39 Tomlin Commission, *Report*, para. 465.

40 Tomlin Commission, *Report*, para. 470.

41 Tomlin Commission, *Report*, para. 469.

42 Tomlin Commission, *Report*, para. 469.

43 POST 115/457, *The Post*, proceedings of the Royal Commission, 5 April 1930, p.335; Wellcome Library, SA/MWF/D/1, 'Payment of Medical Women under the Post Office, 1919–1930', statement by the MWF as to why they wanted to appear before the Royal Commission on the Civil Service.

44 SA/MWF/D/1, 'Payment of Medical Women under the Post Office, 1919–1930', Letter to Postmaster General from the MWF, 1 October 1921 and reply 4 November 1921. Further letter, 23 February 1923 re-confirmed the GPO's position. SA/MWF/D/1, letter from Dr Madgshon to Mrs Vince MD, September 1919. BPMA, POST 59/144–171, GPO Establishment Books, 1911–39.

45 *Hansard*, Post Office (Women Doctors) HC Deb 17 March 1925 vol. 181 cc.2042-3. See also the evidence of the Institution of Professional Civil Servants: Tomlin Commission, Evidence, paras 16,407–16,411

46 *Hansard*, Salary Scales (Medical Officers), HC Deb 27 July 1936 vol. 315 c.1097; BPMA, POST 59/168–171, GPO Establishment Books, 1936–1939.

47 Francis D. Klingender, *The Condition of Clerical Labour in Britain* (London: Martin Lawrence, 1935), pp.90–91.

48 LMA, GLSA/1/32–37, LCC Staff Association minutes, 1930–1939.

49 POST 115/90, *Opportunity*, 'The Past and the Future, 1932–3', p.3.

50 WL, 6JCS, Box FL339, Minutes of the Joint Committee on Women in the Civil Service, 10 May 1932.

51 *Opportunity*, 'The Past and the Future, 1932–3', p.3.

52 *Committee on Women's Questions Report*, para. 35.

53 MRC, MSS.148/UCW/3/7/2, Union of Post Office Workers, N[ational] W[hitley] C[ouncil]. Equal Pay (1935 Campaign), Committee Minutes, 26 February 1935; POST 115/91, *Opportunity*, 1935, *passim*.

54 *Red Tape* special issue, 1936.

55 MRC, MSS.148/UCW/3/7/2, Union of Post Office Workers, N.W.C. Equal Pay (1935 Campaign) – Committee Minutes, 18 June 1935.

56 *Hansard*, Salaries and Wages (Sex Equality), HC Deb 7 June 1935, vol. 302, cc.2211–2215.

57 *Hansard*, HC Deb 7 June 1935, vol. 302, cc.2215–2220; Martin Pugh, 'Tate, Mavis Constance (1893–1947)', *Oxford Dictionary of National Biography* (Oxford University Press, 2004) [www.oxforddnb.com/view/article/39185, accessed 5 February 2015].

58 *Hansard*, HC Deb 7 June 1935, vol. 302, cc.2229–2230. For Hills' long-standing support of women's equality issues in the Civil Service, see other chapters in this volume and Takayanagi, 'Parliament and Women', pp.62–78.

59 Philip Ziegler, 'Cooper, (Alfred) Duff, first Viscount Norwich (1890–1954)', *Oxford Dictionary of National Biography* (Oxford University Press, 2004), online edn, January 2011 [www.oxforddnb.com/view/article/32547, accessed 10 July 2012].

60 *Hansard*, HC Deb 7 June 1935, col.2245. For further use of this rhetoric, see WL, 6NCS, Box FL435, 'Equal Pay: Mainly Equal Pay Publicity Sub-Committee', Correspondence between Miss Annie Norris and Mr S. S. Hammersley.

61 *Hansard*, HC Deb 7 June 1935, col. 2244.

62 POST 33/729A, Evidence of Sir Alexander King, col. 31,263; col. 31,394; col. 31,453; col. 31,458–31,461

63 Salaries and Wages (Sex Equality), col. 2244.

64 *Hansard*, HC Deb, 1 April 1936: Orders of the Day: Supply: Civil Estimates and Estimates for Revenue Departments, cols 2018–2019.

65 Orders of the Day: Supply: Civil Estimates and Estimates for Revenue Departments, cols 2018–2019.

66 Salaries and Wages (Sex Equality), col. 2244.

67 See Chapter 3.

68 *Royal Commission on Equal Pay*, para. 467.

69 WL, 6JCS, Box FL339, Minutes of the Joint Committee on Women in the Civil Service, 22 July 1935.

70 MRC, MSS.148/UCW/3/7/2, Union of Post Office Workers, N.W.C. Equal Pay (1935 Campaign), Committee Minutes, 18 June 1935.

71 LMA, GLSA/1/32, LCC Staff Association executive committee minutes, 28 October 1935.

72 LCC Staff Association executive committee minutes, 4 May 1936.

73 Smith, 'Sex vs Class', p.32.

74 A number of women MPs initially supported the motion but fewer lent their support when the issue was turned into a vote of confidence. Jones, *Women in British Public Life*, p.149.

75 WL, 6/JCS/D, Joint Committee on Women in the Civil Service, Joint Committee Leaflets, 1935–1936, letter from LNSWS *et al.*

76 MRC, MSS.148/UCW/2/1/21, UPW executive committee meeting, 13–15 July 1937, 'Sex Differentiation in Pay. Sub-Committee of the Joint General Purpose Committee of the National Whitley Council. Report', para. 2. In addition, the CSCA stated that their participation in the committee left 'our hands completely free to resume the equal pay campaign at the first opportune moment'. See MRC, MSS.415/62/4, CSCA Annual Report, January–December 1937, pp.36–37.

77 MRC, MSS.148/UCW/2/1/21, 'Sex Differentiation in Pay', para. 3.

78 See MRC, MSS.148/UCW/2/13/20/1, Annual Conference Report, 1938, Miss D. Aspden speech on 'Sex Differentiation in Pay', p.27; POST 115/184, *Red Tape*, CSCA Women's Notes, July 1937, p.803; POST 115/92, *Opportunity*, 'The Unequal Pay Agreement', July 1937, pp.123–124.

79 POST 115/92, *Opportunity*, 'The Unequal Pay Agreement', July 1937, pp.123–124; WL, 6NCS, FL435, NAWCS Equal Pay Campaign, 'Equal Pay: Mainly Equal Pay Publicity Sub-Committee'.

80 POST 115/92, *Opportunity*, 'Equal Pay', December 1937, p.218.

81 MSS.148/UCW/3/7/2, Union of Post Office Workers, N.W.C. Equal Pay (1935 Campaign), Committee Minutes 20 February 1939.

82 Harold Smith, 'The Problem of "Equal Pay for Equal Work" in Great Britain during World War II', *The Journal of Modern History*, vol. 53, no. 4 (December 1981), p.654.

83 LMA, LCC MIN/12731, Joint Committee of Members and Staff, agenda paper 300, 17 February 1937.

84 LCC MIN/12731, Joint Committee of Members and Staff, 27 July 1937.

85 *London Town*, 'A Rebuff', September 1937, p.294, p.300; Letters to the Editor, October 1937, p.327; November 1937, pp.361–362; Letters to the Editor, December 1937, p.398.

86 MSS.148/UCW/3/7/2, 3 July 1939.

87 BT Archives, POST 33/1987, Telegraph instrument and counter duties: proportion of men to women, part I.

88 Boston, *Women Workers and the Trade Unions*, p.169.

89 POST 115/467, *The Post*, 'Report of Conference Proceedings' (Supplement to 8 June 1935 edition), p.33; POST 115/469, *The Post*, 'Report of Conference Proceedings', 23 May 1936, pp.54–55; POST 115/471, *The Post*, Report of Annual Conference Proceedings 1937, supplement, p.46.

90 Boston, *Women Workers and the Trade Unions*, pp.168–169.

5

The slow road to victory:
the equal pay campaigns from 1939 to 1954

It may be that we are at a psychological moment when the enunciation
of the principle of equal pay would crystallise sentiments at present
vague, and would have an important influence in breaking down the
non-economic as well as the economic barriers which have hitherto
restricted the sphere of employment of women.

Dame Anne Loughlin, Dr Janet Vaughan and Miss L. F. Nettlefold,
'Memorandum of Dissent', *Report of the Royal Commission on
Equal Pay* (London: HMSO, 1946), p.194

The campaigns for equal pay for female public servants were in an
ambiguous position by 1939. In the Civil Service, in particular, the
vociferous campaigns and the psychological victories of the House
of Commons votes in 1920 and especially 1936 had rendered the issue
prominent and also meant that a considerable amount of the ground-
work – both in terms of organisational alliances and amassing support
amongst politicians – had been completed. However, successive governments and the Treasury remained as opposed as ever to enacting equal
pay. By 1955, the landscape had changed dramatically. Equal pay for grades
on which men and women were employed in the LCC's minor establishment was granted in 1952, bringing these grades into line with the major
establishment. In the LCC as a whole equal pay had remained less of a
volatile issue, in part because a considerable number of women in its professional and administrative grades already received equal pay. The LCC's
decision to grant equal pay to the minor establishment was, as we will see
later in this chapter, a surprise to many, especially given the ongoing saga
of equal pay debates in the Civil Service and the LCC's on-and-off assertions that it needed to pace itself against the Civil Service.

The much more publicised campaign by the staff side and women
campaigners of the Civil Service was finally successful by mid-1954, with

the details of the agreement finalised by early 1955. It was clear from the early post-war years that the balance of ministerial and political opinion had begun to shift in favour of equal pay and whilst considerable campaigning continued until 1952 and 1955, much of this was concerned with the timing and physical implementation of equal pay rather than seeking widespread acceptance of the justice of the claim, although some more conservative and reactionary views on the issue naturally remained. Ultimately the equal pay decision was always going to be political, because it had to be decided by Parliament.[1] The Trades Union Congress (TUC) was at best cautious in any support for equal pay for public employees across much of the first decade after the Second World War and was not prepared to support the same thing for employees in other trades it represented.[2] Thus, this stage of the battle was fought largely by public service associations and their long-standing allies, though both the UPW and the CSCA had re-joined the TUC in 1946 so were also able to use TUC annual conferences as an opportunity to air the issues.

This chapter charts the campaigns from 1939, evaluating the actions of staff, officials and campaign groups and the rhetoric deployed. In so doing, it provides the first comprehensive analysis of the campaigns in this period. Sarah Boston has argued that the campaigns for equal pay in the Civil Service were a 'notable exception' to the general tenor of women and trade unionism in the 1950s and also that they 'challenged assumptions about women's apathy' in the trade union movement.[3] However, her account focuses on some of the more noticeable and creative publicity stunts in the campaign rather than analysing it as a whole or from the perspective of longer-term activism for equal pay in the public service.[4] Harold L. Smith argues that the 1954 agreement brokered by Rab Butler, Chancellor of the Exchequer in Churchill's government, was an attempt to secure a greater number of women's votes ahead of the forthcoming general election.[5] However, the emergence of the equal pay agreement and its evolution and implementation were part of a much longer campaign with much wider significance. Although vote winning may have been the short-term catalyst this hides the fact that it was, in effect, a capitulation by a long series of administrations who had finally run out of excuses to not grant women the equal pay they so desired.

Indeed, it is clear that equal pay for civil servants as a theoretical principle was accepted as a cross-party issue from the mid-1940s. Even if individual ministers did not believe in it, they were outwardly prepared to support the issue. It would be teleological, of course, to suggest that equal pay was a foregone conclusion in the early post-war years, but the broad support for the principle meant that it was questions of timing and implementation which became the most prominent after 1945. Although it was perhaps a more minor issue in the grand scheme of national policy, discussions of equal pay are markedly absent from economic histories of the years after 1945 and from biographies and memoirs of many politicians – especially given that it was the argument of national finance that was used again and again to justify not granting equal pay. This chapter is thus also an attempt to set the equal pay campaigns in the context of broader discussions about finance and the economy in the post-war years.

The equal pay issue and the Second World War

As Braybon and Summerfield have shown, the Second World War, much like the First, saw relatively few women in many industries actually receiving equal pay even if they were theoretically doing the same work as men.[6] In the LCC's manual work grades, women filled vacancies that would have been ordinarily reserved to men, though this was carried out on an as-necessary basis department-by-department rather than as a result of a Council-wide decision.[7] The question of what to pay women on such work naturally arose, particularly if it was perceived that women did not, or could not, carry out all of the men's duties. The Ministry of Labour would offer no advice to local councils when the work in question did not relate directly to the war effort, and the LCC agreed to the proposal made by the Joint Industrial Council for the London region, which meant that women were paid 75 per cent of men's wages for an initial four-month probationary period and then the full male rate thereafter.[8] For clerical work and grades above this in both the LCC and the Civil Service, the fact that women and men already worked in "mixed" or "aggregated" grades meant that the war made no difference: pay scales remained fixed and differentiated along gendered lines as no woman could be said to be doing work that was usually done by men only. This was exactly the same as peacetime and therefore the precedent was already set.

As ever, we might question what difference the war made to attitudes to equal pay both inside and outside the public service. Mark Crowley has examined this question for the Post Office, and particularly for the manipulative grades, tracing some of the complexities of the campaigns but noting that campaigners were ultimately frustrated by many of same issues that had been present in the interwar years.[9] However, women's participation in the war as war workers and, in many cases, as replacements for men, was so prominent – both in and outside public service – that it is conceivable that this had an effect on general attitudes to equal pay among the public. Alix Meynell, for example, argued that 'the obviously equal work of women during the war must have done more than any argument could do to forward the case for equal pay'. By 1942, the CWCS was already thinking about its equal pay campaign strategy for when the war was over, noting that the public mood appeared to be changing.[10]

Specific campaigning for equal pay began in the midst of the war. In 1944, Thelma Cazalet-Keir proposed a now-infamous amendment to Butler's Education Bill to give women teachers – the other stalwarts of the equal pay campaign alongside civil servants – equal pay.[11] This passed by one vote, though ultimately Churchill turned it into a vote of confidence in himself and Cazalet-Keir was forced to abandon support for the amendment.[12] The incident undoubtedly raised the profile of equal pay as an issue, given the coalition government's defeat and Churchill's subsequent actions in the midst of the war. Cazalet-Keir was a member of the Equal Pay Campaign Committee (EPCC), a wartime alliance stemming initially from the campaigns by female politicians and women's groups on issues such as equal compensation for war injuries.[13] The EPCC was, effectively, a more formalised version of the women's alliances and support networks that had existed throughout the interwar years, its membership comprising many of the middle-class or professional organisations campaigning for female equality in other spheres. EPCC campaigns took very much the same form as their interwar forerunners had, and each of the constituent societies gave time, personnel and money to the cause. The initial members included Philippa Strachey, a long-time supporter of the rights of women professionals through the LNSWS, the celebrated female engineer Caroline Haslett, Muriel Pierotti of the National Union of Women Teachers and Hilda Hart of the NAWCS. Dr Edith Summerskill, Labour MP for West Fulham who had become prominent in the war years in the campaign for equal compensation and for the right for women to bear arms, was also appointed.[14] By the late 1940s, the chair was Cazalet-Keir, no longer an MP after losing her seat in the 1945 election. The EPCC voted to grant women-only associations full membership but mixed associations, such as the CSCA, the National Staff Side of the Whitley Council, the National Association of Local Government Officers (NALGO) and the LCC staff association could be part of the advisory council which did have the power to appoint the personnel of the campaign committee.[15] Thus, just as the interwar campaigns had involved the Whitley Council staff side and women's organisations as two distinct but overlapping groups, gender remained a significant component of the campaign structure in the post-war years.

The gendered divisions of the post-war campaign were further cemented when word reached the EPCC that the Whitley Council staff side did not want to co-operate with it, but instead was working with the Civil Service's Equal Pay Committee (CSEPC).[16] This might have been expected given that both the CSEPC and the national staff side were Civil Service-specific, whereas the EPCC was intended to represent female public servants and professionals more widely. However, it was also symptomatic of the long-standing antagonism between the NAWCS in particular and the national staff side. Throughout the late 1940s and into the 1950s, the latter refused to allow the former into discussions over potential equal pay schemes, though this was at least in part because the NAWCS's dwindling membership meant that it had lost official representation rights for women clerks.[17] Thus, in addition to its combined efforts with the Equal Pay Campaign Committee, the NAWCS conducted its own publicity campaign for equal pay for women, which it addressed to MPs in particular.

The Royal Commission on Equal Pay, 1944–1946

The result of 1944 Commons debate and the ensuing furore was the Royal Commission on Equal Pay. William ('Bill') J. Brown of the CSCA and Independent MP for Rugby[18] attempted to bring about another Commons debate on equal pay in the Civil Service in any case in May as a means to continue highlighting the issue. It was recognised that the Royal Commission, like many of its predecessors, was a stalling tactic and a means for the government to claim it was addressing the issue whilst not really addressing it.[19] Chaired by the Honourable Mr Justice Asquith – son of the former Prime Minister – it also featured Dr Janet Vaughan, the Countess of Limerick, Dame Anne Loughlin, DBE and Lucy Frances Nettlefold. Vaughan was the Principal of Somerville College, Oxford, and a doctor with socialist sympathies, and Loughlin the TUC President who believed that equal pay should be given as a reward for women's war work.[20] Nettlefold, one of several women to campaign against the barring of women from becoming solicitors before the First World War, had been a departmental assistant secretary in the Ministry of Food in the First World War. She was then for many years a company director and it was her participation in the Commission which marked a transition from her career in industry to her career in public service. In 1949, she would become an LCC member, holding the St Marylebone seat for the Conservatives, and in recognition of her support for the equal pay cause, was appointed to the EPCC in 1948.[21] Completing the membership were Mr John Brown, the Honourable Jasper Nicholas Ridley, Professor Dennis Holme Robertson, an influential economist,[22] and Charles Stanley

Robinson. The Royal Commission had a relatively narrow remit: it was not asked to make recommendations, and nor did it consider work that was of equal value to be 'equal work'. Thus, its narrow definitions and the fact that it did not need to make a recommendation meant its conclusions were never going to be disruptive to current norms.[23]

During Commission hearings, unions and associations of course gave evidence in support of equal pay. Associations which represented both men and women insisted that there was majority support amongst their membership for equal pay, even if in previous years this had not quite been the case. The staff side of the Civil Service Whitley Council stated that the claim for equal pay was based simply on justice for women workers and the NAWCS's evidence was very much along the same lines.[24] The CWCS continued its campaign to highlight the numbers of dependents its members individually supported, citing that 88 of the 151 members surveyed had dependents, and that on average each was supporting 1.6 people other than themselves.[25]

Although Boston has argued that public employers giving evidence to the Royal Commission universally opposed equal pay, this is not entirely true for the LCC.[26] Its evidence revealed – albeit sometimes reluctantly and backhandedly – broad acceptance of the principle of equal pay. In fact, the Clerk of the Council, Eric Salmon, had privately indicated his support for equal pay in the early 1940s.[27] Of course, the Council was anomalous in many respects because it already paid its major establishment female staff at the same rate as men, but its submitted written and oral evidence revealed that the LCC knew it could not sustain its current practice of paying male and female clerical staff at differentiated rates.[28] Indeed, the original justification for this, based on the apparently different outputs of men and women working for the Council in the First World War, was deemed no longer relevant.[29] This had important implications for the future direction of the campaign in the LCC. The Clerk of the Council was prepared to admit that justification for pay discrimination had no foundation. Whilst doing so, he argued that the LCC would need to keep pace with the Civil Service – even though of course it was already ahead because of the parity of pay between men and women in its higher grades.[30]

The LCC Staff Association's evidence was similarly illuminating. Including a section on the social, economic and financial implications of equal pay, the association tackled the "male breadwinner" argument directly. It argued that the idea of the "rate for the job" – increasingly the more preferable and palatable expression for "equal pay for equal work"[31] – was now a 'fundamental principle of modern economic thought' and that the principle of paying men more because they were assumed to have dependents undermined this principle. Similarly, it was, the Association argued, unfair to punish women on the assumption that all women were less effective workers than all men. This point had been made publicly numerous times and was of course bolstered by the LCC's own admission that men and women were equally accomplished workers. The Staff Association was clearly not without its reservations about the process of equal pay, and in several key respects picked up on points made by the UPW before the war, arguing that whilst equal pay would be of benefit to men and women in roles where both sexes already did the same work, its introduction would otherwise encourage employers to frame other work as either women's or men's so as to avoid giving equal pay. The best solution, the Association argued, was to open all work to both men and women and to establish a national minimum wage at the same time.[32] This had resonance with certain UPW debates of the late 1930s which had emphasised, for different reasons, the granting of equal pay first, before work was made interchangeable between the sexes. These points, though not entirely original to the LCC Staff Association, were not picked up by the Commission during oral evidence. Instead, the Staff Association was able to demonstrate that there was no empirical or logical basis for sick leave creating the disparity between men's and women's pay and to air their frustration that the LCC felt it could not get ahead of the Civil Service on the question of equal pay.[33]

The Treasury argued along economic lines and specifically drew on what it referred to as the principle of fair relativity – that is that it had to pace itself against outside employers and therefore had to calibrate the wages it paid carefully. It had used this argument before, and the reasoning had also been used in parliamentary debates, but always alongside other social arguments against equal pay.[34] However, it was now the principal basis for the Treasury's argument and it backed down on other arguments such as those relating to women's capabilities, though it clearly still felt that the male breadwinner argument had currency. Essentially, the basis of its argument was that women civil servants were well-paid compared to women in outside employment; its critics pointed out, however, that in outside employment women rarely did the same work as men and therefore the comparison in that sense was moot. Sir Alan Barlow, Second Secretary of the Treasury, conceded that he could see the case for paying women in the highest positions the same as their male counterparts, once they were employed there, but argued, as his predecessors had, that this did not necessarily translate to other grades.[35] This may have been because women in the highest positions were identifiable and their work quantifiable; it may also have been a case of elitism or classism, unconscious or not. There was also a question which invited a comparison between the LCC and the Civil Service in terms of the former paying its higher-grade staff equally, but the Commissioners did not push the issue further.[36] Furthermore, the language Barlow used at times revealed some deeper unease about giving women equal pay. For example, when asked what the Treasury would do to make the Civil Service appeal to men in the event that they might be put off from joining the service by women being paid the same as them, Sir Alan Barlow began his response with 'If we were driven to it, if some of the results which we fear from the introduction of equal pay matured, and we found that they were having evil effects...'.[37] The use of "driven" indicates the immovability of the Treasury and the words "fear" and "evil" reveal a deep-seated anxiety about a public service where women were treated and rewarded in the same way as men.

Despite instructions not to make recommendations, the Commissioners nevertheless made it clear that the present state of unequal pay in the public service was untenable and, as Mortimer and Ellis have noted, managed to 'provide much useful evidence to assist the civil service unions in their campaign for the rate for the job'.[38] The report noted that equal pay was already prevalent in professional work outside of public employment and that it was unlikely equal pay would alter the propensity to employ women in the public service. Evidence presented had also, unlike previous Civil Service pronouncements, suggested that women and men performed equally well in the workplace.[39] The Commission, like others at the time, worried that equal pay would result in different standards of living for those with dependents and those without, and argued that this would likely increase the demand for family allowances, legislation for which had been passed the previous year.[40] Vaughan, Loughlin and Nettlefold, three of the four female Commissioners, went further in their criticisms, arguing that much of what had been presented to the Commission as evidence was in fact only opinion, and that if women were allowed to pursue a wider range of careers this would lead to greater productivity. The three co-authored a minority response to part of the report, arguing that women were not demonstrably less efficient than men and that women's wages remained low for a number of social and economic factors, including the fact that employers did not want to compete with one another in offering better wages to women as this would create a general rise in wage bills.[41]

The assumption that men had dependents and women did not had pervaded interwar equal pay debates, as we have seen. The passage of the

Family Allowances Act, one of the seminal pieces of post-war, welfare state legislation, therefore had significant implications for equal pay debates. By guaranteeing that an allowance would be paid to the mother for the second and each subsequent child, family allowances might in theory have divorced the question of provision for "traditional" nuclear families from equal pay. Indeed, several associations continued to argue that family allowances should be treated as irrelevant from the fairness and justice to women of an equal pay claim, as had *The Times* in 1944.[42] However, rather than the new legislation having eliminated the dependents argument entirely, detractors from equal pay tended to now argue that wives were dependents but not provided for in family allowances, or to argue that as family allowances were insufficient, a wage differential was still needed.[43] Thus, the "rate for the job" was still not quite the only consideration.

Given the relative predictability of the Royal Commission's report in light of its remit, the most significant reaction to it was resignation. Florence Key, chair of the Open Door Council, labelled it 'tedious, verbose and inconclusive'.[44] Amongst the other reactions to the report was a pamphlet by Elaine Burton, Labour MP for Coventry South and long-time writer on women's issues.[45] She was adamant, like many of her colleagues in the Labour movement, that equal pay and dependents' allowances should be separate issues. She was also one of the few to articulate that ingrained prejudices against women workers affected wider attitudes to equal pay, stating that the Commissioners 'have under-estimated the force of all the conventions, customs and prejudices perpetuating the tradition that women are unreliable and indifferent workers'.[46] She was clear about what her own party should do, too:

> The Labour Party is committed to the principle of the rate for the job, therefore the Government should give a lead to the country by informing the Treasury that the principle of fair relativity [with outside employers] is no longer to be regarded as paramount over all other considerations. Nothing but a directive from the highest political level will make any impact on the Treasury, where, at the moment, there exists an impossible circle. The Treasury say they believe in the principle of fair relativity, ie the Government should not pay more to their own employees than is paid outside. As the Treasury formulate their rates of pay by first looking outside and then assuming that women should be paid four-fifths of the men's rate, this attitude is not likely to make for progress. Outside employers find the circle useful too: they take the view that the Government pay less to women than to men, so why should they not do the same? In effect, from all arcs of the circle, long live the status quo.[47]

In this short paragraph, Burton managed to sum up the vicious circle and the dominant argument in the debate for the next few years.[48] The way in which this played out is discussed below.

During a 1947 deputation, both the National Whitley Council Staff Side and the Chancellor of the Exchequer, Hugh Dalton, lamented the style and inadequacy of the Commission's report, Dalton labelling it 'a very wibbly-wobbly sort of document'. The meeting was good-natured, and Dalton stressed that the financial position of the country prevented the granting of equal pay. The deputation tried to no avail to argue that increased wages for women would mean an increase in their purchasing power and also a return to the Treasury of a portion of the funds via taxation of the women affected. Several female deputation members went on to stress in particular the psychological and equality implications of equal pay, but Dalton managed to outmanoeuvre these points with rhetoric.[49]

In his formal response to the Commission's report in the Commons, Dalton accepted the principle and justice of equal pay but argued implementation created its own set of challenges in terms of cost and the inflationary risk. The acceptance may have seemed promising, but the statement was little more than one extra assertion of theoretical support which civil servants had been hearing since the early 1920s. Indeed, Dalton's own diary entry conveyed his conservative approach to the issue, and perhaps his misjudgement about the growing Civil Service agitation. He wrote:

> I made, on Wednesday, a Parliamentary Statement about 'Equal Pay', accepting the principle but refusing to apply it now or to give any future date when it could be applied. This was taken surprisingly well in the House as, indeed, it had been at a Party Meeting held earlier the same day. I don't think there is much political steam behind the Equal Pay agitation, and people are becoming better educated to the dangers of inflation.[50]

The public might well have been becoming more aware of inflationary dangers but civil servants would certainly have begged to differ on Dalton's point about the seriousness of the equal pay campaigning. Also, as Thelma Cazalet-Keir pointed out in her autobiography – somewhat partisanly, given that Conservative governments had not been above giving feeble excuses themselves – many other wage increases were actually made that year, rendering the justification about inflation somewhat suspect.[51] Several MPs, including William J. Brown of the CSCA, mooted during the debate the possibility of reducing costs by giving women men's increments each year until they reached equal pay, a suggestion which Dalton claimed to have not heard previously, though it had also been discussed during the 1931 Royal Commission. He offered to consider this, his words coming across as more out of politeness than actual commitment.[52]

Sections of Dalton's own party were also becoming vocal about the equal pay position. At the 1947 Labour conference the month before the Commons debate Mrs E. M. White had proposed a motion that was carried by four votes to one arguing for equal pay for all public servants in central and local government. This was, of course, embarrassing for Dalton and his government. However, as one commentator at *The Spectator* wrote:

> There are various ways of getting out of this dilemma. The issue may be avoided altogether, as it usually has been in the past. There is the expedient of referring the matter to a committee. The Report of the Royal Commission on this subject, six months ago, was a model of evasion. Or again, there is the policy of the present Government of accepting equal pay in principle and postponing it in practice. All these devices are expedients, varying mainly in the degree of cynicism with which they are adopted.[53]

The 1947 discussions in the Commons spurred the LCC Staff Association to question the Council. The staff side wrote asking for an affirmation of support for equal pay, if only in principle, and presented a plan for granting greater increments to the women not currently receiving equal pay, so that in effect the principle would be eased in over a decade or so.[54] The Clerk of the Council's reply argued that this plan actually went further than the Chancellor had been prepared to entertain for the public service and concluded – perhaps somewhat conveniently – that a full financial review was needed and that agreeing to the plan would push the LCC ahead of the rest of the public service.[55] Thus, the see-sawing effect between different factions of the public service was evident, as was the LCC's lack of acknowledgement that it was already ahead of the Civil Service in equal pay terms. Interestingly, the LCC does not appear to have used the inflationary argument as a defence.

In 1948, the Civil Service staff side met with Sir Stafford Cripps, now Chancellor, and proposed introducing equal pay over a 12–18-year period, but this was rejected on the grounds of finance once again. In particular, it conflicted with the Labour government's White Paper on Personal Incomes. The paper, which arose out of the work of the Working Party on Wage Stabilisation, recommended a voluntary wage freeze except for employment sectors where there were staff shortages or which were being particularly productive. The TUC agreed ultimately to endorse this.[56] This, therefore, goes some further way towards explaining why the TUC was so hesitant in pushing forward the call for equal pay, given that the campaign was in direct conflict with the contents of the White Paper. As Dorfman also shows, this support for the White Paper was the only example in the post-war era of the TUC keeping its side of the bargain with the government for more than two years.[57]

The Civil Service Clerical Association saw Cripps' statement and reluctance as a sign to 'pursue a vigorous campaign'.[58] However, the cracks in the blanket refusal to grant equal pay in the Civil Service had already begun to show. When she became Deputy Secretary of the Ministry of Town and Country Planning in 1946, Evelyn Sharp was granted the same salary as her male counterparts, but this remained personal to her only.[59] More significantly as it involved a group of employees in a newly created job, male and female NHS administrators had been granted equal pay in 1949 after representations had been made.[60] Therefore, a considerable number of anomalies now existed, though these remained more hidden compared to higher-grade salaries in the LCC. In addition, some women in provincial local government were granted equal pay after an agreement in January 1946, which also had the potential to be seen as precedent-setting.[61] Thus, a momentum was gathering.

Whilst staff side deputations went to see successive chancellors, equal pay pressure groups continued their public activities. In July 1949, the EPCC held an emergency meeting at which it was decided to accept an offer from Jill Craigie to write and direct a film in support of the equal pay cause.[62] The film cost £5,000 to make and was funded by donations from the EPCC and its advisory council. The NAWCS, CWCS and LCC Staff Association were among the principal donors.[63] The resulting film, *To Be A Woman* (1951), did not have a theatrical release[64] but played in a number of cinemas and elsewhere. Craigie herself, at a difficult point in her career, was not pleased with the result.[65] The short film began with a "state of the nation"-esque assessment of women's lives, emphasising the numbers of women working outside the home, the work that women were already doing, and the desire for women to have equal training and employment opportunities with men. It described the benefits and value to society of women being in the workplace but then warned that 'the old prejudice isn't dead yet. A woman in a job in twentieth century Britain is encouraged to feel inferior. She's not paid the rate for the job. She's CHEAP LABOUR'. The female narrator, who conveyed the woman's point of view, was the acclaimed actor Wendy Hiller and the soundtrack included a series of drumrolls at the points of emphasis. The phrase 'cheap labour' was repeated several times in emphatic tones, the final time being abbreviated for dramatic effect to 'women are cheap'. Significantly, the first example offered of unequal pay was the postwoman receiving nearly £1 per week less than the postman. The prominent argument for equal pay throughout the film was thus that current practice also hurt men as women remained the cheaper employees. There was some discussion, using teachers as the example, of men having dependents and women not, but this was refuted in terms which would be familiar to any viewer who had followed the equal pay debates.[66] In a further attempt to address this line of thinking, towards the end of the film Ian Mikardo, an industrial relations consultant and Labour MP,[67] argued that workers should be paid the rate for the job and that it was the state's responsibility to help pay for dependents. Julien Sommers, the male narrator who introduced points of dissent, then repeated that all of the political parties supported equal pay but the time was not right. Hiller's narration remarked angrily that 'Now never is the time. Women were fighting for the rate for the job even before they were going to prison for the vote'. The footage moved to a shot of Parliament, with a pointed question from Hiller: 'Have some of those women in there, who are getting the rate from the job, forgotten the cause of women?' This was not an entirely fair question, given that successive women MPs had taken prominent roles in equal pay debates and that women MPs alone could not make the difference in the vote because they were numerically so few. Hiller's narration was followed by a clash of cymbals and a further drum roll. Finally, the film featured the idea that equal pay would cause or exacerbate inflation. The retort of Hiller, and by implication the film, was (rather optimistically) that no man would be discriminated against on the grounds of religion, ethnicity, immigrant status or hair colour, but women were paid less because of their sex. The film closed with a continuation of its opening footage of a young woman and the question 'Isn't it time that we in Britain made it a proud thing to be a woman?'[68]

The film highlighted much more than the problem of unequal pay by underlining how such discrimination compounded, and was compounded by, negative attitudes to women. *London Town*, whose readership had of course contributed to the funding of the film, reported that it was '[a]nother powerful weapon in the continued struggled to secure "equal pay" … The film … is notable for the vigour and humour with which it presents an overwhelming case for full recognition of the value of women workers of all kinds'.[69] *Red Tape*, although lauding the concept and existence of such a film, was less complimentary, arguing that 'its message has not been put over convincingly enough' and that the case of the Civil Service should have had a more central place.[70] How much impact the film had on either the general public or those who had the power to bring about equal pay is debatable but it is significant that it was made as the groundswell of support for equal pay was increasing.

The early 1950s

In the early 1950s, the staff side argued that the financial concerns over the introduction of equal pay had abated and began reinvigorated campaigns targeted at Parliament. In January 1951 it told Hugh Gaitskell, Chancellor of the Exchequer, that the country's financial situation was better, that the scheme it proposed for equal pay involved negligible costs and that it would in fact accept any incremental scheme as long as it meant a start on the equal pay process could be made straightaway. This did not make much headway as Gaitskell said that he needed to finance rearmament.[71]

In June 1951 Gaitskell announced in Parliament that he was unable to amend the 1947 decision on equal pay in public services owing to the state of the country's finances. There remained cause for concern, after the sterling crises of 1947 and 1949.[72] However, rather than confining his explanations to finance, he used the well-worn argument that men had dependents and women did not in order to suggest that equal pay would bring further demands for increased family allowances, though Irene Ward, Conservative MP for Tynemouth, tried to challenge him on this. He also suggested that women's supposed lack of dependents would mean that women were in a better position compared to men and that any wages increase would also bring inflationary pressures to bear on the economy. Female MPs responded again, with Ward arguing that Civil Service salaries had already been allowed to increase by £40 million in the years since the Royal Commission on Equal Pay, and Jennie Lee taking him to task on the fact that the City was not being checked on the inflationary pressures it put on the economy.[73] In a sign that the government did not take complete control of the issue, and one which gave the LCC considerable room to manoeuvre, Gaitskell ended the debate by saying that he would not stop local authorities from implementing equal pay if they so wished. It is not clear whether this spurred the LCC Staff Association to further activity, but the Association's donations to the EPCC increased at this time.[74]

It is fair to say that Gaitskell's performance and reasoning appeared weak to his many spectators. By bringing up the familiar reasoning against equal pay – much of which was either now discredited or irrelevant – he made it seem as if governmental support for equal pay was no stronger than it had previously been and that there had been no progress on the issue. As the North Kingston-upon-Hull Labour Party Joint Women's Section told him, '[y]ou used all the arguments against equal pay that are used by people who do not believe in the principle, & we are now wondering what the Policy of the Labour Party is'.[75] The group was one of two women's organisations to warn of the possibility of militancy.[76] The NAWCS's response was notable for its deliberate engagement with socialist ideals when it was a non-party-political organisation as it 'consider[ed] that equal pay would be a powerful incentive to increased production and that it would have a beneficial moral effect at this time when all the community must stand together without any section of it suffering a sense of injustice'.[77] The organisation had circularised MPs ahead of the debate asking them to support immediate and full implementation of equal pay, and had sent a telegram to Gaitskell to the same effect. Elsewhere, the general response to Gaitskell's announcement ranged from tempered criticism to outright vitriol. Stanley Mayne, General Secretary of the Institute of Professional Civil Servants, wrote to *The Times* arguing that the announcement of the government's position on equal pay ran contrary to TUC and Civil Service union policy, and also stated that the question of family allowances was a 'bogy' in the equal pay debate.[78] Groups of women of numerous political and of feminist leanings telegraphed or wrote to the Chancellor. The volume of correspondence testified to the number of organisations which saw female government employees as the key to achieving equal pay more broadly. The National Union of Women Teachers and the National Council of Women each sent two telegrams, one from the President and one from the Secretary, as if to doubly emphasise the point, and the other organisations and groups writing to the Chancellor included the National Union of Bank Employees, twenty-eight teachers from Battersea, the Brighton and Hove branch of the Business and Professional Women's Clubs, the Ministry of Supply section of the Society of Civil Servants, the Barry branch of the National Union of Teachers and the Equal Pay Committee of the South West Essex Technical College and School of Art.[79] The lone letter of congratulation to Gaitskell was from the National Association of Schoolmasters, which, as Alison Oram has documented, had vehemently opposed equal pay from the 1920s.[80]

Boston argues that mid-1951 was the point at which the campaign really coalesced and developed a momentum that continued throughout the following four years.[81] Certainly, this can be seen in the increasing activities of the staff side's equal pay co-ordinating committee and the

EPCC. The CSCA used one of the two motions it was able to send to the TUC conference to demand equal pay in the Civil Service.[82] After the 1951 election and Rab Butler's appointment as Chancellor, the letters of support for equal pay kept coming. The Women's Westminster Union, for example, sent Churchill a map showing all the countries in the world where female public servants received equal pay. There was a brief parliamentary debate about equal pay towards the end of the year, which, though it was symbolically important after the change of party in government, did not really advance the case any further.[83] A Treasury memorandum reveals a further twist in the government's retorts. In November 1951 the Treasury effectively gave £25 million to the City via an increase in the bank rate, and justified this in Parliament partly through the fact that they would recoup a proportion of this in taxation. When the Ruislip-Northwood Constituency Labour Party wrote to question why the Treasury could afford this and not equal pay, Treasury officials had to think carefully how to respond. Several commentators, including, as we have seen, the staff side, had previously argued that equal pay, too, would result in money returning to the exchequer via increased taxation, and the Treasury officials realised that they could not justify the City decision using the taxation argument because this would undermine their stance on not introducing equal pay.[84]

On 16 May 1952, Charles Pannell (Labour) succeeded in the private members' ballot and introduced a parliamentary motion calling for a specific date for the introduction of equal pay in the Civil Service. This was supported by Douglas Houghton, another Labour member and a prominent figure in Civil Service staff associational life. Irene Ward, a long-time campaigner for equal pay, spoke at length and passionately about the issue, and accused the Treasury as a department of being wholly resistant to change.[85] The debate largely revealed that MPs on both sides of the House supported equal pay but once again the issue was down to the precise details of implementation. The financial state of the country continued to carry some gravitas.[86] Suggestions that the introduction of equal pay would cause inflation were debated and refuted.[87] The outcome frustrated the staff side of the Whitley Council even further: although the principle was affirmed they were barred from going to arbitration and Butler still refused to negotiate. Their only recourse was to continue putting pressure on MPs.[88]

Meanwhile, the campaign in the LCC had been reignited by a Staff Association petition on the subject in February 1952. The Staff Association reported in *London Town* that it had recently come to light that the UK government had told the International Labour Organization that equal pay in local government service in Britain should be settled by collective bargaining. The Association had then used this as a justification for proceeding.[89] The petition essentially argued that were it not for the "miscalculation" in 1919 that clerical women could not do the same work as efficiently as clerical men (which of course the Clerk of the Council had "owned up to" recently), all main grades of LCC established employment would have been granted equal pay there and then. Thus, the staff side tried to argue that this was all about remedying an error of three decades ago and that the clerical grades had hitherto been anomalous in the LCC in not having equal pay. This was a clever attempt at the argument, particularly because the Council had previously justified unequal pay in terms of efficiency and output and had not really engaged with the wider social debates about fairness and assumed male breadwinners. The Council's representatives continued to insist that their evidence to the Royal Commission had not constituted a recommendation for equal pay, but they were seen to have crossed the line into supporting equal pay.[90]

Whilst there is no surviving evidence of the thought process of the key Council figures, it is clear that the LCC Staff Association essentially won the war without much of a final battle. Importantly, though, the Association threatened to take the Council into arbitration, and the Council was clearly mindful of the fact that the claim for equal pay for housemistresses, which had been taken to arbitration in 1951, had gone against them.[91] Although the Council offered a thin defence of its stance by arguing that equal pay would be ahead of the government's position, it soon began working out formulations of a gradual introduction of equal pay after an initial outline idea by the LCC Staff Association. The staff side proposal had to be approved by three Council committees – the General Purposes Committee, the Establishments Committee and then finally the Council itself on 1 July – but it was clear from spring 1952 that the Council was preparing seriously for equal pay and indeed expected it to be implemented.[92] Thought was given, for example, to how the press should be briefed on the issue: preliminary discussions took place largely away from public view – so were not known about, at least officially and publicly, when Pannell's mid-May Commons debate took place. However, the fact that the LCC was discussing equal pay was leaked to the press in late May.[93] The smoothness of the negotiations should not be taken to imply that all were in favour. Informal minutes of a meeting of officials record arguments about women's capabilities and married women's family responsibilities being a distraction as reasons for differentiated pay.[94] This was one of the first times such "social" arguments were made by

LCC officials, but this was clearly too little, too late when the decision elsewhere in the Council was largely a foregone conclusion.[95]

The Council predicted that the financial implications of introducing equal pay would not be great, as teachers' pay would be unaffected and the scheme was intended to be gradual, but argued that other local authorities might not be pleased.[96] Not all LCC constituents were happy of course, including 'R Gray', a Middlesex resident, who argued that 'higher pay has already caused a great increase in the divorce rate & equal pay will, like a festering sore, rot the very heart out of marriage & our social structure.'[97] Much of the reporting in the national press was a factual account of the process, but several newspapers took some delight in noting that there were only five women present to hear the outcome of the decision at 11 p.m. on the night it was announced, though given it was a Tuesday, presumably most of the women concerned had to work the next morning. The *Daily Telegraph*, in predicting the passage of equal pay on 28 June, pointed out that the LCC was socialist-controlled, hinting at the widespread perception that the Labour-dominated LCC had agreed to equal pay as a means to embarrass Churchill's Conservative government.[98] Most interesting was the article from *Local Government Service*, which pointed to the fact that 'this is the first substantial breach in the wall of "inopportunism" which public service employers have raised against adoption of a principle enshrined in the Charter of Human Rights and accepted by successive Parliaments since 1920' and that '[t]he victory removes the last shred of the argument of other employers that they cannot meet the claim until the government has granted it to the civil service.'[99] Although the campaign for equal pay had been long-standing and the LCC victory was clearly not something that took place in a vacuum, it is important to see this as a momentum-generating moment: it was obviously incredibly difficult for the government to ignore, and it severely disrupted the "fair relativity" argument. The only thing that arguably saved the government was Gaitskell's announcement in mid-1951 that local authorities could implement equal pay if they so wished: this had, in some respects, neatly divided the Civil Service from local authority public servants.

So what made the LCC grant equal pay in June 1952 but not before this point? In so doing, it had seemingly overridden its previous concern about getting ahead of the Civil Service and the government's wishes. However, a number of things had coalesced by this point: a Labour LCC during the first post-war Conservative government, the statement by Gaitskell about local authorities and equal pay, as well as the fact that through arbitration – a process denied, of course, to civil servants – a group of LCC employees had won equal pay. This point, in particular, meant that the writing was on the wall and a sense that equal pay was inevitable sooner or later appears to have pervaded the Council's discussions. The LCC's decision to grant equal pay left the Treasury in an awkward position. It argued that the 'giving of equal pay by the Socialist controlled LCC was in the nature of a political stunt to embarrass H M Government over the Civil Service'.[100] Staff wages in several LCC departments were funded in part through Treasury grants to the LCC as a local authority, and the LCC therefore had to ask Treasury permission to use grant funds to pay women staff more – though in many cases the numbers concerned were quite small. The Treasury, the Ministry of Housing and Local Government and the Home Office had a long and involved discussion about whether to agree to this, given the implications of agreeing to equal pay for employees it paid for indirectly and still refusing it for those it paid directly. Eventually, it was decided that it would be difficult to refuse the LCC staff equal pay, not least because the Treasury in effect already funded equal pay for women in the higher grades of the LCC departments concerned and also because of the fear of wider political reactions by the LCC.[101] The government was effectively backed into a corner. As the Treasury feared, the affirmative LCC decision created some new fire for the Civil Service equal pay campaign. In October 1952 Irene Ward, whom the Treasury had already predicted would 'sho[o]t at [the government] as inconsistent', tabled a parliamentary question which assumed that the decision about the LCC was now precedent-setting for, at least, women staff working for local authorities around the country.[102]

In late 1952 Butler stated publicly that he could not promise equal pay in the near future, having told the staff side this in early 1952.[103] Butler's parliamentary announcement elicited an angry response from Thelma Cazalet-Keir, who argued that the statement

is astounding because it is contrary to the spirit of the Financial Secretary's speech winding up the House of Commons debate … last May; contrary to the wishes of the House of Commons itself on that and many former occasions; contrary to the view of all the main women's organizations; and above all, contrary to justice. It is often said – and rightly – that in politics it requires strength to do unpopular things if you believe them to be right. But can it be possible that the Government still feel their opinion on this matter is the only right one, thought it conflicts with practically the entire organized opinion of the country, including the three political parties?

She pointed out, as others before her had, that, despite the Chancellor's pronouncement about the country's finances, many other groups of workers were receiving wage increases and she reminded readers that civil servants were prevented from entering arbitration.[104] Butler did permit the staff side to discuss with him how equal pay might be gradually implemented but would not accompany this with a declaration of when equal pay could be enacted. The staff side eventually turned this down, seeing such discussions as pointless and, perhaps, as creating only false hope and disappointment.

In many respects, 1953 was used as a year in which to generate publicity with nationwide campaigns by the staff side[105] and ongoing campaigns by the EPCC. In February 1953, Lord Pethick-Lawrence instigated a debate from the House of Lords in which he called on the government to state its intentions for equal pay. Given that, as Pethick-Lawrence himself argued, it was not protocol for the Lords to intervene on financial matters, the question was raised as a matter of both policy and publicity.[106] Three days later, three women from the CSCA delivered a Valentine's card to the Chancellor inscribed 'Remember your promise of 16th May/Be true to us on Budget Day'.[107] This was a prominent publicity stunt which changed nothing. The 1953 Budget came and went and in late 1953, the Priestly Royal Commission was set up to examine the issue of pay in the Civil Service. Equal pay campaigners, as Boston notes, saw this as another delaying tactic.[108]

By early 1954 the mood had changed somewhat as the Labour Party announced that it would grant equal pay to women in the Civil Service should it be returned at the next election. Serious discussions began in the Conservative ranks and in Cabinet. As Harold Smith argues, Cazalet-Keir played an important role in maintaining the pressure on Butler over equal pay.[109] She reported in her autobiography that '[t]he main thing was to transform into a definite commitment the vague approval of my party … Winston had never been exactly a crusader in our cause, but he and R.A. Butler did yield to my plea that the wording of the party's views on the subject should be clarified'.[110] In February 1954, she asked last-minute for a deputation with the Chancellor in order to state the views of the EPCC. Butler felt he could not refuse Cazalet-Keir, a colleague in his own party, though he would certainly have preferred to refuse the deputation as a whole. The attitude of Barbara Sloman, his Private Secretary, was symptomatic of the Treasury's longer-term attitude to women's organisations: she referred to the meeting as the 'equal pay jamboree', the deputation as 'equal pay girls' and suggested that the Chancellor might like a Treasury civil servant there to protect him.[111]

This gendered infantilising of the campaigners suggests an attempt to belittle the issue and to deflect anxieties.

In March 1954, two massive petitions – one from the staff side and one from the women's EPCC – were delivered to Parliament.[112] On 9 March, Butler announced that he had offered to begin talks with the staff side of the National Whitley Council on a scheme for gradual implementation, but that this had been declined.[113] This was, as Douglas Houghton suggested, somewhat disingenuous: the discussions had been refused previously because Butler had not agreed that equal pay could actually be implemented.[114] The parliamentary debate was full of submitted questions about the timing of equal pay and the promises previously made as well as the precise economic conditions on which equal pay would be granted. Butler conceded that '[t]here is no precise criterion by which to judge whether the financial and economic situation of the country is such as to justify the step desired. This must be a matter of judgment' – a statement which was perhaps seen to highlight that the passage of equal pay was still dependent on government whim and subject to the wider political context.[115] As Dr Horace King pointed out, the government was treading a fine line: on the one hand it was arguing that it had improved the economy; on the other, it was arguing that it could still not finance equal pay for women civil servants. Butler was also challenged on the fact that women MPs received equal pay but women civil servants working in Parliament did not. He ended the session reminding parliamentary colleagues he had accepted the principle of equal pay – something which campaigners had of course heard before from previous chancellors.[116]

The significance of the equal pay question to women civil servants was not lost on several political cartoonists, suggesting that, amongst other possibilities for satirical comment, the plight of women civil servants had captured the attention of at least some of the newspaper-reading public. Victor Weisz's illustration in the *Daily Mirror* on 9 March 1954 perhaps best summed up the campaign by depicting an imagined 9 March 1994 where women were being told once again by 'Mr Butskell' that the time was not yet opportune.[117] Lee in the *Evening News* three days later perhaps anticipated a favourable outcome on equal pay, but offered a seemingly ambivalent view on the women's struggle, depicting men with larger teacups than the women and a caption which read 'See that girl? We win the Battle for Equal pay in the Civil Service and now we've got to start a new one for equal-size tea-cups and digestive biscuits!'.[118]

Away from public view there was much discussion amongst the Cabinet and the most senior Civil Service officials. Butler told Florence Horsbrugh, Minister of Education, that '[i]f we don't move, someone will' and Harold Macmillan, Minister of Housing and Local Government, that '[i]f we don't pipe up, others will witness our Party resolutions and theirs'.[119] It is clear that Labour's promise had been influential, as Harold Smith has also argued,[120] and it was felt that it would be better to proceed at an early date in anticipation of a general election the following year.[121] Although the women civil servants affected made up a relatively small proportion of the electorate, the issue had been well publicised and was believed to have currency among women more generally.[122] The point Dr Horace King had made in Parliament also carried weight: it was contradictory for the government to argue it had improved the economy and to use the argument of finance to continue denying equal pay.[123] Significantly, too, several officials pointed to the fact that equal pay had been accepted as a principle repeatedly, and thus to the inevitability of it coming into being sooner or later. Notably there remained real resistance by the (male) senior Civil Service representative to the idea of women being worthy of equal pay.[124] Although the eventual scheme would have to be agreed with the Whitley Council, ministers and senior civil servants appear to have spent much of their time working out which of several schemes they wanted to advocate. The charmingly named 'Old Ladies Scheme', under which older women in the Service would be given equal pay first, was rejected as too complicated; the incremental implementation, described by one official as 'beautifully simple', was the preferred scheme.[125]

On 12 April in Parliament, as part of the Budget, Butler offered again to open negotiations with the staff side of the National Whitley Council to create a scheme for gradual implementation of equal pay for women in the Civil Service and this was accepted.[126] Thus, 1954 was the "moment" for the decision but it was backed by years of campaigning and near-successes or moral victories, outward cross-party support, broken political promises and a fair share of last-minute politicking. Equal pay had, therefore, been a long war of attrition.

The early years of equal pay

Despite the long years of activism, the final implementation of equal pay nearly a year later was met with a somewhat lacklustre and anti-climactic feeling and *Red Tape*, the magazine of the CSCA, suggested that it was seen by some to be no different to an ordinary pay claim.[127] There were divided opinions over the gradual implementation: under the Whitley scheme devised, women would proceed to men's maximum over a period of seven years, starting in 1955. However, many felt marked sympathy with the older women in the Civil Service who had been campaigning for equal pay for years but who would retire before feeling the full benefits, both in terms of their pay and their pensions.[128] The National Whitley Council report noted that several solutions to this had been proposed, but none could be found to be legal.[129] The EPCC, CSCA and NAWCS continued to campaign for a more advantageous solution for older and retired civil servants, but this proved to be to no avail.[130] Len White of the CSCA reported that the staff side had considered rejecting gradual implementation completely, but had realised that this would jeopardise the whole agreement. David Low's *Manchester Guardian* cartoon of 28 January 1955 depicted the 'seven ages of woman', satirising the seven-year implementation period until 1961. The 'equal pay woman' stands formally to salute Butler and a companion who are depicted as walking proudly by. The image was undercut by the caption 'Of course it takes millions of years before they reach perfection', highlighting the fact that women were still thought of as inferior.[131]

Thus, it was under the government of Winston Churchill, who had once written 'refuse, resist, and in the last resort, defy' about equal pay claims, that equal pay for women civil servants was now passed. Equal pay was not, of course, accepted by all commentators with equanimity. To take one example, in early 1955, Hilda Hart of the NAWCS was forced to write a robust letter to *The Times* in response to an article published criticising the implementation of equal pay for female civil servants.[132] The editorial had criticised, along now-familiar lines, the extra expenditure on public funds to bring this about and the fact that women without families would be better off than married male civil servants supporting families. In a pointed comment, it ended with the remark that '[t]he ghost of Eleanor Rathbone's "disinherited family" is not yet laid'.[133]

The EPCC also did not entirely know how to greet the news: in fact, it passed a resolution confirming that it would not make a definitive statement either way.[134] When the dust had settled a couple of months later, the Committee decided to have a so-called "Milestone Dinner" to symbolise the fact that the gradual schemes did not, in fact, satisfy the Committee's aims but were achievements in themselves.[135] There was a real debate as to whether the organisation should wind up its endeavours, as its main aim, equal pay, had been achieved in some form albeit with delayed gratification. Indeed, notes for the speech on disbandment, probably given by Philippa Strachey, strike a sad note, suggesting that relations in the Committee had been harmonious hitherto but that members would only be inviting dissent by continuing and trying to come to a conclusion as to whether gradual implementation of equal pay constituted the victory they had been working for. Eventually, disbandment was agreed to.[136]

For the women's grades where there was no male equivalent, there was of course a longer postscript. In the LCC, women typists and other women in women-only grades received so-called "sympathetic increases" of 16 per cent in October 1952.[137] Female typists in the Civil Service had to wait considerably longer after the Civil Service equal pay settlement.[138] In the Post Office, because women employed on telephones, in particular, did not undertake nightwork, and therefore did not undertake the same duties as men, a new agreement had to be found. Eventually, it was agreed that women who volunteered for nightwork should receive 100 per cent of men's pay, and those who chose not to should receive 95 per cent. However, as Alan Clinton has shown, in the other manipulative grades where equal pay did not apply until the enforcement of the 1970 Equal Pay Act, the UPW continued to "ring fence" jobs for men.[139] Thus, the equal pay settlement in both the LCC and the Civil Service highlighted the compounding effect of issues of gender and class for women in these positions: the lowest-paid work, despite sympathetic increases, continued to be largely women's work. Occupational segregation, which had limited women's opportunities in the public service for so long, was starkly in evidence here. These women had to wait for the 1970 Equal Pay Act and often longer, because their jobs seldom had a direct male equivalent and instead encroached upon the thorny question of 'work of equal value'.

It is fair to say that post-war, the achievement of equal pay for female government employees became something of an obsession for an alliance of women's organisations because it had been promised for so long, it was an often carefully worded manifesto pledge, and the gendered reasons for refusing it were manifestly unfair. This, combined with the ongoing campaigns by the mixed-sex associations of the National Whitley Council staff side, effected a campaign of attrition. The tactics of the campaigns, largely established in the interwar years, remained the same. What was occasionally noticeable was the re-moulding of campaigners' rhetoric and language to chime with, or unpick, current rhetoric and discourse.

That the equal pay issue had lingered for so long was amongst other things a symptom of the fact that successive governments decreed that it could not be discussed by Whitley Councils or conciliation and arbitration machinery. In effect – and especially after the 1926 Trades Disputes Act – this meant that civil servants' only recourse was Parliament – with its publicity possibilities but also its delays. Between party politics in the early years, and then financial pressures and politicking among the party in government in the later years, the issue was, as we have seen, repeatedly shelved, in part because it was feared it would be precedent-setting for private employees. The rhetoric of the Treasury, Civil Service officials and politicians meant that for many years the LCC did not feel comfortable progressing with equal pay for its own staff, though it is significant that the passage of equal pay in the end in the LCC was sudden and straightforward and could only add to the pressure on the government to do the same for civil servants. This aspect of the end of the long equal pay story has been under-appreciated by those historians offering an assessment of the granting of equal pay in the Civil Service, essentially because this period of the LCC's history as an employer has not been examined in detail previously.

However, even with the battle won in the Civil Service, female staff there still often had to negotiate the stereotypes and preconceived attitudes of their superiors, co-workers and union officials. To take just one example, writing a history of the Civil Service in 1956, E. N. Gladden made the following remarks:

> The campaign for equal pay for women has been waged by the staff since the recognition of equality between the sexes following the First World War ... Some women and many men may have had doubts, for rather different reasons, but it was not popular to challenge such an eminently fair principle as equal pay for equal work, although one might cynically ask whether there could be a more difficult principle to apply to the existing Civil Service system ... The long-term effect, of course, is to give unmarried women as a class a larger share of the national income, but whether the equating of a married man who has a non-wage-earning wife with a single unit is altogether equitable or socially desirable is another matter. These afterthoughts may be still to come! Unless the principle becomes universal the long run effect on the Civil Service may be to reduce its pay standards to that of the single woman.[140]

These comments clearly echo a number of the discourses explored in this and the previous two chapters. Still remaining were the assumptions that women civil servants would all be single – when the marriage bar had been abolished for over ten years – and that women civil servants would not have dependents regardless of their marital status. Single men did not figure in this picture.

Equal pay remains a familiar phrase in contemporary society because it has not yet been achieved in full. More research is of course needed on equal pay as a whole and also to establish the effect of equal pay in the public service on campaigns for equal pay in other sectors. In 1955 the Institute of Personnel Management convened a seminar which sought to predict the effect of equal pay in the Civil Service on, variously, women's employment and recruitment, but particularly, the effect on private businesses and industry.[141] In 1967, Edith Summerskill lamented the lack of further progress and the implicit lack of value attached to women as workers and therefore citizens.[142]

Thus, the fight for equal pay was in part about finance, and was often couched in those terms in the post-war years, but it was also a fundamentally ideological fight over the longer term about women's rights to be valued in the workplace as much as men. The campaign of over three decades scored important psychological victories in the interwar years and eventually found, and operated within, a more receptive climate in the post-war years. The victories for equal pay for women public servants therefore need to be seen as the culmination of long years of activism and pressure.

Notes

1 This is also discussed in Parris, *Staff Relations in the Civil Service*, p.157.

2 Boston, *Women Workers and the Trade Unions*, p.228; Solden, *Women in British Trade Unions*, pp.159–163.

3 Boston, *Women Workers and the Trade Unions*, p.248.

4 Boston, *Women Workers and the Trade Unions*, pp.248–251.

5 Harold L. Smith, 'The Politics of Conservative Reform: The Equal Pay for Equal Work Issue, 1945–1955', *The Historical Journal*, vol. 35, no. 2 (June 1992), p.410; p.412.

6 Braybon and Summerfield, *Out of the Cage*, p.159; p.171; pp.175–177; pp.180–182.

7 LMA, LCC/CL/ESTAB/01/5, Women Employed on Men's Work.

8 LCC/CL/ESTAB/01/5, memorandum, 12 March 1941.

9 Mark Crowley, 'Women Workers in the General Post Office, 1939–1945: Gender Conflict or Political Emancipation?' (unpublished PhD thesis, University of London, 2010), chapter 7.

10 Meynell, *Public Servant, Private Woman*, p.172.

11 John Grigg, 'Keir, Thelma Cazalet-(1899–1989)', rev. *Oxford Dictionary of National Biography* (Oxford University Press, 2004), online edn, January 2007 [www.oxforddnb.com/view/article/39850, accessed 12 July 2012].

12 Jones, *Women in British Public Life*, p.199; Smith, 'Equal Pay for Equal Work', p.669.

13 Jones, *Women in British Public Life*, p.198. For a brief discussion of the campaign for equal compensation for war industries, see Boston, *Women Workers and the Trade Unions*, pp.193–195; Smith, 'Equal Pay for Equal Work', pp.661–662.

14 John Stewart, 'Summerskill, Edith Clara, Baroness Summerskill (1901–1980)', *Oxford Dictionary of National Biography* (Oxford University Press, 2004), online edn, January 2011 [www.oxforddnb.com/view/article/31734, accessed 8 February 2015]. On her campaigns for women and home defence, see Penny Summerfield and Corinna Peniston-Bird, *Contesting Home Defence* (Manchester: Manchester University Press, 2007), pp.64–71.

15 WL, 6EPC01, Equal Pay Campaign Committee, 1944–1956, minutes, 26 January 1944; 17 April 1944.

16 WL, 6EPC 01, Equal Pay Campaign Committee, minutes, 6 March 1944.

17 TNA, T 215/485, Equal pay in Civil Service: representations from TUC, staff associations and outside bodies, memo from staff side member to Mr Peck, 9 January 1951.

18 Richard Temple, 'Brown, William John (1894–1960)', *Oxford Dictionary of National Biography* (Oxford University Press, 2004), online edn, January 2011 [www.oxforddnb.com/view/article/32118, accessed 21 September 2013].

19 Jones, *Women in British Public Life*, p.200.

20 Janet E. Grenier, 'Loughlin, Dame Anne (1894–1979)', *Oxford Dictionary of National Biography* [online edition, accessed 3 July 2012].

21 See the discussion of Lucy Frances Nettlefold in Rosemary Auchmuty, 'Bebb, Gwyneth Marjory (1889–1921)', *Oxford Dictionary of National Biography* (Oxford University Press, May 2011), online edn, January 2012 [www.oxforddnb.com/view/article/101944, accessed 12 July 2012]; Cheryl Law, *Women: A Modern Political Dictionary* (London: I. B. Tauris, 2000), p.22; WL, 6 EPC 01, minutes, 29 January 1948.

22 Gordon Fletcher, 'Robertson, Sir Dennis Holme (1890–1963)', *Oxford Dictionary of National Biography* (Oxford University Press, 2004) [www.oxforddnb.com/view/article/35776, accessed 16 August 2014]

23 Boston, *Women Workers and the Trade Unions*, p.226.

24 *Royal Commission on Equal Pay*, Appendices to Minutes of Evidence taken before the Royal Commission on Equal Pay, Appendices I–V (London: HMSO, 1945), Evidence submitted by the National Association of Women Civil Servants, paras 2306, 2312; evidence submitted by the National Staff Side, para. 1655.

25 *Royal Commission on Equal Pay*, Appendices, Evidence submitted by the Council of Women Civil Servants, paras 105–111.

26 Boston, *Women Workers and the Trade Unions*, p.229.

27 LMA, LCC/CL/ESTAB/01/5, Memorandum on 'female porteresses', 3 March 1941.

28 *Royal Commission on Equal Pay*, Appendices, Evidence of Sir Eric Salmon, paras 701–702.

29 Evidence of Sir Eric Salmon, para. 699.

30 Evidence of Sir Eric Salmon, paras 760–761.

31 Smith demonstrates that fewer emotions were aroused from questions in a 1954 survey about 'the rate for the job' rather than about 'equal pay', despite the fact that the two were actually the same thing. However, the shift in language and the sense of

egalitarianism implied in the former phrase is widely evident from the later stages of the war. Smith, 'Politics of Conservative Reform', p.409.

32 LCC/CL/ESTAB/1/6, Royal Commission on Equal Pay (1944), Written evidence from LCC Staff Association to the Royal Commission on Equal Pay.

33 *Royal Commission on Equal Pay*, Evidence, paras 1168 and 1209.

34 *Royal Commission on Equal Pay*, Evidence, para. 1360–1367.

35 *Royal Commission on Equal Pay*, Evidence, para. 1517.

36 *Royal Commission on Equal Pay*, Evidence, paras 1387–1388.

37 *Royal Commission on Equal Pay*, Evidence, para. 1551; para. 1562.

38 James E. Mortimer and Valerie A. Ellis, *A Professional Union: The Evolution of the Institution of Professional Civil Servants* (London: George Allen & Unwin, 1980), p.160.

39 *Royal Commission on Equal Pay, 1944–1946: Report* (London: HMSO, 1946), paras 418–421.

40 *Royal Commission on Equal Pay*, para. 433.

41 *Royal Commission on Equal Pay*, 'Memorandum of Dissent', pp.187–196.

42 See, for example, the NUWT's position as quoted in *The Times*, 'Equal Pay Enquiry Opened', 17 February 1945; *The Times*, 'Equal Pay', 17 April 1944; *Clerical Grades Monthly*, Official Organ of the Civil Service Clerical Association (Ministry of Health Branch), March 1944, p.1. As we have seen, the argument of the NAWCS and its predecessors had always been based on the idea of justice to women workers for doing the same work as men.

43 *Hansard*, Equal Pay (Government Policy), HC Deb 11 June 1947 vol. 438 col. 1070. For an argument against this, see TNA 215/487, statement from CWCS to Treasury, October 1951, with accompanying report by Marian E. A. Bowley, and TNA, T 215/489, Equal pay in Civil Service: representations from TUC, staff associations and outside bodies, letter from NAWCS to Butler, 1 March 1954. This was still a question debated about equal pay more widely after the 1955 settlement. See LMA, LCC/CL/ESTAB/1/10, Equal Pay, invitation for 23 March 1955 meeting and accompanying document: 'Some possible implications of the Civil Service Equal Pay Scheme for industry, commerce and other fields of employment'.

44 *The Spectator*, Letters to the Editor, 'The Rate for the Job', 24 January 1947, p.16.

45 Duncan Sutherland, 'Burton, (Frances) Elaine, Baroness Burton of Coventry (1904–1991)', *Oxford Dictionary of National Biography* (Oxford University Press, 2004), online edn, May 2012 [www.oxforddnb.com/view/article/49597, accessed 12 July 2012].

46 Elaine Burton, *What is She Worth? A Study on the Report on Equal Pay* (London: Fitzroy Publications, 1947), p.5.

47 Burton, *What is She Worth?* p.11.

48 This had already been noted by some involved with the Royal Commission on Equal Pay. Boston, *Women Workers and the Trade Unions*, p.227.

49 TNA, T 215/484, Equal pay in Civil Service: representations from TUC, staff associations and outside bodies, Verbatim report of the national staff side deputation to the Chancellor, 17 February 1947.

50 Ben Pimlott (ed.), *The Political Diary of Hugh Dalton, 1918–1940, 1945–1960* (London: Jonathan Cape, Ltd/LSE, 1986), entry for 13 June 1947, p.394.

51 Thelma Cazalet-Keir, *From the Wings: An Autobiography* (London: Bodley Head, 1967), p.119. See also T 215/486, letter from NAWCS, 8 May 1951. There were also wage increases made across the LCC in 1947. See *The Times*, 'Higher Pay for L.C.C. Staffs', 8 February 1947, p.2.

52 *Hansard*, Equal Pay (Government Policy), HC Deb, 11 June 1947, vol. 438, cc.1069–75.

53 *The Spectator*, 'Women's Wages', 5 June 1947, p.2.

54 LCC/CL/ESTAB/1/9 Equal Pay, memorandum by the Staff Side to the Joint Committee, 1 October 1947.

55 LCC/CL/ESTAB/1/9, Memorandum to the Official Side members of the Joint Committee, 6 October 1947.

56 Nicholas Woodward, *The Management of the British Economy, 1945–2001* (Manchester: Manchester University Press, 2004), p.36. See also Boston, *Women Workers and the Trade Unions*, p.228.

57 Gerald A. Dorfman, *Wage Politics in Britain, 1945–1967* (London: Charles Knight & Co., 1974), p.52.

58 WL, 6 EPC, Box 2, Equal Pay Campaign Committee, Campaign Newsletter, July 1950.

59 Kevin Theakston, 'Evelyn Sharp (1903–1985)', *Contemporary Record*, vol. 7, no. 1 (1993), p.145; *Hansard*, HC Deb 16 May 1952 vol 500, 'Equal Pay (Public Services)', Miss Irene Ward, col. 1793. Sharp had been one of the first female entrants to the Civil Service administrative grades in the 1920s.

60 WL, 6 EPC 01, Equal Pay Campaign Committee, minutes, 7 March 1950.

61 Boston, *Women Workers and the Trade Unions*, p.231.

62 June Purvis, 'Jill Craigie (1914–1999)', *Women's History Review*, vol. 9, no. 1 (2000), pp.5–8; 6 EPC 01, emergency meeting 20 June 1949.

63 WL, 6EPC 01, 'To Be A Woman' donations list, 25 January 1951.

64 Carl Rollyson, *To Be A Woman: The Life of Jill Craigie* (London: Aurum Press, Ltd, 2005), p.132.

65 Rollyson, *To Be A Woman*, pp.132–133.

66 *To Be A Woman*, dir. by Jill Craigie (Outlook Films, 1951).

67 Rollyson, *To Be A Woman*, pp.132–133.

68 *To Be A Woman*.

69 *London Town*, January 1951, p.27.

70 *Red Tape*, 'Whitehall Notebook', September 1951, p.491..

71 T215/486, memorandum on a staff side deputation of 3 January 1951, dated 3 April 1951

72 Peter Hennessy, *Having It So Good: Britain in the Fifties* (London: Penguin, 2007), p.200.

73 *Hansard*, HC Deb 20 June 1951 vol. 489 Civil Service (Equal Pay) cc.526-33.

74 LMA, GLSA/1/43, LCC staff association executive committee meetings.

75 TNA T215/486, letter from Mrs L Kennedy, Honorary Secretary, 26 June 1951; letter from Birmingham Branch of the NUWT, 26 June 1951.

76 TNA 215/486, letter from Mrs L Kennedy, 26 June 1951; letter from Birmingham Branch of the NUWT, 26 June 1951.
77 TNA 215/486, letter from NAWCS to Gaitskell, 21 June 1951.
78 *The Times*, Letters to the Editor, 22 June 1951, p.7.
79 TNA 215/486, telegrams and letters to Gaitskell dated late June 1951.
80 Oram, *Women Teachers and Feminist Politics*, p.166. The NAS also wrote to Butler in 1952 asking him not to give in to the pressure for equal pay. TNA 215/487, letter from NAS, 7 January 1952.
81 Boston, *Women Workers and the Trade Unions*, pp.248–249.
82 *Red Tape*, 'Association Notes', September 1951, p.492.
83 *Hansard*, Equal Pay, HC Deb 13 November 1951 vol. 493 cc.816-7.
84 TNA, T 215/487, letter from Ruislip-Northwood Constituency Labour Party, 17 December 1951; internal memo from Armstrong to Rhodes, 14 January 1952.
85 *Hansard*, HC Deb 16 May 1952 vol. 500, 'Equal Pay (Public Services)', col. 1791.
86 Hennessy, *Having It So Good*, p.200.
87 *Hansard*, HC Deb 16 May 1952 vol. 500, col. 1781; 1799.
88 See, for example, *Civil Service Argus*, letter from A. J. T. Day, Chairman of the Staff Side to MPs, January 1953, p.13.
89 *London Town*, April 1952, p.62.
90 CL/ESTAB/1/10 Equal Pay, memorandum from the Vice Chairman of the Staff Side of the Joint Committee, 16 February 1952.
91 LMA, LCC/CL/ESTAB/1/10 Equal Pay, memorandum to the Clerk of the Council, addressing issues raised in the staff side memo, n.d.
92 LCC/CL/ESTAB/1/10 Equal Pay.
93 LCC/CL/ESTAB/1/10 Equal Pay, Memo 1952 from the Director of Establishments, 22 May 1952. The LCC Staff Association denied responsibility for this. GLSA/1/44, Executive Committee Meeting of 19 and 26 May 1952.
94 LCC/CL/ESTAB/1/10 Equal Pay, notes on a discussion at the E.O.C., 7 March 1952.
95 *Daily Telegraph* and *Daily Mirror*, 2 July 1952.
96 LCC/CL/ESTAB/1/10 Equal Pay, memo to the Clerk of the Council [n.d.].
97 LCC/CL/ESTAB/1/10, letter from R. Gray, 27 June 1952.
98 *Daily Telegraph*, 28 June 1952.
99 *Local Government Service*, 'LCC's Equal Pay Lead', July–August 1952, p.201.
100 T215/243, Equal Pay. Treatment by London County Council, memorandum (unsigned), 9 July 1952.
101 T215/243, Equal Pay. Treatment by London County Council.
102 T215/243, memo by 'AW', undated [October 1952?]; *Hansard*, Equal Pay (LCC Award), HC Deb 28 October 1952 vol. 505 cc.1714-5.
103 *Hansard*, HC Deb, 14 October 1952 vol. 505 cc.11-2; TNA T215/486, letter from Rab Butler to A. J. T. Day, 29 January 1952.
104 *The Times*, Letters to the Editor, 26 September 1952, p.7.
105 Parris, *Staff Relations*, pp.154–155.
106 *Hansard*, Equal Pay for Equal Work, HL Deb 11 February 1953 vol. 180 cc.353-69.
107 *Red Tape*, March 1954, p.176.

108 Boston, *Women Workers and the Trade Unions*, p.250.

109 Smith, 'Politics of Conservative Reform', p.406.

110 Cazalet-Keir, *From the Wings*, p.194.

111 TNA, T 215/489, internal memo by 'MBS' [Barbara Sloman], 1 February 1954.

112 Civil Service societies circulated the petition widely, and sought signatures from friends, family and members of the public. T 215/489, copy of Society of Civil Servants memo, 2 February 1954.

113 *Hansard*, Equal Pay, HC Deb 9 March 1954 c.1906.

114 *Hansard*, Douglas Houghton, Equal Pay, 9 March, 1954, vol. 524, c.1907.

115 *Hansard*, Butler, Equal Pay, March 1954, vol. 524, c.1910.

116 *Hansard*, Equal Pay, HC Deb 9 March 1954 vol. 524 cc1905-19.

117 *Daily Mirror*, 9 March 1954, p.3.

118 *Evenings News*, 12 March 1954.

119 TNA, T171/439/18, circulars to Horsbrugh and Macmillan, 20 March 1954.

120 Smith, 'Politics of Conservative Reform', p.401; p.415.

121 T171/439/18, minutes of cabinet meeting, 24 March 1954; memo by Mr Fraser, 30 March 1954.

122 T171/439/18, minutes of cabinet meeting, 24 March 1954.

123 T171/439/18, Rab Butler, paper for cabinet meeting, 19 March 1954.

124 T171/439/18, minutes of cabinet meeting, 24 March 1954; memo by Mr Fraser, 30 March 1954.

125 T171/439/18, note by Sir T. Padmore, 4 March 1954; memo to Chancellor, 10 March 1954.

126 *Hansard*, Budget Proposals, 12 April 1954, vol. 526, col.920. There had been debates about whether this should include women in the industrial civil service as well during cabinet discussions (see T171/439/18). For a summary of the government's justification of the eventual decision to not include them, see T 215/489, 'Equal Pay and the Institute of Personnel Management'.

127 *Red Tape*, 'Talking Shop', March 1955, p.164.

128 BPMA, POST 122/207, File 8, Equal Pay: Gradual Introduction of Scheme, Report of Joint Committee of National Whitley Council, paras 11–15.

129 POST 122/207, para. 15.

130 T 215/489, Memo by AJP to Treasury, 15 July 1954; letter from NAWCS, 10 August 1954; letter from NAWCS, 16 February 1955; letter from NAWCS, 9 May 1955; and T 215/490, Equal pay in Civil Service: representations from TUC, staff associations and outside bodies, letter from NAWCS, 15 July 1955.

131 *Manchester Guardian*, David Low, 'Seven Stages of Woman', 28 January 1955, p.9.

132 *The Times*, Letters to the Editor, 1 February 1955, p.9.

133 *The Times*, 'Regardless of Sex', 26 January 1955, p.9. See also *Daily Mail*, 'Women and their Pay', 15 March 1954, p.4.

134 WL, 6EPC 01, minutes, 10 February 1955. See also the resolution from the Fawcett Society condemning the gradual implementation: T 215/490, 21 July 1955.

135 6EPC 01, minutes, 2 May 1955.

136 6EPC 01, minutes, 29 February 1956.

137 LCC/CL/ESTAB/1/10 Equal Pay, petition from driving licence machine typists and reply 19 July 1952, and correspondence from LCC Staff Association, 11 September 1952. E. Leopold, *In the Service of London: The Origin and Development of Council Employment from 1889* (London: Greater London Council, 1986), p.58.

138 Eric Wigham, *From Humble Petition to Militant Action: A History of the Civil and Public Services Association* (London: Civil & Public Services Association, 1980), pp.130–132.

139 Clinton, *Post Office Workers*, p.434.

140 Gladden, *Civil Service or Bureaucracy*, p.55.

141 LCC/CL/ESTAB/1/10, Equal Pay, letter to Director of Establishments and programme for discussion for 23 March 1955.

142 Edith Summerskill, *A Woman's World* (London: Heinemann, 1967), pp.141–143.

6

Lark rise to spinsterhood? Women, the public service and marriage bar policy, 1900–46

As earlier chapters have shown, there was an assumption in the Civil Service in particular that women's careers would be shorter and of far less significance than men's. This assumption was rooted in gender and marriage norms of the day but it was bolstered and seemingly confirmed by the existence of the marriage bar, which enforced the departure of married women from the workforce. Although considerable numbers of women had lifelong public service careers, the suppositions and discourse around the marriage bar were so all-consuming that it was difficult for such women to be able to re-shape the assumption that all women's work was inferior and typified by a short, pre-marital career. The Civil Service marriage bar in particular – because it was so rigid and affected so many women – had very much set a standard early in the twentieth century for other employers to copy. Furthermore, the 1920s and 1930s constituted the height of marriage bars in public and private employment and the various bars in operation reinforced each other. This chapter surveys the debates and discourses surrounding the marriage bar and the attitudes of unions and associations, as well as tracing the emerging policies in both organisations. It argues that the marriage bar permeated all other aspects of women's employment because it helped to trivialise women's presence in the workplace. The chapter charts how marriage bar debates were at the heart of conceptions of female public service, of women's employment more generally, and of women's position in society as a whole.

The Post Office was the first Civil Service department to create a marriage bar in the 1870s, in consultation with the Treasury. As the first department to employ women, its views remained influential until the mid-1930s, when the culmination of several campaigns by women's organisations and the deliberations of the Tomlin Commission brought about minor changes ahead of the abandonment of the bar – at first temporarily in the Second World War and then permanently in 1946. By 1920, the LCC and all other Civil Service departments operated marriage bars. The Civil Service marriage bar would prove the most resilient, whereas the LCC marriage bar had less rigid terms and was at times applied more flexibly. However, it is clear that the Civil Service influenced the LCC, with informal dialogue between the two organisations on the issue at various points.

With its self-proclaimed pioneer status as an employer of women, the GPO decided to institute a bar in 1876 which forbade the employment of married women and compelled female employees to resign on marriage. In the 1890s this policy was reviewed and eventually further entrenched by the implementation of a "marriage gratuity", supposedly in lieu of a pension, for those women leaving for marriage after at least six years' established service. A bar was also instituted for all Civil Service typists in 1894. By 1903, virtually all female civil servants were subject to the marriage bar, though there appears to have been some flexibility at departmental level.[1] With the exception of the First World War, the bar remained in place and was introduced across those Civil Service departments which did not already conform to it in the early 1920s. The LCC put in writing its expectation that married women would retire from employment in 1906. However, women teachers and doctors remained exempted from this requirement until the 1920s.

Motivations and justifications for the marriage bar before the First World War

With the exception of the marriage bar in teaching nationally, the implementation and implications of marriage bars have not been explored in depth by historians, though there has been more discussion of the Civil Service marriage bar compared to the LCC's.[2] Historians and sociologists studying the origins of the Civil Service marriage bar have emphasised economic motivations to varying degrees. Samuel Cohn has suggested that the marriage bar was a means to facilitate staff turnover whilst also being an ideologically acceptable reason to dismiss staff, and that marriage gratuities were an 'enormous financial commitment to creating short female careers'.[3] However, it needs to be remembered that marriage gratuities were much cheaper than the pensions that women would have been entitled to if they had stayed in the service. Zimmeck sees the bar as being more socially motivated but also demonstrates that one of the justifications for the marriage bar in the 1890s, amongst others, was to generate a turnover for routine work.[4] Whilst turnover clearly could be financially advantageous – but might have been somewhat negated by marriage gratuities and training costs for replacements – what is striking about the original GPO debates over married women's right to work in the 1870s is the fact that financial advantages to the service were not mentioned once. It is therefore worth looking at the individual debates more closely and the social discourses in which they were steeped.

Frank Scudamore, in his now-infamous 1871 advocacy of women's employment in the Post Office, had suggested that women voluntarily leaving for marriage would save the GPO money but the terms of the discussion when the marriage bar was instituted in 1876 were very different.[5] When the GPO secretary wrote to senior colleagues for their opinion he received a wide variety of responses. One official argued that the service 'rather gains than otherwise by the presence of married women', several stated that it was difficult to give a definite answer and that cases should be dealt with individually, and others stressed the difficulties that might be encountered by married women having time away from work to have children, appearing in public whilst pregnant or being influenced by their husbands. The responses were clearly rooted in either the personal experience of the administrators with their female staff or in wider late nineteenth-century ideologies about marriage, including the assumption that this would automatically include child-rearing. Most striking, perhaps, was the fact that none of the respondents advocated outright dismissal of married women. Although the exact decision-making process thereafter was not recorded, the marriage bar was instituted shortly after, seemingly in spite of some of these responses.[6] It applied to all established – that is, permanent – female postal employees, so postmistresses were subject to the regulation but sub-postmistresses were not.[7]

The social motivations for the marriage bar were further borne out in the early 1890s when a review of the marriage bar was ordered by an unconvinced Postmaster General. Again, women's presumed requirements for confinement leave, their inability to carry out heavy lifting during pregnancy and their ongoing childcare responsibilities were brought to the fore in the resulting report. The report's authors – five senior men in the GPO – argued that in the case of family illness 'she would be an unnatural wife or mother who did not ask to be allowed to stay at home, and the department could hardly refuse permission'.[8] The authors continued, '[i]f, on the other hand, means be adopted to prevent the birth of children there is a risk that still more serious evils might result'.[9] The report was steeped in gendered norms and also general anxieties about any change to women's conventional roles. It questioned how far a public department was wise to encourage women to 'neglect their home duties' and to affect the upbringing of children by encouraging the mother to be absent. It argued that married women with irregular attendance at work would bring harm to the public service, whereas for a private employer, her absence would affect only him and his business. In light of the fact that many women civil servants – in the lower rungs of the service – were employed interchangeably with one another, this argument did not necessarily wholly stand up as work could be covered with relative ease. The report concluded that that there was no desire among women to continue employment after marriage: 'marriage they appear to regard as promotion ... a woman who ... retain[ed] her appointment would be regarded by her companions as having to some extent lost caste'. A marginal note from a reader – possibly the Postmaster General – highlighted the committee's lack of evidence from women.[10]

With women's Civil Service employment policy not yet solidified across all departments, the marriage bar was not extended much beyond the GPO by the turn of the century. It is also clear that there was some ambivalence about it, though clearly not sufficiently strong views to change the status quo. In 1903, the Royal Commission on Superannuation in the Civil Service stated that 'the ineligibility of married women as Civil Servants has not been universally regarded' and the 1912 MacDonnell Royal Commission was torn between the idea that marriage and domestic duties were not compatible with state service on the one hand, and the loss of expertise when a woman was forced to resign on the other.[11]

The LCC marriage bar appears to have developed piecemeal in the course of the late 1890s and very early 1900s. By 1906, Laurence Gomme, the Clerk of the Council, could report that numerous departments and committees required their female staff to resign on marriage, and this was followed shortly by a standing order which formalised the marriage bar for all female employees except teachers and any others the Council chose to specially exempt.[12] Therefore, there was some in-built flexibility into the Council's marriage bar, presumably to help handle labour shortages. Although there is no documentary evidence that the Council looked to the Civil Service for inspiration or a policy to draw upon, the Civil Service marriage bar was widely known so it is inconceivable that this was not also taken into consideration. However, controversy was caused when the marriage bar was applied to female assistant medical officers when they were appointed in the

Public Health department of the LCC from 1913. As qualified doctors and one of the highest-profile occupations for women, this was perceived as an attack on their professional freedom. The Women's Freedom League asked to bring a deputation to the Council on the matter, but were refused.[13] The female doctors, and sympathetic male staff, protested the decision a year later, though again to no avail.[14] When the Council agreed the introduction of several three-year medical assistant posts, it was again discussed whether the female post-holders should be exempted from the marriage bar. The suggestion was put to a Council vote, and thirty voted for the exemption and seventy-two voted against.[15] Although ultimately in favour of a marriage bar by a significant majority, the vote revealed that opinions of LCC members were not unanimous on the issue.

The First World War, bringing with it new demands for replacement labour, created changes to the marriage bar in both the Civil Service and the LCC. In 1915, married women were allowed to undertake employment in the Post Office for the duration of the war, though they lost their "establishment" rights and benefits if they had previously been employed on the establishment whilst single.[16] In March 1915, an Establishment Committee decision allowed married women to remain in the LCC provided that their husbands were on war service.[17] Later in 1915, there was some discussion as to whether married women with no previous LCC or clerical experience could also be employed, though LCC officials judged this prospect remote. By 1916, the question of temporarily employing married women was effectively put to a vote, and the division of opinion was roughly even. In a reflection of the ongoing saga regarding how to implement the marriage bar in the medical officer's department, the Chief Medical Officer declared himself in favour of employing married women medical officers and assistants, but not clerical staff.[18] By mid-1916 the Clerk of the Council decreed that married women could be employed as long as suitable single women were not readily available; any children of the proposed employee would be properly cared for in her absence and that preference be given to cases where family resources seemed to be '*prima facie* inadequate'. Any doubtful cases had to be submitted to the Establishment Committee for its consideration. It is not clear that the requirement for childcare was intended to be benignly out of concern for the children rather than a means for the LCC to ensure that it would not have absent mothers through childcare issues. However, the instance of giving preference to households in the greatest financial need was seemingly an attempt to use such temporary employment for the greatest possible good.[19]

The marriage bar after the First World War

After the armistice, the marriage bar was re-established in the Civil Service. The fact that Murray, GPO Secretary, did not mention its existence to the War Cabinet Committee on Women in Industry might indicate that it was so normal as to be unremarkable, or that he was sure that the Civil Service would revert to the status ante.[20] Similarly, the Gladstone Report (1919) mentioned that women left for marriage but did not explain that they were compelled to do so.[21] Therefore, official reports did not really offer any new discussion on the issue, nor suggest that there was any need to re-think the existence of the marriage bar. The Sex Disqualification (Removal) Bill eventually made it legitimate to exclude married women from the Civil Service, despite efforts from Major Hills and others to support married women's right to work during the parliamentary debates. Though the first line of the eventual Act – 'A person shall not be disqualified by sex or marriage' – seemed outwardly to mean that married women could work in the public service, the all-powerful proviso (a) meant that the government could overturn this for the Civil Service, as a number of historians have noted.[22]

The existence of a marriage bar alongside the Act was challenged almost straight away by the FWCS.[23] In 1921, a government solicitor confirmed the way in which the Act could be interpreted:

> when the Sex Disqualification (Removal) Act says that a woman is not disqualified by sex or marriage, it means that the woman is not under an inherent disability from holding certain posts because she is a woman or because she is married. In other words, the appointment of a woman or a married woman to these posts if made would not be invalid. It is quite another thing to say that a woman is entitled to be appointed to or to hold any of the specified posts on exactly the same terms as if she were a man, and this in fact is precisely what the Act refrains from saying.[24]

Undoubtedly, the pre-existence of a Civil Service marriage bar in many departments, the Act proviso and this legal opinion were instrumental in confirming the ruling for the entire service by 1921. Treasury officials argued, seemingly without much evidence either way, that the existing marriage bars did not cause complaints; that 'the whole trend of modern social reform is to make it possible for married women not to have to go out to work'; and that '[t]he efficient administration of Government Services would be jeopardised if there were no bar to the employment of married women' as the work required 'continuous service'.[25] The point about continuous service could arguably only be supported so far: at this time, most women in the Civil Service did routine work – as officials were quick to point out on occasions where it suited them to do so. More significantly the point about absence was based on an assumption which was entirely unproven – because the marriage bar had been in existence for over forty years – that married women would be away from work to a significant degree.

The Sex Disqualification Removal Act and the legal advice subsequently given to the Treasury on this were so important because they fed directly into the August 1921 House of Commons declarations for the Civil Service, which included a reconfirmation of the marriage bar. The operation of the bar was the same as previously, but it was agreed that exceptions could be made to the requirement to resign if retention of the woman in question was believed to be 'in the interests of the Public Service'. Exceptions had to be authorised by the Treasury and the Civil Service Commissioners, in the case of new appointments, and the Treasury only for existing employees. These individual exceptions had to be published in the *London Gazette*, and those female officers appointed or retained under the exceptions became ineligible for a marriage gratuity.[26]

The LCC was not as quick to reinstate its marriage bar. The wartime resolution allowing married women to work was extended several times after the armistice whilst deliberations continued. The marriage bar was eventually put back into place in July 1920 but, importantly, women doctors and teachers remained exempted. Throughout the interwar years, certain very specific exemptions were also made in response to shortages of single women for the type of work concerned: for example in 1926, married women attendants at public baths and conveniences were permitted.[27] Other exemptions were also occasionally possible: Susan Lawrence, a Labour member of the Council, managed to get some married women school cleaners reinstated in their former posts as she proved that they were dependent on their wages.[28]

In 1923, the Council re-imposed the bar for women teachers. The regulation was not made retroactive, so any woman currently serving was free to marry and continue her career if she wished, meaning that there was a mix of both married and unmarried women teachers on the LCC's staff in the interwar years.[29] The implication of this is significant, as it meant that it was a number of years before the new cohorts could demonstrate the true effect of the marriage bar on staff turnover and career length. Furthermore, as Oram has shown, a great deal of attention was paid to the marital status of women teachers in the interwar years: marriage bars existed in the LCC and other local authorities but at the same time vehement anxieties were expressed in some quarters about 'spinster teachers' and the negative example they were deemed to be setting to pupils.[30] As women civil servants also would be, teachers were criticised because of the regulations they were working under.

Although a final decision was not taken on women doctors until 1924, there was much debate in the immediate post-war years about whether to include them in the reinstated marriage bar. There had been correspondence and even a deputation from the Medical Women's Federation in the latter half of 1919 emphasising the fact that marriage was not a bar to women doctors being able to continue their careers.[31] In the event, the LCC continued to permit the employment of married women doctors on account of the shortage, due to the war, of women graduating from medical school and then gaining sufficient experience. This was not enough to save Dr Miall Smith, Medical Officer for St Pancras, who was dismissed in her district because she was married.[32] The decision to not apply the marriage bar was reviewed several times in the early 1920s, including by a sub-committee devoted to the issue of married women staff. The committee in 1920 found three reasons for the continued employment of married women doctors: the relative lack of availability of female doctors; the fact that married women with children (the committee rather assumed that marriage would lead to children) were more suitable employees for the LCC's needs; and the fact that marriage should not be a reason to stop women working in roles for which they were qualified. Two counter-arguments were also made: that married women's employment in the LCC as a whole had to be considered first, and that married women absent because of domestic needs would mean that temporary women had to be employed to the Council's detriment.[33] The continued employment of married women doctors came under even closer scrutiny in 1923 and 1924. Although its experience of married women's employment – three doctors out of a female staff of thirty-four (a mix of part-time and full-time appointments) – had been good, the LCC was particularly conscious of the fact that women doctors were now the only LCC employees not subject to a marriage bar. When it came to the vote on doctors, Council members do not appear to have been convinced that the apparent lack of suitably experienced women doctors was enough to keep the marriage bar anomalously lifted. In July 1924, it was decided that the Council would no longer offer appointments to married women doctors from the forthcoming November, though, as with teachers, those already married and employed were permitted to stay in the service.[34]

Once the decision came into effect, there was considerable publicity against it. At the start of November, the Council received a letter from the

Women's Local Government Society condemning the decision.[35] Florence May Dickinson Berry, Secretary of the Medical Women's Federation (MWF), wrote to the *British Medical Journal*. She argued that the marriage bar struck 'at the very foundations of the position women have won through the long struggle of recent years for emancipation and citizenship'. Though she conceded that there might be occasions where marriage affected a woman's work, she also argued that there were 'undoubtedly many instances where the special value of the individual outweighs the risk of temporary drawbacks'. She explained the MWF's own policy, which decreed that individual married women should only be dismissed if it became clear that their work was being adversely affected, and argued that 'sweeping regulations' deprived public authorities of the full range of the best candidates. She pointed out, as remarkably few others did, that '[t]he mere fact that a woman wishes to continue ... after marriage often indicates special devotion to her profession and love of her work'.[36] However, her later assertion, like that of those at the Council who supported married women's work, that married women could be better doctors than single women also came close to the trend Oram has identified with regard to women teachers: that women's special abilities, and in particular the motherly qualities embodied by the wife and mother following a profession, made them better at their profession.[37] Finally, on a note of exasperation, Dickinson Berry signed off:

> If this movement against married women as worker is progressing it may well be asked: Does the public desire all professional women to be celibate? Must a girl who takes up a profession be faced with the prospect that she can only marry at the price of that profession and the loss to herself and the public of the time and money spent on her training?[38]

The MWF continued to write to the Council in the late 1920s and the early 1930s to protest the policy, but all to no avail.[39]

Perceptions of married women working in the interwar years

Marriage bars were therefore entrenched across the LCC and the Civil Service by the early 1920s. Furthermore, the interwar years became the era of the British marriage bar. Marriage bars were common for women teachers across the country as the 1920s wore on, though they varied by location and length of operation.[40] The four main railway companies did not employ married women,[41] and the Bank of England and clearing banks only did so in very rare cases.[42] Unilever and Imperial

Chemical Industries Ltd had a marriage bar, Rowntree and Co. Ltd and Cadbury Brothers Ltd allowed married women to work for them only in exceptional cases.[43] Other private firms operated marriage bars, and in many cases there was also the expectation that women would resign from their jobs when they married in any case. In 1938 and 1939, *The Times* ran a series of articles entitled 'Careers for Girls'. The fact that some of the articles mention the need, or not, to resign on marriage reveals both the prevalence of restrictions on married women's work and the fact that such restrictions might be a factor in decisions about careers.[44] The numbers of married women in employment according to the 1911, 1921 and 1931 censuses were small, hovering consistently around 10 per cent, though the proportions would have varied significantly according to social class and would have risen during the First World War. This said, vagaries of census compilation often did not of course take into account part-time, casual or freelance work or paid work done in the home.[45]

Marriage bars remained, of course, controversial in some circles, particularly but not exclusively among feminists. For others, though, marriage bars were simply a formal announcement of what was expected of women, of what women wanted to do or – at least – of what women had been nurtured and socialised into believing was their natural role. For the decades before the First World War it had been largely expected that middle-class women, when they married, would devote their attentions to being full-time wives and mothers. This discourse was largely rooted in notions of class: it was a marker of social status if married women did not work for pay. Thus, the marriage bar backed up, and was backed up by, these notions of gender and of class. It also had some debatable financial advantages in terms of pension savings and payment of replacements at starting pay but at the same time, as we will see, Civil Service and government officials moaned repeatedly in the interwar years that women left inconveniently for marriage and were not committed to careers. It was therefore also seen as problematic by the very people who were enforcing it.

The interwar feminist and labour movements discussed married women's right to work and marriage bars in public service roles were at the heart of these debates. The issue was divisive in the labour movement. On one side were those who felt that married women would be taking away jobs either from single women or married men – a fear that was heightened in the context of unemployment. On the other hand, it was argued that allowing married women to work followed the principle of economic equality and, perhaps more significantly, if women were denied the right to work on the grounds that they did not need to, this could have serious implications for other trade union arguments about workers' rights in the future.[46] Support for married women's right to work was the official labour movement line, but this was honoured almost as much in the breach as in the observance, as parts of this chapter will exemplify. By the mid-1930s the arguments had shifted, as Graves shows. Formal labour movement support for married women's was adjusted to include the argument that, unlike fascist Germany and Italy, Britain gave its women a choice. At the same time, supporters of the marriage bar in the Labour movement used the 1930s notion of citizenship and the idea that women would be better citizens if they were able to devote themselves to the home and voluntary work.[47]

Although it did not quite reach the levels of discourse on equal pay – possibly because a woman giving up work on marriage was considered the social norm in this period – the marriage bar was discussed from time to time by policymakers and the women's press.[48] Edith Morley's *Women Workers in Seven Professions*, published by the Fabian Society in 1914, took a quasi-feminist perspective on the marriage bar. She lamented the fact that the marriage bar forced a woman to abandon the profession for which she had trained.[49] Rooted in the discourses of eugenics and fears of a falling birthrate, Morley argued women civil servants were by definition good childbearers as they had to pass a medical exam in order to join the service. If they then chose a career over marriage, they would be depriving the nation of healthy children. She suggested that women be allowed to rejoin the service between or after having children as a solution to this.[50]

The alignment of femininity and domesticity remained powerful in the interwar years and emerged each time the marriage bar was discussed. At the same time, interwar feminists campaigned for women's rights to pursue a career alongside marriage. Despite its split on other issues, the National Union of Societies for Equal Citizenship (NUSEC) remained committed to married women's right to work. The National Union of Women Teachers, the St Joan's Political Alliance and the LNSWS all campaigned against the marriage bar.[51] The basis for many feminists' arguments was the right of married women to choose whether they did paid work or not. As Vera Brittain wrote in the late 1920s, there was deep frustration with the fact that 'employers … invent moral reasons for refusing to a woman the right to separate her public and private affairs as every man is permitted to separate his'.[52]

Women public servants and attitudes to the marriage bar

Women who worked in the Civil Service or the LCC in the early twentieth century knew that they definitely could not marry at the same time as having a career. The impact of this knowledge is impossible to gauge.[53] Some women may have planned a career, or had no interest in marrying; others might have intended their service as a "stop-gap" between education and marriage, though romance and matrimony were of course notoriously difficult to plan for. Some also met their husbands through public service employment.[54]

Qualitative evidence of women's attitudes to the marriage bar is harder to find and often relies on the individual having felt strongly enough to commit their feelings to paper. Not surprisingly, women's own opinions tended to encompass the full social spectrum of ideas about women's position in society. Winifred Oakley of the Post Office Savings Bank argued that 'if … posts … are retained by married women, then the chances of young women and girls fresh from school will be seriously hampered, indeed, their chances of entering the service would be practically negligible, and I think that on these grounds alone the marriage bar should remain'.[55] However, as will be discussed later, the perception of the turnover rates generated by the marriage bar was often different to the reality. Another female civil servant wrote an article in favour of retention of the bar in late 1929, and left for marriage less than a year later. She too drew upon the fact that promotion prospects would be improved, the usefulness of the marriage gratuity payment and the fact that a married woman would be distracted and affected by her home life.[56] By contrast, Miss A. E. Holden, employed at the District Manager's Office in Liverpool, could not 'reconcile [her]self with the idea that marriage should be a full-time job for a woman, and a sort of part-time business for a man … [L]et us be fair and allow that women in common with men, can run a career hand in hand with marriage'.[57] There was a similar divide amongst women UPW members regarding the marriage bar, and male postal employees were prepared to share their views too. In 1935, for example, "GNC" published an article entitled ' "A Woman's Place is in the Home" ' arguing against women working in the home full-time. One respondent called a married couple having two wages 'a scandal' and others made vitriolic assumptions about the ill-effects of growing up with a mother who worked.[58]

There was another side to the marriage bar which was seen more rarely. We will never know how many women civil servants did what Alison Oram has uncovered about women teachers and took off their wedding rings at work and pretended to be single.[59] In the LCC, it was discovered in 1936 that two women employees had been "living in sin". The LCC took, in light of its own rules, the easy way out: it was argued that no action should be taken because neither woman was actually married and had never claimed to be. It seems that officials ultimately wanted to retain both women in employment but also did not want to attract attention to the case: they did not want to make any sort of public statement about their decision for fear of appearing that they encouraged cohabitation.[60] Ida Mann, who worked at the Post Office Savings Bank for a short time, stated in her autobiography that one way that women could – and did – get around the marriage bar was by living 'in sin'.[61] On several occasions, outside commentators also questioned whether the marriage bar effectively encouraged women to live 'in sin'.[62] Although archival records do not indicate that any women civil servants were found to be living in sin it is unlikely that this did not happen. Lilian Gertrude Wolfe, a suffragist-turned-anarchist and a telegraphist, fell pregnant whilst unmarried and decided to leave the Post Office before her pregnancy became obvious because she 'didn't want to be thrown out'.[63] Her story is not isolated.[64]

Union, staff associations and the marriage bar

Whilst the marriage bar provided the copy for plenty of sentimental news items in staff magazines,[65] there was a diverse reaction amongst unions and staff associations to the re-establishment of the marriage bar after the First World War. The FWCS was dismayed that the marriage bar remained but did not launch a further protest, pointing to the post-war dismissals of temporary staff and the priority given to ex-servicemen for employment and concluding that 'it was hardly an opportune moment to press for the retention of married women'.[66] Although the Federation's more vocal interwar activism was concentrated around equal pay and opportunity, it remained staunchly against the marriage bar. In 1933, its successor, the NAWCS, deplored the term "bar", arguing that '[i]t conveys to our mind a stout barrier to keep us herded together in "single blessedness", which to cross is annihilation'. It encouraged its members to attend a public meeting where 'the non-supporter will [realise] that attacks on the right of the married woman to work for payment are attacks on the right of the working woman to marry'.[67] Thus the NAWCS turned the common perception of women's social role on its head: a woman was not to be defined first and foremost by her marital status but should be given the option of conducting several roles. Although the membership of the NAWCS and the way it positioned itself was lower middle class, the use of the term "working woman" was also perhaps a means to ally itself with a more working-class constituency and to indicate that, in the Civil Service at least, the marriage bar affected all women regardless of class.

The UPW executive had long, drawn-out debates about what its stance on the marriage bar should be, which in many ways mirrored the wider debates in the labour movement. The members of the UPW's 1921 sub-committee on women's issues declared themselves 'emphatically' of the opinion that given the current industrial climate, 'women on marriage should leave the Service'. When the report was debated, Mary Herring, the most overtly feminist executive committee member, disagreed, arguing that the right to work after marriage was of 'tremendous importance' to women for three reasons: their human rights, their choice of occupation and right to participate in the workforce, and their right to be economically independent if they so wished. Arguing that technology reduced domestic duties in the home and that new work, such as clerical posts, had opened up for women, she stressed that women were not expected to perform the duties of motherhood alone and that it was a 'terrible thing' to tell women to relinquish all else when they married when this was not expected of men. Furthermore, she argued, '[t]heir education had been developed in [the] direction of employment, and they could not now be expected to confine their duties to the home' – a point which was likely to have also resonated with a number of middle-class women campaigners. She argued that making a woman economically dependent on her husband increased antagonism between the sexes, and that the marriage bar would not solve the unemployment problem. Another executive member argued that whilst capitalism existed, so would current conditions, but Herring countered that 'they had no right to ask women to wait until an ideal system arose'.[68]

The divisions on the issue within the UPW's executive committee were not gendered and they encapsulated the differing points of the labour movement with regard to the issue, as Graves has identified. Mary Herring supported married women's work from a feminist standpoint; others supported the married woman's right as a class issue and others, still, opposed married women's work on the grounds that the wage of the male breadwinner was the most important.[69] Miss Cox spoke fervently in favour of the bar, arguing that '[i]f a woman married she did it with a full knowledge of the responsibility she was undertaking in regard to home duties' and thus was duty-bound to bring up her children, something which could not, she felt, be done as well by an outsider. She argued further that '[w]omen should be educated in the direction of home life and duties' rather than going out into the world and leaving their children to be cared for by others. It is possible to only speculate whether it occurred to her that without a broader education, she might not have been able to be part of a committee making such pronouncements. Mr Wallace argued that the marriage bar was a dangerous precedent, as it might lead officials to argue that married men should have preference over single men for appointments. It was also argued that women helped to earn their husbands' income by running the household. J. W. Bowen, the General Secretary, on the other hand, returned to discussions about double incomes when married women worked and the unfair distribution of wealth that it was felt came about as a result. It was, he argued, a lesser evil to deprive married women of work than single women – and indeed this view was held by others throughout this period and permeated the debate.[70] In the end, support for the marriage bar became union policy by thirteen votes to nine; few other votes in UPW executive history were so close.[71] It was noted that the contents of the report would be presented to the next annual conference, but this does not appear to have happened.[72] The UPW executive had a reprise of its debate when the Standing Joint Committee on Industrial Women's Organisations (SJCIWO) produced its report on the employment of married women in 1922. The SJCIWO wanted to advocate married women's employment but this was contrary to agreed UPW policy. Edith Howse, UPW woman organiser, found herself in a difficult position as a SJCIWO member and a UPW executive council member. In the UPW debate on the report, it was noted that UPW executive members who were also MPs would find themselves in an awkward position if they advocated women's dismissal on marriage. The UPW's own delegates at Labour conferences had argued that there should be 'no sex disqualification against women'. Opposing the SJCIWO's report, therefore, also meant defying the Labour Party's position, to which the UPW would remain affiliated until the Trades Dispute Act of 1927. Eventually, a motion was passed to secure the only outcome which would – just about – prevent the UPW from performing an about-turn and possibly alienating sections of its membership: Howse was to oppose the report and 'express the view that the employment of married women in industry is generally undesirable'.[73] The report was published with a note stating the UPW's opposition and belief that allowing married women to work 'would merely increase the number of people on the Labour market at the mercy of capitalist employers'.[74]

The CSCA, as an organisation which admitted women from only 1921, took longer to formulate a definite policy and was less public and dogmatic about its stance than the UPW or the FWCS. However, it remained in support of the bar in the 1920s, as we will see. The Association of Women Clerks and Secretaries (AWCS), representing temporary women civil servants in the early 1920s in particular, argued that 'women solely dependent on their earnings, whether married or not, should have preference in employment during times of excessive depression'.[75] This, then, was not actually support for the marriage bar but in practical terms the position manifested itself as such and any application of such a position would have entailed developing a system to gather this information, which may have been seen as either intrusive or unnecessarily bureaucratic.

1927–1935: debates, continuity and change

The Civil Service marriage bar was debated in Parliament for a second time in a decade in 1927 when the NUSEC drafted a Private Members' Bill for Robert Newman MP arguing for married women's right to work. The LCC Staff Association, which until now had not had a defined marriage bar policy, decided not to support the Bill but did not record why.[76] Officials at the Council decided to take no action regarding it after advice that it was unlikely to pass to a second reading but the General Purposes Committee did vote by nineteen votes to nine to oppose the Bill. Significantly, the grounds for doing this were not the contents of the Bill itself, but the fact that married women's employment in local authorities should be decided by the authorities themselves.[77] The Joint Committee on Women in the Civil Service also felt that it could not support the Bill as it contained no provision to retain the existing marriage gratuity arrangements, which were important to women who did want to leave for marriage.[78] The Civil Service Confederation, of which the UPW was part, also opposed the Bill for this reason, as well as the detrimental effect on recruitment and promotion prospects it was felt that the employment of married women would have.[79]

What ensued was a debate largely about the social desirability of married women working and the extent to which they could remain efficient workers, ending in defeat of the Bill by eighty-four votes to sixty-three.[80] Only one or two MPs came close to realising that if women MPs, in their roles as public servants, were allowed to be wives and mothers, it seemed nonsensical and contradictory to place restrictions on women civil servants.[81] The Financial Secretary to the Treasury, Ronald McNeil, gave a pointed preamble about his support for previous women's causes and proceeded to argue that the Bill should not come from a private member as the government of the day had to run the Civil Service; that the Bill was not in the best interests of women civil servants and might result in women not being employed at all; and the catch-all Treasury argument that the Bill was not in the interests of Civil Service efficiency.[82] It was also argued that the marriage bar was needed in order to help the falling birthrate.[83] An attempt to draft a Private Members' Bill was made in 1928, with the intention abolishing the marriage bar in the higher grades only of the Civil Service. However, this was not well-supported by the lower grades of the service and came to nothing.[84]

The 1927 Bill was also the occasion for the CSCA first establishing a definite marriage bar policy, in a hastily organised vote in reaction to the Bill. Christine Maguire, the woman organiser, campaigned vociferously against the Bill.[85] The poll of women members only found in favour of keeping the bar by a significant majority. William Brown, CSCA General Secretary, told the annual conference in 1927 '[w]e took the view that retirements on marriage should be compulsory. We took that view not because we are anxious to get rid of the women, or because of sex bias, but because we held the view that having regard to the mass unemployment in this country it is better that what employment there is should be distributed as widely as possible rather than concentrated in one family. (Hear, hear.)'.[86] This was a clear reiteration of the "double wages" argument, to which the UPW had alluded earlier in the decade. When the Royal Commission in 1929 was appointed and the CSCA executive was preparing its evidence, it had shifted and softened its argument somewhat, espousing the right of women to choose whether they worked or not when married, though it argued that many women would choose not to work.[87] This was backed by a flurry of opinion pieces and letters in *Red Tape*, the association's journal.[88] This time a lengthier ballot procedure was instituted and the paper asked three questions, the two related to the abolition/retention resulting in the following responses (see Table 6.1).[89]

What emerged from this was the overall support for the marriage bar, but within this, the importance of the marriage gratuity. For women who wanted to relinquish their position when they married, the gratuity would have been a welcome payment to meet the costs of setting up a new home. The second question thus reveals that some of the anxiety about the marriage bar being abandoned actually arose from the fear of loss of marriage gratuity. In response, Winifred Holtby wrote an exasperated piece for the *Manchester Guardian* in which she argued that the single women clerks who voted had a 'grass is greener' attitude to marriage. She argued, instead, for far-sightedness and for a more flexible service

Table 6.1 Results of the CSCA ballot of women members on the marriage bar

	Yes	No
Are you in favour of the retention of women in the Service after marriage, if the marriage gratuity is thereby forfeited for all?	112	4,352
Are you in favour of the retention of women in the Service after marriage in the event of the gratuity being retained for those who retire on marriage?	1,245	3,219

Source: *Red Tape*, January 1930, p.224.

which allowed maternity leave, one that did not force women to choose between marriage and a career and thereby ultimately 'raised [women's work] from its status at the bottom of the labour market'.[90] Three days earlier, Brown had told the same newspaper that the 'normal woman' looks forward to marriage.[91]

Between 1929 and 1935 the marriage bar principally came into focus on two occasions. The first of these was the Tomlin Royal Commission and the debate it fostered about the significance of the marriage bar. As might be surmised, the views on the marriage bar presented during evidence sessions of the Royal Commission were ambivalent and contradictory from both the staff associations and Civil Service officials. Many women's organisations external to the Civil Service, as well as the FWCS, told the Commission that the abolition of the bar was in women's best interests.[92] The AWCS told the commissioners that it supported the removal of the marriage bar for cases of desertion and separation, but that it wished to see the bar continue as a whole until all the temporary women staff, whom it chiefly represented, had been awarded full-time posts in the service.[93]

A submission by the Treasury spoke volumes about its attitude to women's work and how the marriage bar became a self-fulfilling prophecy within this. The memorandum argued that:

> In the Civil Service, as in outside industry, a marked feature in connection with women's employment as compared with men's is the tendency for women to be found in the manipulative processes. The cause is undoubtedly to be found in the difference of attitude towards a career. In the Civil Service, as the marriage statistics show, the average career of a woman is comparatively short. This makes them in many cases unwilling to spend time and money in fitting themselves for superior occupations, with the result that they tend to seek positions where

they can earn a reasonably satisfactory wage as soon as possible. There can be no doubt that work is often looked upon as a temporary career which occupies the period between school and marriage and is best filled in quickly by repetitive work. So long as this attitude is prevalent there will be found a disparity between men and women in the twin fields of enterprise and ambition.[94]

This statement was made with no discernible research and in fact was more of a statement of what the Treasury wanted to believe the situation to be. According to officials, women's careers were shorter because of marriage (though they of course neglected to mention that the reason for this was the enforced marriage bar) and because careers were shorter women as a group were universally opposed to 'spend[ing] time and money in fitting themselves for superior occupations'. By not mentioning the marriage bar outright and by insisting that women were less ambitious, this distorted the picture of women civil servants' careers horribly. As we have seen throughout this book, many women civil servants were clamouring for wider opportunities to progress but were consistently denied them, in part because of the reasoning that the marriage bar made them less valuable as employees. The Ministry of Labour, as discussed, had firm ideas about the women it wanted to employ: mature, experienced women with whom other women would feel comfortable talking at employment exchanges.[95] It did not mention married women outright – and of course it was not just married women who were mature and experienced – but the lack of marriage bar, allowing women to stay in the service after marriage if they so wished, might have alleviated this situation to a degree.

The Tomlin Commission reported that none of the official witnesses wanted the marriage bar to be abolished and felt that the efficiency of the service was best served by having married women resign, alongside judicious use of the power enabling departments to retain some women in the interest of public service. It reported some suggestions of having the marriage bar abolished for the higher grades but kept for the lower grades,[96] something which would have had clear class implications and sent a message to clerical grade, typist and manipulative grade women about the value of their contributions. Such sentiment was mirrored in the division amongst the majority signatories of the report as to the future of marriage bar policy. The possibility of having a bar for lower grades but removing it for the higher was eventually dismissed, however, on the grounds that the service would not always want to retain all women in administrative or higher grades and whilst high turnover was considered 'an advantage', 'the disadvantages which would result from the removal of the bar outweigh the disadvantages which result from its retention'.[97]

The minority report signatories wanted the marriage bar abandoned on the grounds of 'a fair field and no favour', arguing that such 'sex differentiation' was 'objectionable in itself' and also that it 'militat[es] against efficiency in so far as it prevents women from looking to the service as a life career'. However, the minority argued that removing the bar would be contrary to the wishes of the lower ranks of the service and so it, too, argued for a marriage bar for the lower grades but not for the higher. Ultimately, with the minority agreeing to accept the majority report as a whole, the marriage bar did not become the contentious issue it might have been.[98] The rest of the report as a whole called for the discretionary power to retain married women to be more readily available.[99] In keeping with this, the Committee on Women's Questions arising out of the Tomlin report confirmed the desirability of a more usable discretionary power.[100]

The Tomlin Commission process also highlighted a number of noteworthy points about the quantitative impact of the marriage bar. The official Civil Service position, most of the time, was that the marriage bar created a high turnover rate, but that this high rate of departures for marriage (enforced by policy) also created an inconvenience. The issue of the rate of departure was so formative in perceptions of women civil servants because it was used, as we have seen in previous chapters, to justify both lower pay and fewer opportunities for women. However, the available evidence suggests that the impact was far less than officials like to contend. One of the 1912–14 (MacDonnell) Royal Commission members had expressed surprise that between only 2 and 3 per cent of the female staff left to marry each year and asked Sir Alexander King if the marriage bar kept the figure so low. He replied saying that he felt the regulation encouraged marriage.[101] Data supplied by the Treasury to the Tomlin Commission revealed that over the total three-year period from 1923 to 1926, 9.6 per cent of the female staff in the typist grades and above left the service with a marriage gratuity. It was noted that the percentage may have been higher due to former temporary staff now having reached the requisite number of years' service for a marriage gratuity. It was also noted that there was some evidence for women remaining in the service long enough to build up a substantial gratuity and thus that 'financial considerations now make a marriage gratuity a factor of considerable importance'. No data was supplied for women leaving without the gratuity, but they may have constituted some of the 4.2 per cent leaving for other reasons.[102] Equally, this number of women leaving for other reasons is striking, showing that departure with a marriage gratuity, whilst the highest cause of exits, did not seem so high a figure compared to other reasons. Furthermore, data compiled about the sizeable number of women in the GPO's Money Order Department for 1926–29 had revealed that although resignation for marriage was the most consistent reason for leaving across all the grades, more women left per year in the writing and sorting assistants grades as a result of transfers to other grades or Civil Service departments than for marriage.[103] This therefore undermined arguments about the impact and inconvenience of the bar.

The best data we have comes from the years 1930–33, possibly when the Treasury realised as a result of the Royal Commission that it would be useful to have data on these issues.[104] Resignations for marriage and for which a gratuity was paid comprised 3.5 per cent of established female staff in the Civil Service as a whole, with figures for the GPO of 4 per cent of its established female staff. Marriage resignations without gratuity comprised 0.6 per cent of the female staff. In comparison, 2.7 per cent of the male staff left for a variety of reasons including retirement and ill health, compared to 5.5 per cent of the female staff leaving for reasons including marriage.[105] Seen in this perspective, it is clear that women were not leaving in huge numbers, as officials sometimes liked to claim. Although data such as this needs to be treated with caution it perhaps indicates that considerable numbers of women chose work over marriage – though the possibility remains of course that some co-habited or hid marriages. It is far from the case that Civil Service departments were having to systematically replace large numbers of their female staff, as officials often liked to assert.[106] Given that they maintained the marriage bar and then blamed the female staff for leaving, what the figures reveal is illuminating. On the rare occasions that the figures were examined, this never led to any serious reconsideration of the notion that all women would leave for marriage. In the mid-1930s, women MPs refuted marriage wastage notions in equal pay debates in Parliament: Ellen Wilkinson argued that 'taking 100,000 men in the administrative and clerical classes, 14,000 men withdrew voluntarily from the service as compared with 7,900 women. That is a pretty high relative wastage'. Similarly, Nancy Astor argued that "wastage" due to death was higher than marriage wastage in the service as a whole.[107]

Besides the opportunities presented via the Royal Commission to evaluate and reconsider the marriage bar, the other public airing of the issues in this period was the campaign in the LCC to have the marriage bar removed for women teachers and doctors. In 1931, the MWF tried again to have the marriage bar abolished for women doctors but the

Council refused on the grounds that it did not want to have different policies for different groups of staff – even though it already had minor exemptions to the bar in operation.[108] However, by mid-1935 married women doctors (except those in residential posts) and teachers could both be employed again by the Council. The story of this change is the activism of certain LCC members, particularly Agnes Dawson, an LCC Councillor sponsored by the National Union of Women Teachers, and the pressure and politicking of women's organisations.

From mid-1934 pressure had been applied to the LCC to consider lifting the marriage bar for women employees generally rather than teachers and doctors specifically.[109] Furthermore, Labour had regained the majority on the LCC and the National Conference of Labour Women had passed a resolution in favour of married women's work in May 1934.[110] Monica Whately – a Labour activist who had clashed with the leadership on a number of occasions – pointedly told the Council in a letter written on behalf of the Six Point Group that it would therefore be appropriate and opportune to see that the policy was carried out for the Council's employees.[111] A report on the marriage bar was commissioned as a result of these deputations for the general sub-committee of the General Purposes Committee. The Committee also considered current Civil Service practice.[112] The report's summary argued that although the current LCC regulations were framed in such a way as to allow exemptions where necessary and that no difficulties had occurred in getting the required staff, the Committee needed to debate the issue of policy. The Clerk of the Council asked the Committee to bear in mind issues such as confinement leave and leave for childcare or domestic reasons, which he assumed would increase; what to do about marriage gratuities if there was to no longer be a marriage bar; and how the increased employment of married women might affect cleaning and other domestic work available to widows.[113]

In 1935 Agnes Dawson, the NUWT/Labour member, was Chair of the General Purposes Committee and also a member of the Establishment Committee. She was therefore prominently placed to apply pressure for the removal of the marriage bar. In fact, sources suggest that she threatened Herbert Morrison, the LCC leader, with her resignation if he did not eliminate the marriage bar for women teachers.[114] Notably, Morrison was present at each meeting of the sub-committee which discussed the possible removal of the bar, whereas he did not attend the General Purposes Committee itself.[115] In the event, the marriage bar was removed for women teachers and doctors only by the Council by a vote of seventy-six to thirty-seven. Although the Council's minutes usually recorded only decisions made rather than discussions had and it is therefore difficult to reconstruct the debate in full, Dawson's arguments for allowing married women teachers ranged from the fact that teacher training was often wasted when married women left, to the fact that marriage gave women a new perspective that was useful for teaching, and that forcing women to stay unmarried was not necessarily healthy for the teaching profession.[116] The same arguments were used about women doctors: marriage might, it was argued, 'enrich' the qualities needed by good women doctors, and public money had already been invested in their training, which would be wasted if they had to leave.[117] These echoed some of the arguments against the bar in the early 1920s for these two specific groups. Retrospectively, the Clerk of the Council used the point about wanting married as well as single teachers to explain the decision to remove the marriage bar, though this does not appear to have been the driving factor in the interwar years.[118]

Evelyn Joyce Denington, a teacher and later an elected LCC member, married one day after the bar was lifted.[119] That there were other women like Denington who wished to combine career and marriage was made evident by the fact that in November 1935 the General Purposes Committee had to back-date when the new rules had come into effect: a sufficient number of women teachers had married after the announcement but before the marriage bar was actually lifted that it was administratively easier to change the date than consider applying any other sanctions.[120]

The available statistics on the effect of lifting the marriage bar, given in Table 6.2, reveal the impact that it had even in the relatively short period before the outbreak of the Second World War.

The lack of marriage bar for two numerically significant groups of female workers meant that the LCC once again had to define policies for confinement leave. Teachers were required to take leave of seventeen weeks, which was to include four weeks before the expected confinement. They were given half-pay for the duration of their maternity absence, but the half-pay for the final two months was withheld until they had completed three months back at work. For doctors, the required period of leave was thirteen weeks, including four weeks before the expected confinement. Providing they had given seventeen months' service before the latter date, they were awarded, in contrast to teachers, four weeks at full pay with the remaining weeks at half-pay. They, too, had to work three months on their return to work before receiving the final four weeks' half-pay.[121] The development of explicit arrangements for confinement leave suggest that it was naturally expected that marriages would lead to

Table 6.2 Women teachers leaving for marriage before, during and after the existence of the marriage bar in the LCC

Year	No. of women teachers leaving for marriage	Total women teachers	Percentage of women teachers leaving for marriage
1920	102	No data available	-
1921	96	No data available	-
1922	76	13,090	0.58
Jan–Feb 1923	6		
Marriage bar put in place for women teachers 6 March 1923 (not retroactive)			
March–December 1923	74	12,919	0.62 (for 1923 as a whole)
1924	66	12,927	0.51
1925	87	12,693	0.68
1926	88	12,919	0.68
1927	88	12,934	0.68
1928	110	12,743	0.86
1929	122	12,653	0.96
1930	120	12,473	0.96
1931	133	12,289	1.08
1932	140	12,102	1.16
1933	177	12,914	1.37
1934	170	12,689	1.34
Marriage bar lifted 1 August 1935			
1935	137	12,349	1.11
1936	77	12,263	0.63
1937	65	11,882	0.55
1938	66	11,464	0.58
1939	63	11,115	0.57

Source: LCC/CL/ESTAB/1/6, 'Statement for the Royal Commission on Equal Pay: effect on wastage of removal of marriage bar – teaching staff only.'

children, and that the women entitled to confinement leave were of the social class and salary group to be able to finance private childcare, or that mothers would be able to source childcare on their return to work. Available data on confinements suggests consistency across a long time span. In 1922, there were 14,377 women teachers and 200 took confinement leave, comprising 1.4 per cent of all women teachers. By the end of 1944 8,437 women teachers were in post and 120 (1.66 per cent) of them had taken confinement leave, the slight increase being attributed to the increase in marriages during the war.[122] Data does not appear to exist regarding the numbers of women who returned to work after childbirth.

The marriage bar in the late 1930s

Whilst the debate about the marriage bar for doctors and teachers was drawing to a close, the LCC Staff Association issued ballot papers to its members with the question 'Are you in favour of the retention of women in the service after marriage?'. Out of the 2,082 respondents, 617 were in favour of the retention of married women, whereas 1,465 – of whom 1,218 were men – were against this. Overwhelmingly, men were against the presence of married women in the workplace, whereas women's responses were slightly in favour of married women staying (305 in favour; 247 against). Significantly, these findings did not chime with those of the Staff Association sub-committee appointed to consider the marriage bar further in 1936.

The committee made some interesting points in support of the abandonment of the bar. It argued that although the marriage bar was generally held to help with the country's unemployment problems, the dismissed married woman would only seek work outside the public service and would thus crowd other employment sectors. More widely the committee argued on the grounds of justice that married women should not be deprived of the chance to be self-supporting. It argued, too, that any 'needs test' to determine which groups of employees needed work the most would be 'unjust and haphazard', pointing also to the illogicality of the insistence that two incomes should not go into one household by arguing that the public service paid people who lived with friends and family who also had incomes, and paid people who also had additional private incomes. In plain language and rhetoric that foreshadowed the women's movement of the 1960s and 1970s, the committee also argued that it should be a woman's choice whether or not she worked after marriage and that work could be positive and fulfilling. 'To sum up', the

Committee said, 'we consider that, although the majority of women will not wish to continue in the Council's service after marriage, if only one woman in the service desired to do so, she should not be prevented'. As a whole, then, the sub-committee appeared to have more enlightened views than the majority of respondents to the poll. The report and the referendum results were referred to the staff side of the Joint Committee of Members and Staff with a request for action, where they appear to have stalled.[123]

In the Civil Service, little was discernibly different now that the 1934 Committee on Women's Questions had agreed to use the discretionary exemption powers for the marriage bar more liberally. This was probably not helped by the fact that the early applications of the power were not without controversy. One case in the Ministry of Labour in 1932 made the national press when the Ministry of Labour Staff Association argued that the woman concerned was not sufficiently important to the public service to be retained, particularly as she had only recently been promoted to her position.[124] In response, Sir Francis Floud told *The Times* that the real reason for this officer's retention was that the department thought it desirable to have a reasonable number of women in the higher ranks, and, owing to the strict enforcement of the marriage bar in the past, there had been too small a supply of qualified women to fill the higher ranks in the departmental class. The department had acted in the interests of the public service, and he thus 'had no intention of altering his decision'.[125] This, then, was an interesting example of affirmative action.

A sample compiled by the Treasury of women applying to stay after marriage indicates how strictly the discretionary exemption was applied. There were eleven successful cases between 1934 and 1939 though several of these had to defer their marriages after their applications were unsuccessful at the first attempt.[126] One applicant was an Assistant Principal, so already in the highest echelons of the Civil Service, and she applied to be retained on marriage in 1934 aged twenty-seven. She was refused, and applied again in 1938, by which point she was serving as Private Secretary to the Director-General of the GPO (and was the first woman to hold this position).[127] This time the application was successful, and a further reference in the same paperwork suggests that she was promoted to the position of Assistant Secretary by 1940. Clearly, the exemption rules for the marriage bar were highly class-based: only upper-middle-class women with education and of sufficient rank in the service were going to be able to meet the criteria and to be considered valuable enough. Writing in a careers' guide for girls in 1938, Alix Kilroy and Evelyn Sharp, two high-ranking women civil servants, struggled to be positive about the way the exemptions worked even at the highest levels: '[W]e believe that while a woman administrative officer who wanted to marry would probably be retired if her experience was still short, she would probably be allowed to remain if she were already a Principal, provided that her Department considered her fully efficient.'[128]

The other dimension to married women's employment that came to the fore in the 1930s was the temporary re-employment of former female staff who had left to be married in the GPO. This can be seen, as Veronica Beechey has argued, as married women serving as a 'reserve army of labour.'[129] Long-term, temporary employment had become a bone of contention amongst individual staff members and associations alike in the late 1920s and 1930s; the married temporary female civil servant became even more so.[130] The temporary staff filled vacancies around the country during busy periods, including some of the women who found themselves in broken marriages, as discussed in Chapter 7. The practice of using married women as temporary labour caused consternation on two grounds: firstly, amongst those who wanted the GPO to cut down on temporary labour and reward all workers with full benefits, and, secondly, amongst those who used the now-familiar argument that married women working took away a potential income from a family with an unemployed breadwinner. The UPW began to complain, at the height of the depression, that 'married women, who have no necessity to go out to work' were being employed.[131] The Post Office insisted that married women were only employed where other 'suitable unemployed persons' were not available, that where they were employed, their number was kept to a minimum and that preference was given to women with unemployed husbands or whose 'domestic circumstances call for sympathetic consideration.'[132] The UPW, however, was unconvinced that these guidelines were being followed.[133] However, temporary employment of married women could sometimes be the only viable – if frustrating – solution to the family finances if the man was unable to find work, as this letter shows:

> I was a telephonist before I married. After some years of marriage, things went wrong and my husband lost his job. He has not been able to get another for four years, although he has tried hard. Every job I apply for I am asked the question, 'What experience have you?' Of course I have none after spending most of my life in a telephone office. My work is as good now as ever it was. Why should a married woman be grudged the opportunity to earn a living? Do we commit a crime when we get married? I would be very pleased if I can manage to live without going inside a telephone office again, but unfortunately rates have to be

paid and expenses met. Good luck to the few married women who have the grit to try to help their men when necessary.[134]

By 1935, married women who were former telegraphists were being employed to meet the telegraph traffic demand when new rates were introduced: a workforce was needed quickly and the Post Office argued that they 'are really the only source of trained staff available at short notice'. Ultimately, the UPW did not resist, but rather than raising the "two incomes in one household" argument, Mr Hodgson, an executive committee member, instead divided women into two groups, using the argument that employing married women 'did not seem to be in the best interests of society' when single women were looking for work.[135] The union's position on married women working and their place in a perceived hierarchy of workers remained clear.

The Second World War and the end of the marriage bar

Just after the outbreak of war, the CSCA cancelled a planned members' ballot on the marriage bar.[136] In recent years there had been a flurry of correspondence on the issue in *Red Tape*, seemingly not prompted by the editors or executive committee.[137] Reading the journal gives the sense of a tide turning or a generational shift making itself known. The ballot was cancelled because the marriage bar had already been lifted because of the war, but by 1944 the CSCA voted for the permanent abolition of the bar in any case.[138]

The Civil Service marriage bar was lifted without fanfare as the war broke out, possibly as a result of the experience of the previous war. In the LCC, the process was more gradual. Individual departments lifted the marriage bar throughout 1940 – particularly those connected with public health and welfare which needed senior staff – and by March 1941 a blanket decision was introduced removing the marriage bar for all grades into which women were normally appointed.[139] This decision took some considerable time to agree to, however, seemingly because of fears about the precedent this would set for when the war was over.[140] Furthermore, one of the reasons given for not abolishing the marriage bar straightaway was the somewhat flimsy argument – based presumably only on guesswork – that the marriage bar was a deterrent to marriage and that by allowing women to marry this would not create a greater female workforce but rather a greater proportion of the female workforce would be married.[141] An increased workforce of married women was, by implication, a problem.

Nevertheless, Eric Salmon, the Clerk of the Council, appears to have been broadly supportive of women's employment. In mid-1945, he wrote a memorandum discussing what the future of married women's employment in the LCC should be. He supported lifting the marriage bar, and appears to have carried this without much opposition.[142] In response, the LCC Staff Association was keen to stress that married women should be held as accountable as other employees in the performance of their jobs, and that women who had served in the LCC for considerable years and thus expected to get a marriage gratuity if they married should be treated fairly.[143] Correspondence from Sir Henry Wilson-Smith at the Treasury to Salmon – who himself had been a high-ranking civil servant in the Ministry of Health until joining the LCC[144] – asked for the LCC's position on the employment of married women. Wilson-Smith's subsequent letter revealed that the Treasury was less than keen to make the same provisions for the Civil Service.[145]

In the event, a special National Whitley Committee was convened to discuss the marriage bar in the Civil Service. The final removal of the bar, in 1946, needs to be seen partly in the context of post-war labour supply shortages, though numerous women and their supporters had also argued for the rights of married women during the Committee.[146] Some women credited the war itself for helping to show that there need not be a marriage bar. The wartime staffing exigencies exemplifed the contributions that married women could still make to the Civil Service despite being a wife and often also a mother.[147] The opinion of associations on the staff side remained somewhat divided, however.[148] E. N. Gladden's comment in 1956 that the lifting of the bar 'can be adjudged a logical outcome of the failure of the Service to recruit sufficient numbers of young girls for routine work' must have rankled with the large numbers of women who had indeed spent the previous years confined to routine work, as must the assumption that it was women who needed to do the routine work.[149] The UPW, as Clinton documents, campaigned for a number of years to have the bar reinstated. Some of the campaigners included women concerned about promotion prospects and availability of work for single women and indeed the UPW continued a marriage bar for its own paid staff until 1963.[150]

The marriage bar, in its years of operation, meant that the vast majority of women public servants were forced to choose between a career and their personal lives – assuming that personal fulfilment meant marriage (and the heterosexual relationship this implied), which of course for some it would not have done. The marriage bar was pervasive and had an effect on all women. Although not necessarily perceived in these terms by all women at the time, the marriage bar was a discriminatory practice which had an impact on the way in which women's employment and prospects were perceived.[151] Public service officials made judgements about women's work based on the existence of the bar, and in turn it strengthened any existing assumptions officials might have had about women and their attitudes to romance and marriage. The strength of wider social attitudes about women's roles in the home and as mothers further allowed officials to legitimise their case for the bar, and with some women opting to leave paid employment on marriage anyway, this normalised the marriage bar's existence. Ultimately, the marriage bar worked because it could be justified on social grounds and could be argued to make sense on business grounds. The varying attitudes to it amongst unions and associations – in contrast to the outwardly uniform attitudes to equal pay – meant that there was no cross-associational campaign to remove the marriage bar and therefore less of a challenge to the status quo.

The marriage bar remains a fascinating and complicated subject but perhaps because of its omnipresence it has been largely overlooked by historians hitherto. For officials – whatever they thought privately about the requirement to resign – the marriage bar was variously justified economically as a means to attempt to increase staff turnover in what was otherwise employment for life, a means to keep the already bulging promotion lists a little shorter and to reduce the funds needed to pay pensions. The deliberately vague concept of 'the interests of the public service' was also available to be invoked when officials desired.

The question of married women's right to work in the public service remained significant because each time it was discussed it unleashed a potential challenge to the idea of what a (female) public servant should be. Marriage – intrinsic to popular understandings of womanhood – was seen in some circumstances to dampen or temper whatever attributes a woman could bring, or had already been bringing, to the service. Indeed, although the marriage bar was effectively abolished in both the LCC and the Civil Service by the early years of the Second World War, the social expectations of women becoming wives, homemakers and potentially mothers remained sufficient to induce employers to continue to debate women's worthiness for promotion. For example, the Royal Commission on Equal Pay – composed, as we have seen, of individuals prominent in public and private employment – posed questions to Sir Eric Salmon as to whether women were less likely to put themselves forward for promotion on account of marriage, and whether the Council was less likely to promote a woman to the highest grades of work on account of the fact that she might marry.[152] He answered in the negative to both questions, but the fact that they were asked speaks volumes about the general, embedded attitudes to the notions of married women continuing careers. The marriage bar, in its conception and the ways it operated bureaucratically, was also based on the assumption that women's lives fell into one of two neat and mutually exclusive categories: married or single. There was no provision for marital breakdown, a fact which left considerable numbers of women in the interwar years in difficult situations and unable to resume their former employment in order to earn an income. The completeness of Civil Service and LCC records on these women's cases allows us to explore these issues in depth in the next chapter.

Notes

1 TNA, T162/329, E22833, 'Introductory Memorandum no. VIII relating to the Employment of Women in the Civil Service', October 1929, p.29.

2 Discussions of the LCC's marriage bar have chiefly been offered in relation to teaching. See Copelman, *London's Women Teachers* and Oram, *Women Teachers*. For brief discussions of the marriage bar in the Civil Service see Zimmeck, 'Jobs for the Girls'; Robert Bennett, 'Gendering Cultures in Business and Labour History: Marriage Bars in Clerical Employment' in Margaret Walsh (ed.), *Working Out Gender: Perspectives from Labour History* (Aldershot: Ashgate, 1999); Kay Sanderson, ' "A Pension to Look Forward To....?": Women Civil Service Clerks in London, 1925–1939' in L. Davidoff and B. Westover (eds), *Our Work, Our Lives, Our Words: Women's History and Women's Work* (Basingstoke: Macmillan Education, 1986). For a discussion of the marriage bar at the BBC, see Catherine Murphy, ' "On an Equal Footing with Men?": Women and Work at the BBC, 1923–1939' (unpublished PhD thesis, Goldsmiths, University of London, 2011), pp.129–182.

3 Cohn, *Occupational Sex Typing*, pp.97–102.

4 Zimmeck, 'Jobs for the Girls', p.162.

5 BPMA, POST 82/197, 'Report by Mr Scudamore to Postmaster General'.

6 BPMA, POST 33/329, File I (1875), responses to the Secretary's memorandum.

7 TNA, T162/50, E3754/08, 'Women in the Civil Service', 'Employment of Married Women, 1 January 1930'.

8 POST 33/329, File VII, Post Office Service Employment of Married Women Committee Report, 25 March 1892.

9 POST 33/329, Post Office Service Employment of Married Women Committee Report, 25 March 1892.

10 POST 33/329, File VII, Post Office Service Employment of Married Women Committee Report, 25 March 1892, p.25.

11 As quoted in Martindale, *Women Servants of the State*, p.149 and Tomlin Commission, *Report*, para. 418. Still, the marriage bar became more prominent in the Civil Service.

12 LMA, LCC/CL/Estab/1/1, Women – resignation on marriage. Employment of married women. Memo from Sub-Committee of the General Purposes Committee to the General Purposes Committee, 12 November 1906.

13 LCC/CL/Estab/1/1, letter from WFL 19 March 1913, and reply from Council, 14 April 1913. See undated document in the same file regarding the discussion of exempting female medical staff from the marriage bar.

14 LCC/Estab/1/1, Memo from officials in Public Health department decrying apparent staff petition, 24 June 1914.

15 LMA, LCC Minutes, 7 April 1914, pp.901–902. Interestingly, one of the Council members voting against was Kingsley Wood, who would be appointed Postmaster General in 1931.

16 POST 33/329, 'Married Women: Employment in Post Office, Part 1', File XX.

17 *LCC Staff Gazette*, March 1915, p.39.

18 LCC/CL/Estab/1/1, Employment of Married Women: Establishment Committee: Report by Clerk of the Council summarising reports by heads of departments, 14 March 1916.

19 LMA, LCC Minutes, 4 July 1916.

20 *Report of the War Cabinet Committee on Women in Industry*, Appendix, pp.157–158.

21 Gladstone Committee, *Report*, para. 34.

22 For a thorough discussion of the passage of the Bill through Parliament and its relationship to the continuance of marriage bars, see Takayanagi, 'Parliament and Women', pp.54–63. Zimmeck, 'Strategies and Stratagems', p.908.

23 TNA, T 162/50.

24 *The Marriage Bar in the Civil Service*, Report of the Civil Service National Whitley Council Committee (London: HMSO, 1946). para. 6, p.4. For more on the Sex Disqualification Removal Act and the fact that it was merely enabling rather than proscriptive, see Takayanagi, 'Women and Parliament', pp.38–77.

25 TNA, T162/50, 'Women in the Civil Service'. Untitled memo dated 17/11; TNA, T162/50, 'Women in the Civil Service'. Memo addressed to Mr Craig and Mr Scott from W. R. Fraser, 16 November [1920?], point 4; TNA, T162/50, 'Women in the Civil Service'. Untitled memo from R. R. Scott to Sir Malcolm Ramsay, 19 November 1920.

26 Tomlin Commission, *Report*, para.421.

27 CL/ESTAB/1/6 Royal Commission on Equal Pay (1944), Evidence, statement B.

28 Graves, *Labour Women*, p.126.

29 LCC/CL/ESTAB/1/6 Evidence of Sir Eric Salmon to the Royal Commission on Equal Pay, col. 764.

30 Oram, *Women Teachers*, pp.51–57.

31 LMA, LCC/MIN/06276, Minutes of the LCC General Purposes Committee, 1918–1919; 26 May 1919; 14 July 1919; 24 November 1919.

32 Graves, *Labour Women*, p.126.

33 LCC/CL/ESTAB/1/2, Employment of Married Women, Sub-Committee on Staff (Married Women), report of 13 July 1920, as quoted in memo by James Bird, Clerk of the Council, 14 July 1924 (General Purposes Paper no. 654).

34 LCC/CL/ESTAB/1/2, memorandum from General Purposes Committee, 28 July 1924.

35 LMA, LCC/CL/ESTAB/1/2, extract from minutes of General Purposes Committee, 17 November 1924.

36 *British Medical Journal*, vol. 2, no. 3335 (29 November 1924), letter from F. May Dickinson Berry, 'Married Women in Professions', p.1025.

37 Oram, *Women Teachers*, p.49. Dickinson Berry made the point as a joint signatory to a MWF letter in 1927. British Medical Journal, vol.1, no.3467 (18 June 1927), 'Employment of Married Women', p.245.

38 'Married Women in Professions', p.1025.

39 LCC/CL/ESTAB/1/2, letter to Clerk of the Council from the MWF, 22 December 1930.

40 Oram, *Women Teachers*, p.26; p.41.

41 Wotjczak, *Railwaywomen*, p.133.

42 *The Marriage Bar in the Civil Service*, Report of the Civil Service National Whitley Council Committee (London: HMSO, 1946), Appendix.

43 *Marriage Bar in the Civil Service*, Appendix.

44 *The Times*, 'Careers for Girls I – The Probation Officer', 12 October 1938, p.9. See also, for example, *The Times*, 'Careers For Girls XV: The Hospital Almoner', 1 May 1939, p.19.

45 Robert Price and George Sayers Bain, 'The Labour Force', in A.H. Halsey, *British Social Trends since 1900* (Basingstoke and London: Macmillan, 1988), Table 4.6, Female participation rates by age and marital status – Great Britain, 1911–81, p.172.

46 Graves, *Labour Women*, pp.126–131; p.189; Smith, 'Sex vs Class', pp.28–29.

47 Graves, *Labour Women*, pp.189–191.

48 In addition to the examples quoted in this chapter, see, for example, *Good Housekeeping*, Mrs Alfred Sidgwick, 'Should Married Women Work?', February 1924, p.15.

49 Morley (ed.), *Women Workers*, p.273.

50 Morley (ed.), *Women Workers*, pp.273–274.

51 Law, *Suffrage and Power*, p.85; Oram, *Women Teachers*, p.47; Janet Courtenay, *Recollected in Tranquillity* (London: Heinemann, 1926), pp.246–247; pp. 251–252; Graves, *Labour Women*, pp.126–130.

52 Brittain, *Women's Work in Modern England*, p.194.

53 See also Sanderson, 'A Pension to Look Forward to?', p.151.

54 See, for example, POST 115/444, *The Post*, notice of the marriage of Mr O. T. King and Miss B. Snagg, both postal employees, 23 November 1923, p.421; *London County Council Staff Gazette*, October 1925, p.242.

55 *Red Tape*, Correspondence, letter from Winifred E. Oakley, October 1929, p.54.

56 *Red Tape*, 'The Marriage Bar Ballot. Why I Favour Retention' by Violet M. Knock, pp.93–94; *Red Tape*, 'Violet Knock', September 1930, p.788.

57 *Red Tape*, Correspondence, letter from Miss A. E. Holden, July 1937, p.820.

58 POST 115/467, *The Post*, GNC, ' "A Woman's Place is in the Home" ', 12 January 1935, p.34; Letters to the Editor, letter from 'Experienced', 26 January 1935, p.91; Letters to the Editor, letter from GNC, 9 February 1935, p.128; letter from Marjorie Webb, 23 March 1935, p.268.

59 Oram, *Women Teachers*, p.56. Interestingly, Oram also notes that cohabitation and concealment of marriage were used as reasons why the marriage bar should be removed. See also Courtenay, *Recollected*, p.250 and *Manchester Guardian*, 'Women Civil Servants: Secret Marriages', 9 July 1938.

60 LCC/CL/ESTAB/2/1, letter dated 10 December 1936.

61 Elizabeth Imlay Buckley and Dorothy Usher Potter (eds), *Ida and the Eye: A Woman in British Ophthalmology: From the Autobiography of Ida Mann* (Tunbridge Wells: Parapress Ltd, 1996), p.14. I am grateful to Mari Takayanagi for drawing my attention to this source.

62 *Hansard*, Married Women (Employment) Bill, cc.1212.

63 IWMSA, 668, interview with Lilian Gertrude Wolfe, 27 February 1974.

64 In the Second World War, Doreen Bates, who worked for the Civil Service in London and then Belfast, had an affair with a married man and became pregnant. She encountered mixed reactions among her colleagues – notably her woman establishment officer was unsupportive but her immediate (male) supervisor was – but was allowed to remain in the service. Amongst other things, she argued that as the sole breadwinner supporting two children she should be accorded the same rights as male colleagues. See Elizabeth McClair, 'Single Parenthood and the Civil Service' in Sybil Oldfield (ed.), *This Working Day World: Women's Lives and Culture(s) in Britain, 1914-1945* (London: Taylor & Francis, 1994), p.71.

65 See, among many, *The Post*, 'P.O. Woman Swimming Champion Marries', 30 April 1927, p.408.

66 BPMA, POST 115/86, *Opportunity*, 'The Debate', September 1921, p.94.

67 POST 115/90, *Opportunity*, 'The Married Woman's Right to Earn', May 1933, p.79.

68 MSS.148/UCW/2/1/5, UPW executive council minutes, 19–21 October 1921.

69 Graves, *Labour Women*, p.131.

70 Graves, *Labour Women*, pp.130–131. UPW executive council minutes, 19–21 October 1921.

71 UPW executive council minutes, 19–21 October 1921.

72 MSS.148/UCW/2/13/3, Third Annual UPW Conference Report, May 1922.

73 MSS.148/UCW/2/1/5, executive council meeting, 26–28 January 1922, p.23.

74 MSS.138/UCW/2/1/5, executive council meeting minutes, 19–21 April 1922, letter from Marion Phillips of the Standing Joint Committee of Industrial Women's Organisations dated 16 February 1922.

75 MSS.148/UCW/2/1/5, letter from Marion Phillips of the Standing Joint Committee of Industrial Women's Organisations dated 16 February 1922.

76 LMA, GLSA/1/30, meeting of 29 March 1927.

77 LCC/CL/ESTAB/1/2, Employment of Married Women, news clipping about the Bill and record of General Purposes Committee decision, 4 April 1927.

78 WL, 6/JCS/A1, minutes, 18 February 1927.

79 *The Post*, 'Married Women and the Civil Service', 4 June 1927, p.534.

80 *Hansard*, Married Women (Employment) Bill, HC Deb 29 April 1927 vol. 205 cc.1171–1233.

81 *Hansard*, HC Deb 29 April 1927 vol. 205 c.1177; 1198.

82 *Hansard*, HC Deb 29 April 1927 vol. 205 cc.1220–1227.

83 *Hansard*, HC Deb 29 April 1927 vol. 205 cc.1208–1211.

84 WL, 6/JCS/A1, minutes, 19 January 1928, 25 April 1928 and 11 July 1928.

85 *Hansard*, HC Deb 29 April 1927 vol. 205, c.1187. See also MSS.415/63/12, CSCA-issued leaflet entitled 'The Parliamentary Debate on the Civil Service Marriage Bar, April 29th, 1927'.

86 *Red Tape*, Report of Annual Conference Proceedings, June 1927, p.445.

87 *Red Tape*, 'The Tape Machine. Another Royal Commission', May 1929, p.445.

88 *Red Tape*, Stanley Mayne, 'Women, the Service and Petruchio: A Plea for the Removal of the Marriage Bar', July 1929, pp.649–650; J. Paterson Bryant, 'Maintain the Marriage Bar! A Reply to Last Month's Article', August 1929, p.712; 'Why the Marriage Bar Should Go!', September 1929, p.773; readers' letters, September 1929, pp.798–800; Stanley Mayne, 'Treat Men and Women Equally', October 1929, p.15; 'Women Should Decide', p.19; p.23; p.43; Violet M. Knock, 'The Marriage Bar Ballot: Why I Favour Retention', November 1929, pp.93–94; Dorothy Evans, 'The Case for Abolition', pp.95–96.

89 These were not the final results, but were published because, as Chris Holock, the interim woman organiser pointed out, they were 'decisive'. See POST 115/177, *Red Tape*, 'Women's Notes: Marriage Bar and Superannuation: Decisive Figures in CSCA Ballots', January 1930, p.224.

90 Winifred Holtby, 'The Wearer and the Shoe' [*Manchester Guardian*, 31 January 1930] in Berry and Bishop, *Testament of a Generation*, p.66.

91 *Manchester Guardian*, 'Married Women in Civil Service: Should They Retire?', 28 January 1930.

92 Tomlin Commission, 1929–1931, para.429. See also, for example, the comments of the St Joan's Political Alliance as reprinted in POST 115/91, *Opportunity*, 'The Outlook', June 1934, pp.97–98.

93 T 162/50, 3754/09/1, Women in the Civil Service. Supplementary Memorandum for the Royal Commission, 'Summary of the Proposals made to the Royal Commission on the Civil Service by the Association of Women Clerks and Secretaries' [n.d.].

94 T162/50, 3754/09/1, Supplementary: Women on routine work [n.d.]

95 TNA, Lab2/1911/S&E699/1932, 'Report of Duties of Women Officers in the Departmental Clerical Class Employed in Three Typical Employment Exchanges in the South Eastern Area', p.5. The insistence on single women – largely out of the hands of the Ministry itself – resonates with earlier decisions in the LCC's public health department, as documented by Susan Pennybacker, to uphold the marriage bar for female inspectors even though experience as a mother might have stood them in good stead as the criteria for employment included domestic hygiene knowledge and child management. See Pennybacker, *A Vision for London*, p.162.

96 Tomlin Commission, *Report*, para. 428.

97 Tomlin Commission, *Report*, para. 436 (i); para. 436 (ii).

98 Tomlin Commission, *Report*, para. 437.

99 Tomlin Commission, *Report*, para. 440; para. 438.

100 *Committee on Women's Questions Report*, para. 20.

101 POST 33/729A, Evidence of Sir Alexander King, 1913, paras 31,571–31,575. The Fabian Committee felt the same as the Royal Commissioners. See Morley (ed.), *Women Workers*, p.273.

102 TNA, T162/329, 'Women: Exits from the Service with special reference to resigna-tion (with gratuity) on marriage, 1923–1926'. POST 33/3237B, File III, Extract from Whitley Bulletin, March 1944; 'Women Clerical Officers Appointed from Open Competition of 1925'.

103 POST 33/3237B, file II, Money Order Department 1926–1929.

104 On the lack of so-called 'wastage' data for the Civil Service generally, see Kelsall, *Higher Civil Servants*, p.8.

105 T162/329, 'Table showing exits from the Service as expressed as % of the numbers of established men and women employed, based on figures for the years 1930/1933'.

106 See, amongst numerous other instances, POST 115/92, *Opportunity*, 'Fantasy on Marriage', February 1937, p.32.

107 *Hansard*, Civil Service Women (Pay), HC Deb 01 April 1936 vol. 310 c.2020; c.2049.

108 *British Medical Journal*, 'Employment of Married Medical Women by the London County Council', 19 December 1931, p.1154.

109 LCC/CL/ESTAB/1/2, notes of deputations by Open Door Council, 2 July 1934, and London and National Society for Women's Service, 4 July 1934.

110 LCC/CL/ESTAB/1/2, copy of resolution passed at National Conference of Labour Women, May 1934.

111 LCC/CL/ESTAB/1/2, copy of letter from Monica Whately of the Six Point Group to the Clerk of the Council, 6 February 1935. Linda Walker, 'Whately, (Mary) Monica (1889–1960)', *Oxford Dictionary of National Biography* (Oxford University Press, 2004) [www.oxforddnb.com/view/article/63900, accessed 8 February 2015].

112 CL/ESTAB/1/2, 'Employment of Married Women. General Purposes (General) Sub-Committee. Report by Clerk of the Council, 22 November 1934', p.7.

113 'Employment of Married Women, General Purposes (General) Sub-Committee. Report by Clerk of the Council, 22 November 1934', pp.8–9.

114 Oram, *Women Teachers*, pp.170–171.

115 LMA, LCC/MIN/06292, Minutes of the LCC General Purposes Committee, 1935.

116 *The Times*, 'Marriage Bar Removed', 17 July 1935, p.16.

117 *British Medical Journal*, 'Married Women Doctors and the LCC', 20 July 1935, pp.130–131.

118 LCC/CL/ESTAB/1/6 Evidence of Sir Eric Salmon to the Royal Commission on Equal Pay, col. 764.

119 Duncan Sutherland, 'Denington, Evelyn Joyce, Baroness Denington (1907–1998)', *Oxford Dictionary of National Biography* (Oxford University Press, October 2005) [www.oxforddnb.com/view/article/70683, accessed 12 July 2012].

120 LCC/MIN/06292, minutes of meeting, 4 November 1935.

121 LCC/CL/ESTAB/1/6 Statement E to the Royal Commission on Equal Pay.

122 LCC/CL/ESTAB/1/6 Memo from E. G. Savage to S. A. Jewitt (Clerk of the Council), 6 March 1945.

123 GLSA/1/36, LCC Staff Association committee, minutes, 22 June 1936.

124 *The Times*, 'Woman Civil Servant. Protest Against Retention After Marriage', 13 July 1932, p.8.

125 *The Times*, 'Woman Civil Servant. Retention After Marriage "In Public Interest"', 4 August 1932, p.7.

126 *Marriage Bar in the Civil Service*, Report of the Civil Service National Whitley Council Committee (London: HMSO, 1946), para. 13; para. 19. TNA, T162/822, 3754/03/01, 'Women in the Civil Service: Retention in an established capacity after marriage. Individual applications', Women Retained on Marriage [n.d.].

127 POST 115/92, *Opportunity*, 'A Pioneer', April 1937, p.69. TNA T162/822, 3754/03/2, 'Women in the Civil Service. Employment of Married Women. General Policy'. 'Information collated for Mr Temple Morris's P.Q. of 18.7.38'.

128 Alix Kilroy and Evelyn Sharp, 'The Civil Service' in Cole (ed.), *The Road to Success*, p.55.

129 Veronica Beechey, *Unequal Work* (London: Verso, 1987), pp.88–89.

130 One of the post-Tomlin Whitley Committees ('Committee B') discussed temporary staffing issues. Parris, *Staff Relations*, p.93.

131 POST 115/458, *The Post*, 'Mr Hodgson's Letter: Employment of Married Women', 21 June 1930, p.615.

132 Letter from Mr E. Raven at the GPO, dated 4 April 1930, reprinted in POST 115/458, *The Post*, 'Mr Hodgson's Letter: Employment of Married Women', 21 June 1930, p.615. See also POST 33/330A, File 31, memo dated 25 November 1929.

133 Letter from Mr J. Paterson, Acting Assistant Secretary, dated 2 May 1930, reprinted in POST 115/457, *The Post*, 'Mr Hodgson's Letter: Employment of Married Women', 21 June 1930, p.615.

134 POST 115/458, *The Post*, Letters to the Editor, 'A Telephonist Who Married', 5 July 1930, p.4.

135 POST 33/330A, File 43, correspondence between GPO and UPW, May 1935.

136 *Red Tape*, Association Notes, October 1939, p.6.

137 This began with Dorothy E. Nicholas' article 'Down With The Marriage Bar' in *Red Tape*, August 1937, p.861 and spanned numerous following issues. See, for example, Vivien Batchelor, 'No, Miss Nicholas! A Defence of the Marriage Bar', September 1937, p.955; C. Haycocks' letter on the marriage bar, p.978; 'This Marriage Bar Business: Miss Nicholas Replies to Critics', October 1937, pp.57–58; M. F. M. Hodgson, 'If the Marriage Bar were Removed', p.127; Stanley Mayne, 'A Man's Views on the Marriage Bar', November 1937, p.209; *Red Tape*, Arthur S. Limmer, 'The Marriage Bar and All That: A Reply to Mr Mayne', January 1938, p.295; M. A. Byrd, 'Marriage and the Marriage Bar: Another Woman States Her Views', February 1938, p.337.

138 *Marriage Bar in the Civil Service*, para. 30.

139 LMA, LCC/CL/ESTAB/1/3, record of Civil Defence and General Purposes Committee, 3 September 1939.

140 See, in particular, LCC/CL/ESTAB/1/3, memo to the Clerk of the Council, 22 January 1941.

141 LCC/CL/ESTAB/1/3, memo to Clerk of the Council, 22 January 1941.

142 LCC/CL/ESTAB/1/4, Employment of Married Women, memorandum by Clerk of the Council, 5 July 1945.

143 LCC/CL/ESTAB/1/4, memorandum by Clerk of the Council, 5 July 1945.

144 Tom Caulcott, 'Salmon, Sir Eric Cecil Heygate (1896–1946)', *Oxford Dictionary of National Biography* (Oxford University Press, 2004) [www.oxforddnb.com/view/article/35913, accessed 22 October 2012].

145 LCC/CL/ESTAB/1/4, letter from Wilson-Smith to Eric Salmon, 24 October 1945.

146 Parris, *Staff Relations*, p.152. POST 122/2373, Employment of Married Women: Abolition of the Marriage Bar in the Civil Service.

147 Meynell, *Public Servant, Private Woman*, p.171.

148 *Marriage Bar in the Civil Service*, para. 30.

149 Gladden, *Civil Service or Bureaucracy?*, pp.78–79.

150 Clinton, *Post Office Workers*, pp.432–433.

151 Martin Daunton and Kay Sanderson have made similar points. See Daunton, *Royal Mail*, p.221 and Sanderson, 'A Pension to Look Forward to...?', p.151.

152 LCC/CL/ESTAB/1/6 Evidence of Sir Eric Salmon to the Royal Commission on Equal Pay, cols. 756–757; 759.

7

Disabled husbands, deserted wives, working widows: the marriage bar in public servants' private lives until 1946

W hilst the last chapter sought to examine the socio-political context of the marriage bar and employers' rationalisations for largely keeping it in place in peacetime, this chapter examines the marriage bar in relation to women undergoing marital breakdown, or facing economic difficulties because their husbands were unable to work. In so doing, it reveals the way in which the marriage bar as an institutional ideal was unsustainable and inflexible in terms of some women's lives and the economic realities they faced. This chapter highlights both the rigidity of marriage bar legislation as well as providing a new window on the experiences and challenges faced by women whose marriages proved not to be lifelong or whose husbands were in difficult circumstances. Furthermore, this study contributes not only to understandings of the marriage bar, its limitations and the profound effect it could have, but the testimony used also provides understandings of the lives of women who faced these circumstances, which might otherwise not be glimpsed. This chapter examines the ways in which policies were gradually evolved in both the LCC and the Civil Service. As the employer of the most women in the Civil Service, the GPO was particularly significant as the site of several "test cases".

Disappointed fiancées

Perhaps the greatest symbol of the marriage bar's rigidity – but in many ways the most nonsensical symbol – was the group quaintly termed "disappointed fiancées". This term was applied by the Post Office to women whose engagements, rather than their marriages, had broken down. They were in a uniquely difficult position in that they had resigned their Post Office employment, only for their engagements to be broken off shortly thereafter. The Treasury, which of course had to be consulted on such issues, initially suggested treating "disappointed fiancées" as widows, despite the inherent ironies in doing so. Widows were permitted to re-join the service in the same role minus one pay increment. To its credit, the Post Office fought hard for the rights of "disappointed fiancées", emphasising in 1913 for example the difference between resigning for a few weeks, which a "disappointed fiancée" was likely to do, and being out of the service for a "fairly considerable" time, which was likely to be the case for widows. Post Office officials argued that the value of a disappointed fiancée was thus much greater than that of a widow.[1] In 1916, they stated their case more strongly to the Treasury:

> We do not seem to have considered specially the case of women who resign to get married and whose marriage is postponed or broken off through causes beyond their own control. Seeing that resignation on marriage is compulsory we are inclined to think that a woman in this position should not be held to have severed her connexion with the Civil Service, but should be allowed to return to her former position without penalty, the period of her absence being treated as special leave without pay.[2]

GPO officials' strength of feeling about this issue, which stood in contrast to their often officious attitudes to women's employment otherwise, was revealed in paragraphs of a draft letter to the Treasury. To take one example:

> As you wish to treat disappointed fiancées in the same way as widows, I can only assume that not only do you propose to reduce the pay by one increment but also you propose to delete all service before resignation for purposes of pension and marriage gratuity. The analogy between disappointed fiancées and widows appears to me a false one. The widow at least has her marriage gratuity to set against the loss of her previous service for pensionable purposes, and she has carried out the object for which she left the service. The disappointed fiancée, on the other hand, has nothing to set against the loss of her previous service and the reduction of her pay, and as she has been prevented by circumstances beyond her own control from carrying out the object for which she left the service, she seems to have a moral claim to return without penalty.[3]

The Treasury eventually relented. The first "disappointed fiancée" suffered from having been the first case of her kind,[4] but thereafter "disappointed fiancées" were reinstated at their former levels of pay, but did have to undergo several weeks of bureaucracy to return to their jobs. Interestingly, it was decided that it would be improper for officials to pry into the circumstances of individual broken-off engagements and weigh up one case against another. This was in stark contrast to the pages of evidence that were sometimes accumulated about separated women, as we will see later in this chapter. This difference is likely explicable by the fact that "disappointed fiancées" were on the "right" side of the marriage bar in the sense that they had never been married and officials seemingly knew that it was hard to justify not reinstating these women.

Widowhood, marital breakdown and challenges to the marriage bar

The rationale and severity of the marriage bar was continually tested by situations involving women who were technically not single but not married either. The breakdown of marriages and engagements was clearly not a new phenomenon in the early twentieth century, though relaxations of the divorce laws in 1923 and 1937 prompted noticeable rises in divorce petitions nationally, particularly by women.[5] As the discussion of "disappointed fiancees" reveals, there were long, bureaucratic and, in this case, often intrusive processes through which women had to go if they wanted to be reinstated into the public service following a broken marriage.

The question of women's entitlement to re-employment in the case of marital breakdown appears to have emerged earlier in the LCC than in the Civil Service. In 1914, Laurence Gomme, Clerk of the Council, produced a memorandum regarding women cleaners, in which he suggested that they should be permitted employment if they were married to a man who was 'permanently, or for a lengthened period, incapacitated from supporting them'. He also suggested that the existing rulings did not prevent divorced women from holding LCC employment. '[T]he case was not so clear', he suggested, for women deserted by their husbands – an argument which was mirrored in later GPO and Civil Service discussions – and he suggested that a period of two years should serve as sufficient proof of desertion. He was taken to task on this issue by workers in Central Hackney who argued that it should be a period of only several months. Significantly, Gomme drew a line between women who had *chosen* to separate from their husbands and cases of desertion: in the cases where women had made the decision, he felt that reinstatement in LCC employment should not be permitted.[6] This distinction would remain important in the LCC throughout the interwar period. It was a hugely problematic distinction which seemed to rest on notions of agency: if a woman had been deserted (and therefore remained "passive") she could be re-employed; if she had taken the decision to initiate a separation, she was not entitled to reinstatement whatever the circumstances.

It was after the First World War that applications for reinstatement in the Post Office's established service were received more regularly. Such applications, and the resultant decisions, reveal the bar's pervasiveness, the concerns of the Treasury and the Post Office, and the nature of the women's circumstances. Whilst the Post Office was certainly not the only Civil Service department where former women staff had either undergone marital breakdown or who had husbands no longer able to provide for them, by virtue of its being the department employing by far the largest number of women (including women from more working-class backgrounds, where financial resources might render marital breakdown situations particularly precarious), a large proportion of the cases appear to have emerged here. In addition, the separate keeping and survival of records in the GPO allows us to see these circumstances in GPO women's lives much more readily than in other departments. The records reveal how a few principles guided early decisions about reinstatement and how a policy subsequently evolved for the whole Civil Service as further cases were considered. The applications came from around the country and whilst these were sometimes accompanied by a testimonial from GPO staff who had supervised the woman in question, the records are too varied to allow any significant conclusions about consistency, leniency or variation among regions. For the period before mid-1934, when new regulations were introduced for the Civil Service as a whole, twenty-nine cases were discussed between the GPO and the Treasury, which had to give final approval, and a number more were rejected by the GPO without any further discussion. The debates about each case formed part of an attempt to formulate a policy for the whole Civil Service for dealing with cases of marital breakdown. In a number of cases, the women who applied for reinstatement were working in their pre-marriage roles in a temporary capacity, but sought to re-gain a position in the Post Office establishment to qualify for the benefits these appointments brought. There were, however, also benefits for the Treasury and the Post Office in keeping women in temporary employment, as we have already seen.

Though widows' circumstances were clearly different from women whose marriages had ended, it is significant that the reinstatement policy for widows formed the initial basis of a policy for women in broken marriages in the Civil Service. The marriage bar rulings contained provision for widows to enter, or indeed to re-enter, the service in established positions, but in practice, matters were less straightforward. Whilst widows had a more automatic right to reinstatement than other groups of women discussed later, they were subject to certain criteria. In particular, the length of a woman's original GPO service was weighed by the Treasury against the number of years she had been out of the service, together with her age and health at the proposed point of re-entry.[7] Therefore although reinstatement policy towards widows appeared benign and straightforward, entitlement to re-enter the Civil Service as established staff was not absolute. In the LCC, there was also some suggestion that some women might take advantage and try to claim widowhood under false pretences. In 1924, there was a debate as to whether widows should be asked to prove their widowhood but this was rejected on the grounds that single women were never asked to prove that they were single.[8]

After the First World War, Treasury policy appeared to be that a divorced woman could be readmitted to the service if she had not been the 'guilty party' in the divorce.[9] An early case of a divorced woman seeking re-establishment in the Post Office indicates that morality was a relevant factor and that the Treasury aimed to keep "guilty" women out of the service. There was a clear resonance here with the stigma and publicity attached to divorce. In June 1920, a former counter clerk and telegraphist applied to be re-established in the service, but when it emerged that she had not instigated divorce proceedings, officials decided that she could not re-enter the service.[10] The context of divorce law nevertheless made it more difficult for her to instigate divorce proceedings. In 1920, the only legal ground for divorce was adultery, and gender inequality in the law meant that women could only divorce their husbands if they could prove adultery together with one other offence. Moreover, divorce remained expensive, making it additionally difficult for women to instigate proceedings. Although the reasons for divorce from the applicant's husband were not included in these papers, the fact that the former counter clerk and telegraphist had not instigated divorce proceedings was evidently inferred to imply guilt on her part. Similarly, in July 1929, another former counter clerk and telegraphist sought reinstatement, being temporarily employed in her former role. As she wrote to the head of the London Postal Service:

> I beg to enquire if it would be possible to reinstate me on the permanent Staff, I resigned on my marriage in 1904. For private reasons a divorce took place between my husband and self, the decree absolute was pronounced on June 14th 1920. I should have made this application before, but my family arrangements have been very unsettled, I thought I should have to be leaving England to join my relatives in America.[11]

The Post Office ruled that she could not be reinstated and, a month later, she asked them to explain the reasons for the decision. Significantly, she was aware that her status as a divorcee would have been a factor in the decision and thus attempted to distinguish between her personal and working lives:

> May I be allowed to know the precise reason for refusal please? Is it due to any inability to perform official work or to circumstances that have connection with private business. My husband was a brute and a drunkard and I left him owing to his habits. When he commenced divorce proceedings I did not defend, I welcomed any opportunity of being free from him. The office of the Kings [sic] Proctor endeavoured to intervene. I did not welcome this, my solicitor advised me not to as I wished for my freedom. I could not get sufficient proof against my husband to bring an action although I was privately convinced of his misconduct. I apologise for introducing these particulars but the circumstances seem to demand it. May I be permitted to know the exact reason for refusal?[12]

One of the Post Office officials who read her letter underlined her phrase 'When he commenced divorce proceedings I did not defend' and wrote 'assumed role of guilty party' beside it.[13] Hence although she had alleged that her husband was guilty of misconduct and had judged it best to not defend herself in order to leave her marriage, the fact that she had not begun divorce proceedings had automatically counted against her. The Post Office Secretary declared that 'she has no claim to be considered for reinsta[tement]'.[14] By insisting on women who had not been the 'guilty party' in divorce proceedings, the Treasury was likely referring to, and insisting upon, standard Civil Service entry requirements that candidates be 'duly qualified in respect of … character'.[15] Since the marriage bar applied only to women, and such questions of reinstatement could therefore apply only to women, the Treasury was, however, effectively imposing a differentiated standard for women. As men were not asked about their private lives, they could not be discriminated against for perceived, or actual, marital indiscretions or problems.

By contrast, an application was received from another woman in December 1925. She had served as a sorting clerk and telegraphist between March 1916 and June 1924. Since her marriage had been annulled by her husband on the grounds of non-consummation, Post Office officials supported the application, stating that the courts had 'decided in effect that there was no marriage'. The Treasury thus ruled that she could be accepted back into the service 'on the usual terms appropriate to the re-instatement of women who have retired on marriage and obtained a divorce'.[16] Her treatment as a divorcee, despite the court's ruling she had never been married, suggested that the Treasury and GPO did not have a category for such cases within the operation of the marriage bar. Indeed, her case highlights the extent to which the marriage bar was set up to distinguish between two groups – married women and single women – and that there was no mechanism for dealing with women who did not fall distinctly into either category. In her case too, of course, getting her job back required that she divulge the most personal details of her sexual life.

Divorced women occupied an ambiguous position in society in the sense that they were no longer married but were not considered as single women. Officials could thus find categorisations of such women different from the women's own. In 1925, a Miss Dale achieved first place in a Post Office examination and was placed on the establishment, before it transpired that she had previously been married and had divorced her husband. When questioned she indicated that her solicitors had advised her that she could use her maiden name again. Her Post Office supervisor vouched for her character and skills. It was eventually agreed that she would not be penalised for not disclosing her marriage.[17] In legal terms, and clearly in Dale's self-perception, she was regarded as single, but this conflicted with some officials' interpretation of the marriage bar.

The cost of divorce in the interwar period meant that many had to opt for a legal separation and maintenance order instead.[18] The "innocent party" requirement still being upheld, the Treasury drew a strong distinction between divorcees and women separated from, or deserted by, their husbands, which effectively meant that divorced women were often more preferable in officials' minds than separated women. It seems that a divorced woman's marriage was perceived as definitely over whereas a separated woman's was not. In 1920, Treasury officials declared that '[a] divorced woman is unmarried ... but a separated woman is not' and gained legal advice to support their position.[19] Cases of desertion and separation tended to complicate decisions and often made individual officials uneasy.[20] There were concerns that the reinstatement of women separated from their husbands may 'form very inconvenient precedents' together with the possibility that a couple might collude in pretending they had separated in order to secure further income. After some initial cases, the Treasury was happy for the Post Office to exercise discretion, arguing that if 'continuous and efficient' service could be obtained from an 'efficient woman of experience', she would be more valuable than an ordinary recruit.[21] Examination of the ensuing cases indicates that financial need was the chief criterion for reinstatement, but other considerations such as age and length of original service were also relevant. If a maintenance order was in place to provide for a separated woman and any dependents, and it was being regularly paid and was considered sufficient, the woman in question was normally refused a place in GPO service. Thus, the decisions also echoed the family breadwinner model: if a "breadwinner" – even a former husband paying a separation allowance – was in place to provide for a separated woman, she should not be allowed to become a breadwinner herself. In the LCC, financial need also appears to have been a similar, guiding principle for reinstatement cases. In one case a woman who had been deserted by her husband lied about her marital status in order to secure LCC employment to support herself and her children. When it was discovered that she had been deserted, she was treated leniently, despite her untruthfulness on official paperwork, but the outcome may have been different if she had been separated, given the LCC's stance on this.[22] In 1924, there was a query over how a woman could prove she was not receiving an agreed maintenance allowance from her husband. It was agreed that evidence from what might be termed a "respectable" member of the state – a JP, local clergyman, doctor, County Court or Police Court officer – would likely be acceptable.[23]

The case of a former telephonist reveals the concern of the GPO and Civil Service to establish genuine financial need. In January 1929, the telephonist applied for reinstatement having married five years previously. She was now legally separated from her husband, by mutual consent, and a maintenance order was in place whereby her husband paid 15s. per week towards living costs for herself and her child. The payments, however, were not regularly made and the Postmaster Surveyor at Plymouth, who oversaw her application, reported that the chances of marital reconciliation were 'extremely remote'. The Post Office told the Treasury that 'she is a capable and reliable operator from whom continuous and efficient service can be expected [and] she would render much better service to the Department than a new recruit'.[24] Initially, the Treasury deferred a decision, indicating that it was a separation by mutual consent and 'one has to guard against abuse owing to temporary separations'. The mutual decision to separate – even if it was in the woman's best interests – was treated with suspicion by Treasury officials. The Treasury also expressed concern that the maintenance order was not being enforced when they deemed it 'clearly enforceable'. Further details were sent at the Treasury's request, from which it emerged that the maintenance payments were seriously in arrears and County Court action was intended. Other details proved that the case was distressing: the telephonist had been ordered to leave by her husband, had given birth to their second child who had subsequently died, and the couple had had no further contact. After receiving these details, the Treasury consented to reinstatement, and though evidently unlikely, included the proviso that the employment would be ended if the couple reconciled.[25]

The late 1920s and 1930s: the gradual evolution of a policy

Throughout the late 1920s and into the 1930s, as more Post Office cases came before the Treasury, differences between the two bodies started to emerge. In forwarding cases to the Treasury, the GPO was overtly endorsing the capabilities of a woman applying for reinstatement, but the Treasury clearly had wider priorities. Though it never explicitly stated its major concerns about readmitting once-married women to the Civil Service, it was clearly keen to ensure that the system was not abused and that those being readmitted to the Service deserved a place, thus ensuring that the marriage bar remained as preserved as possible. The Treasury therefore asked the GPO to confirm that reinstatement would be 'in the interests of the public service', rather than merely giving 'due regard to the interests of the service' in each recommendation.[26] As GPO officials pointed out, however, the phrase 'interests of the public service' was ambiguous. Internal memoranda suggest that GPO officials simply agreed to use the phrase 'without entering into an academic discussion as to the precise construction to be placed upon it'. It had more sympathy than the Treasury with its former employees who had 'through no fault of [their] own been thrown on [their] own resources' and wanted to re-employ these women on the same grounds as widows.[27] It made such a case to the Treasury in 1933, arguing that, as a department with large numbers of women doing routine work, it could be treated differently from other Civil Service departments. More explicitly, it argued that 'if one of our former employees – say a Telegraphist or Telephonist – is left a widow and has to provide for herself and possibly a young family, her Post Office training is of little or no use to her in the outside market and she would probably find it difficult to get employment of any kind if we refused reinstatement'.[28] The GPO's views clearly revealed a diversity in attitudes among the various echelons of the Civil Service hierarchy and, in some cases, distinct support for individual women amongst Post Office officials. Their attitudes and sympathy towards some individual women contrasted significantly with many of their attitudes towards the rights and abilities of women as a collective group.

Rather than the Tomlin Royal Commission itself having particular views on the employment of women undergoing marital breakdown, it was the 1934 Whitley Committee on Women's Questions that instigated notable change on this issue. The rulings regarding divorce cases were delineated and standardised. The Committee ruling confirmed that divorced women could be readmitted to departments of the Civil Service if in financial need,[29] and the Treasury no longer needed to be consulted.[30] Had the right to work after an unsuccessful marriage been derived from anything other than economic necessity, it would presumably have opened the marriage bar to challenges from other directions. There was no specific reference to an "innocent party" requirement, but this may have been subsumed into the "interests of the public service" clause, which remained prominent.[31] Interestingly, the requirement for demonstrable financial need contrasts with apparent practice for divorced women in the LCC by the early 1930s. The Council declared that alimony should not be counted as income just as income from shares and equity was not.[32]

The Committee also ruled that so long as the reinstatement of a particular individual was 'in the public interest', women separated from, or deserted by, their husbands and without other means of support should be sympathetically considered and reinstated on the same grounds as widows.[33] Around the same time, the LCC decided that a point of policy could not be made to cover all cases of desertion and each had to continue to be dealt with on its own merits.[34] It had, three years previously, confirmed that it would not provide re-employment in cases of judicial separation but only in cases of desertion.[35] Such a policy essentially highlighted that if a woman had married the wrong man, or had a failed marriage for another reason but was still being provided for, she essentially still had no chance at financial independence from her former husband and to move on with her life. Such an attitude was rooted in early twentieth-century views of marriage and also in attitudes to the working wife. However, this contrasts markedly with the LCC's comparably more relaxed policy towards divorced women where alimony payments were disregarded. It was also something with which Council officials were not entirely comfortable. During the Whitley Committee on Women's Questions, W. R. Fraser at the Treasury wrote to Weeks at the Council to enquire how the Council handled cases of desertion and separation. Weeks' reply outlined the harshness of LCC policy and his own discomfort about it:

> Apparently desertion has never been legally defined. We do not pay attention to the fact of desertion, ie a magistrate's order affirming

desertion and ordering payment, but merely to the question whether the whereabouts of the husband are known. Nor do we regard the amount awarded. If the husband is available, any award, even if not paid, disqualifies for employment. The practice is hardly consistent with the rest of [our policy], the principle of which seems to be that married women who are not being supported by their husbands may be employed, nor is it sometimes even humane. Women with several children and getting perhaps only 10s. a week or so, have been discharged or refused employment. Obviously the magistrate has ordered not what is necessary but what he considers the husband can afford, and the amount must be supplemented – by public assistance if everything else fails. Sometimes, however, humanity (or common sense) has triumphed and a few married women in such circumstances have been employed. In my opinion the situation is not satisfactory, being consistent neither with itself nor with the spirit of the [policy].[36]

Any maintenance award, whether paid or not, was enough to ensure that women would not be re-employed. A few years previously the LCC had been presented with a case which hinged on the differentiation between desertion and separation. The case of a woman who received a small but insufficient allowance from her husband requested employment. This was at first refused because she was separated and not deserted; when it emerged that desertion had preceded the separation, the LCC looked on the case more favourably and agreed to employ her upon production of proof that she was deserted, making this perhaps one of the triumphs of common sense that Weeks referred to.[37] This case highlighted the fact that desertion and separation were not mutually exclusive states and one could precede the other.[38]

During the Committee on Women's Questions' deliberations and possibly in light of Weeks' observations, the Treasury also confirmed that it would consider individual cases where some financial support was received from an absent husband but which was insufficient to maintain the woman and any children from the marriage.[39] The Committee's eventual regulation was carefully worded, again using the undefined "public interest" clause to allow room for manoeuvre. Complete documentation of the 1934 Committee has not survived, so the relative role of the Treasury and the staff associations in making this decision cannot be determined. However, a poll amongst CSCA members revealed mass support for women deserted by their husbands and unable to gain financial support, and the AWCS had argued from the early 1920s that married women with no other source of subsistence should be given priority for employment.[40]

The Treasury was also keen to ensure that women were not reinstated after long gaps between their original service and their return. The "interests of the public service" notion thus became intertwined with questions of length of service versus length of time away. Significantly, this stringency had also begun to apply to widows, with one official arguing rather unsympathetically that '[f]or a woman to be left a widow after a long span of married life is a normal expectation and does not amount to special hardship'.[41] On the one hand, this concern stemmed from the regulation that no civil servant could be given an established position over the age of fifty because more than ten years' service was required in order for a pension to be paid. On the other hand, concerns about the length of break in service were also clearly related to perceptions of efficiency and the question of whether a woman with a long break of service could still be valuable. Often, "value" in older widows stretched as far as the Treasury wished it to: to temporary and thus insecure employment, but no further.[42]

Since it employed such significant numbers of women, the Treasury asked the GPO to keep detailed records of received applications for reinstatement.[43] Treasury officials were particularly concerned to ensure consistency and uniformity of treatment. Cases of separation still seemed to be forwarded to the Treasury in the mid-1930s, except in the most clear-cut of circumstances, and there are instances of the GPO and the Treasury viewing individual cases differently.[44] Of the seventy-eight applications for reinstatement made between the 1934 rulings and 1945, twenty were rejected because they were from women who were separated and had a means of support, so the maintenance criterion was clearly respected.[45] Otherwise, few systematic patterns emerge regarding which women were accepted back into the service and which were rejected, though the "interests of the public service" were clearly considered, with reports being gathered on an applicant's performance at work (if she was, as many were, doing temporary GPO work in the meantime) and the length of service and experience accrued. Whilst financial need was definitively made a criterion, the presence of children or elderly parents also needing support appears not to have been regarded sympathetically as a qualifying measure for reinstatement.[46]

In the LCC, the approach was similar, apart from its more relaxed position about divorced women and income, as discussed above. By early 1936, the General Purposes Committee re-worded the marriage restrictions because the Council had started allowing women who had voluntarily left their husbands to return to the service. The LCC did still insist on financial need and on, effectively, the reinstatement being in the interests of its service as well.[47] Although both organisations insisted on financial need and "good character", this still constituted considerable progression in attitudes compared to just after the First World War. This may also be a reflection of the emerging calls for less rigid divorce laws.[48]

The 1934 Whitley Committee on Women's Questions also made significant, but controversial, pronouncements regarding women married to men with either mental or physical health problems which left them unable to work. This was an issue which presumably occurred with relative frequency, though only one example appears to survive from GPO files before 1934. In September 1918, the case of a twenty-four-year-old employee was sent for Treasury approval. She had held an established position in the London Telephone Service before her marriage and had been serving as a temporary telephonist for the fifteen months prior to her application. Her husband had been a postman and had joined the army in the first few days of the war. He was injured in his first month of service and in May 1917 was discharged on account of "insanity" arising from injuries sustained in 1914. He resumed Post Office duties one month later but suffered a breakdown at the start of 1918 and was placed in an asylum, with little chance of recovery. The telephonist had some support: her husband had been awarded a Post Office gratuity of £29.14.2 and an additional allowance of £11.17.8 and she was also in receipt of an allowance from the Ministry of Pensions because of her husband's disability, but she also had a child to support. After considering the case, the Treasury agreed to her reinstatement in October 1918.[49] She was not without financial support, but several other factors were significant in her case. The fact that her husband was a war casualty would have been influential and the fact that both she and her husband had been Post Office employees undoubtedly added an extra sense of duty and responsibility to ensure she had 'an opportunity of taking up a career which will enable her permanently to earn her own livelihood.'[50] Indeed, the GPO later reported that, in cases where a widow and her former husband had both worked for the GPO, 'we feel a double obligation to treat the widow as sympathetically as we can.'[51] In this case, she was not a widow, but was clearly, despite minimal financial support, treated sympathetically. She was also young, and had not accrued a large number of years out of GPO service.

The 1934 Committee attempted to set out conditions for women in cases like this. It allowed women whose husbands resided in mental asylums and who would not recover to be reinstated to established positions on the same terms as widows, providing they met the "interests of the public service" criterion. Three women whose husbands had mental illnesses applied for reinstatement after 1934. One was rejected for not meeting the "interests of the public service criterion" on the basis of her performance in temporary work, one was accepted, and for the third, no decision was recorded. Importantly, the ruling did not allow women whose husbands could not work on account of physical ill-health back into the service and this was an issue over which the Committee divided. The staff side argued that paid employment and job security were important to women, irrespective of the reason why their husbands were unable to work. Furthermore, they felt that 'permanent physical incapacity is no more difficult to define than permanent mental incapacity.'[52] The Treasury was concerned about 'borderline cases' of physical incapacity, and would not permit residence in an institution as sufficient evidence of physical incapacity. When the staff side called for women who were about to marry men with physical disabilities to be able to retain their employment, officials would not make this concession, seemingly arguing, in effect, that women marrying men with disabilities did so in the knowledge that their husbands would be unable to work. The differing policies for physical and mental incapacity thus remained in the final report, with the official side citing fears that any other solution would 'give rise to anomalies and complaints.'[53] It reported, however, that wives of men with physical incapacities would 'always be sympathetically considered from the point of view of temporary employment',[54] which effectively rendered them subject to a life of job insecurity. The same issue and decision had clearly arisen in teaching, as Alison Oram has shown that women teachers with husbands unable to work through illness were employed but had their cases reviewed annually.[55]

The LCC – the employer of some of the teachers in Oram's work – seemed to have varying solutions amongst its staff as a whole to instances where women married physically disabled men. In the mid-1920s, a charwoman who had been hired as a widow had remarried without telling the LCC. This was discovered and she confessed, but she was treated very leniently after she explained that her husband was 'quite disabled and will never work again'. Intriguingly, the LCC insisted she now use her new surname at work, something which may have caused her some embarrassment as she had previously asked the LCC not to make her situation public.[56] By contrast, in 1934, a man wrote to the LCC explaining that he was engaged to an LCC employee but as he was a war pensioner and had a very small income, 'there does not seem to be any likelihood of our marriage for which we are both anxious'. He asked for the marriage bar to be waived for his wife-to-be, but the LCC refused.[57] However, the LCC appeared to offer temporary work more readily to wives with physically disabled husbands, requiring annual certification as to the husband's condition.[58]

The Civil Service's policy differentiation between mental and physical health was challenged almost immediately by a Post Office case. An application was received from a temporary employee whose husband was suffering from encephalitis, a physical injury that affected mental faculties. She was denied a permanent position in the service on the grounds that her husband was still living at home, rather than in residential care.[59] GPO officials pointed out to the Treasury that '[t]he line of demarcation between mental and physical incapacity is pretty thin in some cases' – a point with which the Treasury did not disagree but continued to insist on residence in an asylum as proof of mental incapacity.[60]

Similarly, another employee's husband was partially paralysed and unable to walk, talk and work owing to a "seizure". She had begun work as a temporary sorting clerk and telegraphist three years after her marriage and was in receipt of 9s.6d per week from the state which provided treatment, medicine and food prescribed for her husband by his doctor. She also had her mother to support, whom, she claimed, would be able to manage the house whilst she worked for the Post Office. However, the case was not forwarded to the Treasury: an internal memo stated that, as the incapacity was physical rather than mental, it would be disregarded by the Treasury. It is possible that GPO officials privately sympathised with her position but knew that the Treasury would be immovable. Temporary employment, in which she was already engaged, was offered as the only solution.[61]

Treasury officials never justified their policy about physical disability and wives' permanent employment. In these cases, it may have been felt that it was a woman's duty to remain at home to nurse an invalid husband, no matter how badly an income was needed to provide proper care and support. It might thus follow that, if a woman's husband had been institutionalised on the grounds of mental illness, she would be freer to resume work – and equally as in need of financial support. Furthermore, the context of attempts at divorce reform is important here. There had been discussions for a number of years about allowing divorce on the grounds of insanity coupled with residence in an asylum and, as Stephen Cretney has shown, support for such a change in the law gathered pace from 1930,[62] and the 1937 Matrimonial Causes Act of course permitted divorce on the grounds of insanity. Therefore, there was a perceptible difference between social attitudes to mental and physical incapacity, and the differentiation between them encapsulated in divorce law was seemingly replicated in Civil Service discussions of what could more properly constitute a right to be re-employed in spite of the marriage bar.

This debate did not go away. Although the residence in a mental asylum qualification implied the absence of a breadwinner, it is harder to see the justification for not allowing women back into the service who were married to physically disabled men who were unable to work. When the 1934 Committee's findings were revisited, a Civil Service official argued that women married to men with 'mental incapacit[ies]' were 'more "unmarried"' than women separated from their husbands. At the same time, he argued against any change of the rules affecting women married to men with physical disabilities (which perhaps also suggests that this was being considered at some level).[63] For as long as the marriage bar existed, situations such as the ones documented in this chapter were a real issue for women public service employees. Not only did the marriage bar make it difficult for women to support their husbands and families when they were the only ones capable of working, knowledge of the rules might also affect women's choice of whom to marry as well.

The reinstatement of women who had suffered marital breakdown is significant for what it reveals about the operation of the marriage bar and official priorities. The Civil Service's insistence, and later the 1934 ruling, on divorced and separated women having no other means of sufficient financial support tied re-employment to normative discourses about each household having one breadwinner. The same discourses were used both inside the Civil Service and outside as one of the ways to justify the marriage bar. It also meant that reinstatement was kept firmly on economic grounds only, thus preventing women who had received adequate financial support after a separation or divorce from seeking a return to a career for reason of self-fulfilment. Finally, the clause about a woman's reinstatement being "in the interests of the public service" was so vague as to be open to many and varied interpretations. It reveals the Treasury's desire to both retain ultimate control of who it readmitted to the permanent echelons of the service and to control its workforce and thus its image and identity. Such rulings also, though it may not have been the Civil Service's priority, reinforced stigmas associated with marital breakdown and made it clear that there would be all sorts of consequences for married women who divorced or separated. Although the LCC treated divorced women more leniently and did not always word its policies in terms of "the interests of the public service" in the methodical and stringent way that the Civil Service did, the overall implications of its policy towards separated women tended in the same direction of those of the Civil Service.

One further factor is important: the reliance of both organisations – and in particular the Post Office within the Civil Service – on long-term, temporary labour, which became contentious in the late 1920s and early

1930s.[64] Many of the women who applied for reinstatement in the GPO, for example, did temporary work whilst their applications were being processed. Trained temporary workers were significant: as we have seen, they filled holes in the labour supply and because temporary workers were not entitled to numerous employment benefits, they were also cheaper employees. It is notable how many women were turned down for re-establishment only to be offered temporary, casual employment instead, particularly in the Civil Service but also in the LCC.[65] Clearly, these women were not incapable of doing a good job, but were relegated to temporary ranks because they did not meet exact reinstatement criteria and temporary labour met immediate public service needs. Indeed, the 1892 Post Office committee examining the marriage bar had suggested using married women or women deserted by their husbands as temporary labour, which constituted an extension of a system already in place in the Central Telegraph Office, and this practice was most clearly replicated throughout the interwar years.[66]

As this chapter has demonstrated, policies surrounding divorced and separated women and those married to men in poor health emerged and evolved throughout the interwar years. Through surviving records, it has been possible to trace differing stances of the various interest groups involved in this policymaking. The policies show some gradual acceptance of the notion that marriage was not necessarily forever – and distinct sympathy in some cases – but also confirm that marital misfortune could render a return to permanent work particularly difficult or sometimes impossible for women. Though the need for, and principles of, the marriage bar were questioned by many female public servants and commentators outside the public service, the lengths to which officials went to delineate policy in the cases of marital misfortune reveal the pervasiveness of the marriage bar and the determination to continue to uphold this gendered piece of legislation as much as possible. The impact of the marriage bar was perhaps most starkly perceived when women who had left work because of it were then unable to earn a secure living because of the assumptions surrounding, variously, women's roles as wives after marriage, their status of dependency after marriage, and the stigmas attached to broken marriages. The insistence that certain groups of women could not come back to work in the most dire of circumstances shows the extent to which married women were defined and conceptualised by their domestic role. Divorced women, although still stigmatised, actually had the best chance of reinstatement because the legal process of divorce was deemed to bring about the most definitive break in a marriage. That divorce was only affordable to the middle classes gave this aspect of the marriage bar, too, a real class dimension.

Finally, the most significant point about the debates and cases presented here is that they highlight how deeply and pervasively gendered the marriage bar was: as men never had to resign on marriage they also never had to have their private lives scrutinised when their marriages fell apart.[67] For women public servants, this was another inextricable link between their gender and their private and professional selves. It was only with the ending of the marriage bar in each organisation after the Second World War that this intrusiveness came to an end.

Notes

1 BPMA, POST 30/4009B, 'Female Post Office Servants: resignation with view to marriage, reinstatement where marriage broken off or postponed', File I.

2 POST 30/4009B, File II, letter from GPO to Treasury, 4 December 1916.

3 POST 30/4009B, File II, draft letter to Treasury, 16 December 1916.

4 POST 30/4009B, File I, File VI.

5 David Coleman in Halsey, *British Social Trends Since 1900*, p.80, table 2.24.

6 LCC/Estab/1/1, 'General Purposes Committee Paper, Report by the Clerk of the Council: Resignation on Marriage', 6 April 1914.

7 POST 30/330A, 'Married Women: employment in Post Office, part 2 (end)', file 40, undated Post Office memo. See also POST30/4476, 'Re-appointment of Widows', File I, undated memo.

8 LCC/CL/ESTAB/1/2, November 1924 – series of memoranda.

9 POST 33/329, File 27, letter to the Treasury, December 30, 1925; File 30, correspondence, July 1929.

10 POST 33/329, File 24.

11 POST 33/329, File 30, correspondence, 26 July 1929.

12 POST 33/329, File 30, correspondence, [?]August 1929.

13 POST 33/329, File 30, correspondence, [?]August 1929.

14 POST 33/329, File 30, memorandum from Murray, 7 September 1929.

15 See, for example, TNA, T1/11590, 24198/1913, 'Regulations respecting open competitive examination for the situation of Woman Clerk…', stamped 24 December 1912.

16 POST 33/329, File 27, correspondence between GPO and Treasury.

17 POST 33/329, File 28, correspondence with GPO Secretary, 29 January 1926.

18 O. R. McGregor, *Divorce in England: A Centenary Study* (London: Heinemann, 1957), p.33; p.51; Lawrence Stone, *Road to Divorce: England 1530–1987* (Oxford: Oxford University Press, 1990), p.397.

19 TNA, T162/344, 'Civil Service Appointments: Eligibility of Women Separated from their Husbands', W. R. Fraser's memo dated 3 August 1920; Solicitor's reply received 1 September 1920.

20 For Treasury unease, see, for example, T162/344, 'Civil Service Appointments: Eligibility of Women Separated from their Husbands'.

21 POST 33/329, file 25, letter from Treasury to GPO, 19 December 1924.

22 LMA, LCC/CL/ESTAB/1/2, correspondence of 3 December 1924.

23 LCC/CL/ESTAB/1/2, letter from the Valuer to the Clerk of the Council, 25 June 1924. See also letter from Mrs Biggs, 15 October 1924.

24 POST 33/329, file 29, letter from GPO to Treasury, 24 January 1929.

25 POST 33/329, file 29, letter from Treasury, 18 March 1929.

26 POST 33/330A, file 31, letter from Ryan at the Treasury to Wakely at the GPO, 14 September 1931.

27 POST 33/330A, file 34, memo to the Staff Branch, 29 September 1931.

28 POST 33/330A, file 40, letter from Peel at the GPO to Robinson at the Treasury, 25 July 1933.

29 *Report of the Committee on Women's Questions*, para. 30.

30 POST 33/330A, file 38, letter from Parker at the Treasury to the Establishments Branch, 28 May 1934.

31 *Report of the Committee on Women's Questions*, para. 33.

32 LMA, LCC/CL/ESTAB/1/2, note dated 26 September 1933.

33 *Report of the Committee on Women's Questions*, para. 33. This was confirmed by Treasury Circular 8/34. This would have helped a temporary Post Office employee, who in 1924 had asked to be treated as a widow on the grounds that she had not heard from her husband since 1915. As she could not prove his death, she was denied permission to compete for an established post. See TNA, T162/344, 'Civil Service Appointments: Eligibility of women separated from their husbands', letter dated 21 September 1924.

34 LMA, LCC/CL/ESTAB/1/2, Clerk of the Council's decision, 21 July 1933.

35 LMA, LCC/CL/ESTAB/1/2, memorandum from the Education Officer to the Clerk of the Council.

36 TNA, T275/266, letter from V. A. Weeks to W. R. Fraser, 7 July 1933.

37 LMA, LCC/CL/ESTAB/1/2, correspondence to and from the Clerk of the Council, 8 February 1927 and 17 February 1927.

38 The LCC also pondered in 1933 whether a case of imprisonment in another country could be dealt with as a case of desertion. See LMA, LCC/CL/ESTAB/1/2, discussions of 11, 12 and 13 April.

39 POST 33/330A, File 30, letter from Parker at the Treasury, 28 May 1934.

40 POST 115/177, *Red Tape*, 'Women's Notes: Marriage Bar and Superannuation – Decisive Figures in CSCA Ballots', January 1930, p.244. See also the case made in POST 115/176, *Red Tape*, Violet Knock, 'The Marriage Bar Ballot: Why I Favour Retention', p.19; TNA, T 162/50/23, Establishment. Women: Women in the Civil Service; Supplementary memorandum for the Royal Commission, 'Summary of the Proposals made to the Royal Commission on the Civil Service by the Association of Women Clerks and Secretaries'.

41 POST 33/330A, File 40, letter from Treasury, June 26, 1933. See also File 42, statement by Peel, 28 February 1935.

42 POST 33/330A, File 40.

43 POST 33/330A, File 40.

44 See, for example, POST 33/330A, File 40, case of Mrs Sanderson; case of Mrs Woode.

45 POST 33/330A, File 40, list of reinstatement decisions, 1934–1945.

46 See, for example, the case of Mrs Woode.

47 LMA, LCC/CL/ESTAB/1/2, General Purposes Committee, 3 March 1936.

48 McGregor, *Divorce in England*; Stone, *Road to Divorce*, pp.387–401; Sharon Redmayne, 'The Matrimonial Causes Act, 1937: A Lesson in the Art of Compromise', *Oxford Journal of Legal Studies*, vol. 13, no. 2 (1993), pp.183–200.

49 POST 33/329, File 23.

50 POST 33/329, File 23, letter from GPO to Treasury, 18 September 1918.

51 POST33/330A, letter from Peel at the GPO to Robinson at the Treasury, 25 July 1933.

52 *Report of the Committee on Women's Questions*, para. 34.

53 TNA, T 275/232, National Whitley Council, Joint Ad Hoc Committee to discuss findings of chapter XII of Report of Royal Commission on Civil Service – 'Women's Questions'. 15 July 1932–26 January 1934.

54 *Report of the Committee on Women's Questions*, para. 34.

55 Oram, *Women Teachers*, p.62.

56 LMA. LCC/CL/ESTAB/1/2, letters from employee and her supervisor, 29 May 1925 and memo from Clerk of the Council, 23 June 1925. See also the case of 23 October 1930.

57 LMA, LCC/CL/ESTAB/1/2, letter, 3 August 1934.

58 TNA, T275/266, letter from V. A. Weeks to W. R. Fraser, 7 July 1933.

59 POST 33/330A, File 38, letter from Treasury, 28 May 1934.

60 POST 33/330A, File 38, letter to the Treasury, 17 May 1934 and reply, 28 May 1934.

61 POST 33/330A, File 42. There was a similar case involving a woman who resigned her position to care for her mother and then asked for reinstatement when one of her sisters was able to take on the caring responsibilities. She was refused, and remained confined to temporary work. MRC, MSS.148/UCW/2/1/5, UPW Executive Committee minutes, 26–28 January 1922.

62 Stephen Cretney, *Family Law in the Twentieth Century* (Oxford: Oxford University Press, 2003), pp.226–227.

63 TNA, T275/266, 'Wives of husbands who suffer from total physical incapacity', memo to Mr Whetmath, [undated – early 1940s [?]].

64 One of the post-Tomlin Whitley Committees ('Committee B') discussed temporary staffing issues. Parris, *Staff Relations in the Civil Service*, p.93.

65 See, for example, LCC/CL/ESTAB/1/2, case of E. Dykes, 11 September 1927; POST 33/330A, File 38, memo from Staff Branch.

66 POST 33/329, File VII, Post Office Service Employment of Married Women Committee Report, p.28. The GPO had also argued that married women temporaries should be kept on their pre-marriage wages, but the Treasury had refused. See POST 33/329, File X, letter from Treasury dated 16 July 1892. See also POST 33/330A, File 40, list of separated or deserted women applying for reinstatement.

67 By contrast, as discussed in Chapter 3, the LCC looked into men's private lives in the First World War, but only so that they could be awarded extra war bonus.

Conclusion

Women civil servants spoke of their battles – equal opportunity, equal pay and an end to the marriage bar – as trying to achieve "a fair field and no favour". By this, they meant being treated as though they were no different to men, the central tenet of the "equality" strand of inter-war feminist thinking. This book has examined the ways in which women's public service employment was regulated and how such regulations were challenged by the women themselves, their supporters and trade unions, and how, at times, they were reinforced or amended by the state as their employer. Throughout the period discussed, women's employment remained highly gendered and the continuities in public discourse and officials' approaches are often much more striking than the changes. Women's work in public service employment was affected by many of the debates about women's work and women's roles in society more widely – such as discourses around femininity, motherhood and accepted gender roles – whilst at the same time acting as a barometer of government and wider social attitudes towards women's paid work.

It was often assumed that women who worked in the public service were single and were also supporting only themselves. Although not the only contributory factor, this line of thinking was significant in denying women equal pay for the same work as their male colleagues for several decades. Such thinking also continually assumed that women would be in employment only until they married and therefore that they were not committed to their careers in the way that men were often automatically assumed to be (although it was of course the marriage bar rulings enforced by the employers themselves which made work after marriage next to impossible). Furthermore, notions about both commitment to work and the insignificance of women's wages to household earnings were used to solidify both assumptions about women's capabilities and arguments that men deserved the best and most interesting work. A woman in a so-called gender-neutral post in the higher echelons of either the Civil Service or the LCC, such as an administrative officer, was relatively rare even in the mid-1930s and women's promotion prospects were often subject to restrictions either *de facto* or *de jure* for much of the period considered here. The reasons for excluding women from certain types of work were diverse and at times worked in combination with each other. These included slippery notions of tradition or suitability, most of which could be proven to be irrelevant, or concerns about pushing what the (tax-paying) public would find acceptable for women to be doing. After the Second World War the consensus amongst high-ranking officials in each institution was that it had done enough to open higher posts to women because there remained few formal restrictions on their employment: it would take until the 1970s and 1980s for issues surrounding indirect discrimination to come to the fore.[1]

To date, work on women in public service employment has focused largely on certain groups of women civil servants. However, my inclusion of a comparison with the LCC highlights the broader similarities of the ways in which women's employment was conceived and regulated and how there was an ongoing trans-institutional dialogue in which the values of both institutions were embodied. The LCC's maximum quotas for women in higher positions were a different means of apportioning women's higher-grade work than those of the Civil Service. Ultimately, though, these had a very similar effect and conveyed a similar message to women about their place in the institution. At times, a comparison with the LCC throws the Civil Service into interesting relief: whilst the Civil Service had initially been the "leader" in women's public employment because it had begun employing women first, the LCC also formulated some of its own policies, especially around the issue of equal pay, deliberately not subscribing to some of the discourse of successive governments or, in the end, the timing of implementation of equal pay for women.

By focusing on the most widespread and pervasive aspects of discrimination that women faced, and by tracing the evolution of policy regarding these aspects of women's employment, this book has presented a case study of agency, employer policy and trade unionism, thereby taking further the understanding of, variously, the public service, attitudes to women's employment, feminism, and employee activism. It also, at times, has illuminated the beliefs and actions of individuals as distinct from the institution of which they were part. The study has revealed that the attitudes of the Treasury – and ultimately the Chancellor and the government in power – were paramount in dictating the experiences of women. Therefore, very often, conservative and normative traditions of female employment were held up in the Civil Service (as well as in the LCC on the occasions when it emulated the former's policy). The fact that the government would not allow any arbitration or Whitley discussion of equal pay in the Civil Service shows the issue's economic and social significance. Importantly, though, as the interwar years wore on and there was more experience with employer–employee negotiation via Whitleyism, changes in the Civil Service were enacted via this mechanism – although ultimately it, too, was controlled by the Treasury. The 1931 Royal Commission, inconclusive though it was in some respects, must also be considered an important factor in raising the possibility for change: the replacement of segregation by aggregation in a greater portion of the service and the greater latitude afforded to marriage bar exemptions were both part of the Commission's recommendations, though they had been part of some union and association rhetoric for a considerable time. Between them, then, the individuals comprising the Tomlin Commission and those serving on the Whitley Councils had important power. The make-up of the LCC meant that it was controlled by elected members and, in practice, the majority party. There was somewhat less of an established elite amongst the upper echelons of the LCC staff and decision-making was largely in the hands of elected officials, especially those who were in charge of the committees most concerned with staffing. The employer–employee negotiation machinery was, as a whole, less strong than that in the Civil Service but nonetheless staff petitions were accepted and discussed and there were some notable examples of this leading to change. Consequently, the case studies in this book allow us to examine which individuals and structures retained control and how, but also how change could be negotiated or resisted. Moreover, they highlight some startling continuities in attitudes to women and their employment.

Whilst the LCC Staff Association had some female representation it could not be said to be blazing a trail for women's advancement. Women's issues in mixed-sex Civil Service unions and associations were rarely prioritised either, with the exception of equal pay at various points. However, equal pay was not just a women's issue: a cheaper labour force had serious implications. The more ambivalent attitudes to the marriage bar and, at times, to women's lack of opportunities, were reflected in part in the relative longevity of these issues. However, the marriage bar in particular was a symptom of the fact that considerable numbers of women accepted it – at least until the later 1930s, when a detectable shift began. The work of the APOWC, FWCS and NAWCS – the successive incarnations of the women's clerical organisation in the Civil Service – and the work of the CWCS was formative in keeping women's issues at the forefront of staff association politics.

The fact that the women of the LCC and many women civil servants (outside of the manipulative grades of the GPO) were located in the metropolis was also important in terms of the access to feminist and political networks it could bring them.[2] In terms of pressuring for change, women were able to draw on the resources of London-based unions, feminist associations and the largely London-based national press, though it is notable that LCC women, who were less organised as a collective, did this far less than their Civil Service counterparts. There is also less evidence of women from each organisation corresponding with each other, though that is not to suggest that contacts were not made in other ways.

In both organisations, but particularly in the Civil Service, the point was constantly made that the service needed the best people – or, more often than not, the best men. It is difficult to tell definitively if linguistically "men" was used to mean "men and women" but regardless, it is striking that so often the public service excluded women from employment or from demonstrating their full capabilities. This signals a number of inter-connected issues related to gender, citizenship, work, efficiency and womanhood. Exclusions and restrictions signalled that women collectively were not considered good enough, or that their experiences and skills had nothing to contribute or could only contribute to matters relating to other women or children. It also signalled that men's work was considered to be the most efficient and to offer far more contributions to public life. Although such attitudes were not unusual in employment given they were found outside of the public service as well, the public service's debates and pronouncements foregrounded the real issues behind these rulings and could also act, intentionally or otherwise, as a yardstick for other employers to copy.

Whilst this book has focused principally on conceptions of femininity it is also worth mentioning what these, by implication, suggest about masculinity in these institutions. That these institutions were patriarchal and embraced normative masculinity is self-evident, but many of the issues discussed here also suggest a real resistance to women in public service employment and often, also, fear. To say that such fear was felt by all men would be generalising and to call this fear misogyny would be difficult to substantiate. Yet it is clear that some men in the Civil Service in particular – especially but not exclusively those in the upper echelons – were uncomfortable with the seeming encroachment of women into a hitherto male space. The upper limits on women's employment in the LCC, which were in place for a good deal of the interwar years, were designed to ensure the LCC proceeded cautiously with the expansion of women's employment and may have had the effect of generating less concern among men about the encroachment of women. Masculinity in the public service is a topic worthy of greater historical attention.

Although women enjoy greater equality with men in Britain today, the experience of the later twentieth and early twenty-first centuries reveals the extent to which the battles have endured throughout the century when many women in the early twentieth-century public service would have hoped they would be more quickly won. The most recent UK statistics reveal worrying gender pay gaps[3] and there is still a strong gender demarcation of occupations. Women's employment in many sectors remains profoundly and unfairly limited by their gender.[4] Although the marriage bar no longer exists to regulate women's private lives in the way this volume describes, all available evidence suggests that women are more negatively affected in the workplace by the decision to have children.[5] Recent research suggests that women remain over-represented in the lower ranks of the Civil Service, and concerns remain regarding the extent to which women are actually moving into more senior positions, where they have traditionally remained under-represented.[6] In 1985, the Council of Civil Service Unions produced a pamphlet detailing how equal opportunities for women might be brought about and offering guidance to union representatives on recent anti-discriminatory legislation. The pamphlet ended by stating: '[e]qual opportunities for women in the Civil Service will not be achieved overnight. It will require long and sustained efforts by union representatives at all levels'.[7] These are words with which women campaigners and their supporters in the earlier twentieth century would no doubt have had sympathy, but also feelings of dismay that they still had to be uttered so many years after their own campaigns.

Notes

1 Kemp-Jones, *The Employment of Women in the Civil Service*; Brimelow, 'Women in the Civil Service'; Society of Civil and Public Servants, *Equality: The Next Step. The Changing Role of Women in the Civil Service* (London: SCPS, 1982).

2 Ruth Livesey makes a similar point for women factory inspectors in the 1890s. Livesey, 'The Politics of Work', p.251.

3 Office of National Statistics, *Annual Survey of Hours and Earnings* (2013), available at www.ons.gov.uk/ons/dcp171778_335027.pdf, accessed 13 August 2014.

4 This was explored in depth by the Women and Work Commission. See Women and Work Commission, *Shaping a Fairer Future* (Department of Trade and Industry, 2006).

5 Fawcett Society, *What about Women?* (2013), pp.16–20, available at www.fawcettsociety.org.uk/wp-content/uploads/2013/02/Fawcett-Society-What-About-Women-report-low-res.pdf, accessed 13 August 2014.

6 'Fewer Women Getting Senior Civil Service Jobs', *Guardian*, 15 July 2008, www.guardian.co.uk/politics/2008/jul/15/whitehall-women, accessed 27 August 2009; 'MOD Needs to Put Women in Senior Positions, Says Top Civil Servant', *Guardian*, 2 December 2011, available at www.guardian.co.uk/uk/2011/dec/02/mod-needs-women-senior-positions, accessed 2 December 2011; House of Commons Library, Parliamentary Briefing papers, *Civil Service Statistics* (2013), p.7, available at www.parliament.uk/briefing-papers/SN02224.pdf, accessed 13 August 2014.

7 Council of Civil Service Unions, 'Equal Opportunities for Men and Women in the Civil Service' (London: Council of Civil Service Unions, 1985), p.38.

Bibliography

Archival sources

British Library

Council of Women Civil Servants (Higher Grades), *Statement Prepared for the Royal Commission on the Civil Service (1929–1930)*, October 1930.
Federation of Women Civil Servants, *Women in the Civil Service: Grading – or De-Grading?* Undated (1921)[?].

British Postal Museum & Archive (BPMA)

POST 30 Series: Post Office: Registered Files, Minuted papers (England and Wales).
POST 33 Series: Post Office: Registered Files, Minuted papers (General).
POST 47 Series: Post Office: Army Postal Series.
POST 57 Series: Post Office: Staff Recruitment.
POST 82 Series: Post Office: Telegraphs, Post Office (Inland).
POST 92 Series: Post Office Publications.
POST 115 Series: Post Office: Staff Association and Union Publications.
POST 121 Series: Post Office: Registered Files, Minuted and Decentralised Registry Papers (Miscellaneous Papers).
POST 122 Series: Post Office: Registered Files, Minuted and Decentralised Registry Papers (Miscellaneous Papers).

BT Archives

POST 33 Series: Post Office: Registered Files, Minuted papers (General).

Imperial War Museum Sound Archive

IWMSA, 668, interview with Lilian Gertrude Wolfe, 27 February 1974.
IWMSA, 676, interview with Mrs Thomas, 1975.
IWMSA, 3151/1, interview with Mary Madden, 1977.
IWMSA, 8889/3, interview with Eileen Johnston, 1985.

London Metropolitan Archives

18.3 LCC Staff Examination Papers.
GLSA Records of the LCC Staff Association.
LCC Minutes.
LCC Establishment Committee Minutes.

LCC General Purposes Committee Minutes.

LCC Staff Lists.

LCC/CL/ESTAB Clerk of the Council's department establishment papers.

Modern Records Centre, University of Warwick

MSS.148/PA Records of the Postal & Telegraph Clerks' Association.

MSS.148/PF Records of the Postman's Federation.

MSS.148/UCW Records of the Union of Communication Workers [formerly the Union of Post Office Workers].

MSS.415 Records of the Civil and Public Services Union and its predecessors.

The National Archives

T1: Treasury Board Papers and In-Letters.

T162: Treasury: Establishments Department, Registered Files.

T 171: Chancellor of the Exchequer's Office: Budget and Finance Bill Papers.

T 215: Treasury: Establishment General Division: Registered Files (EG and 2EG Series).

LAB 2: Ministry of Labour and predecessors: correspondence.

The Wellcome Library

SA/MWF: Records of the medical Women's Federation.

The Women's Library

6APC: Records of the Association of Post Office Women Clerks.

6JCS: Records of the Joint Committee on Women in the Civil Service.

6EPC: Records of the Equal Pay Campaign Committee.

6NCS: Records of the National Association of Women Civil Servants.

Online resources

Oxford Dictionary of National Biography.

Newspapers and periodicals

British Medical Journal

Civil Service Argus

Clerical Grades Monthly

Daily Mail

Daily Mirror

Local Government Service
London County Council Staff Association Gazette
London Town
Manchester Guardian
The Post
Red Tape
The Times
The Spectator

Published reports and evidence

Committee on Recruitment for the Civil Service After the War Final Report (HMSO, 1919).
Hansard.
The Marriage Bar in the Civil Service, Report of the Civil Service National Whitley Council Committee (London: HMSO, 1946).
Report of the Civil Service National Whitley Council Reorganisation Committee (London: HMSO, 1920).
Report of the Royal Commission on the Civil Service (London: HMSO, 1931).
Report of the Royal Commission on Equal Pay (London: HMSO, 1946).
Report of the War Cabinet Committee on Women in Industry (London: HMSO, 1919).
Royal Commission on the Civil Service 1929–1931, Evidence, (London: HMSO, 1930).
Royal Commission on Equal Pay, Minutes of Evidence taken before the Royal Commission on Equal Pay (London: HMSO, 1945).

Published primary sources

Barton, Dorothea M., 'The Course of Women's Wages', *Journal of the Royal Statistical Society*, vol. 82, no. 4 (July 1919), pp.508–553.
Beauchamp, Joan, *Women Who Work* (London: Lawrence & Wishart, 1937).
Bondfield, Margaret, *A Life's Work* (London: Hutchinson & Co, 1949).
Bowley, Ruth, 'The Cost of Living of Girls Professionally Employed in the County of London', *The Economic Journal*, vol. 44, no. 174 (June 1934), pp.328–334.
Breckinridge, S.P., 'The Home Responsibilities of Women Workers and the "Equal Wage"', *The Journal of Political Economy*, vol. 31, no. 4 (August 1923), pp.521–543.
Brittain, Vera, *Women's Work in Modern England* (London: Noel Douglas, 1928).
Brown, W. J., *Civil Service Compendium* (London: CSCA, 1927).
Burton, Elaine, *What is She Worth? A Study on the Report on Equal Pay* (London: Fitzroy Publications, 1947).
Cazalet-Keir, Thelma, *From the Wings: An Auobiography* (London: Bodley Head, 1967).
Council of Civil Service Unions, *Equal Opportunities for Men and Women in the Civil Service* (London: Council of Civil Service Unions, 1985).
Council of Women Civil Servants (Higher Grades), *Higher Appointments Open to Women in the Civil Service* (London: P. S. King and Son, Ltd., 1928).

Council of Women Civil Servants (Higher Grades), *Higher Appointments Open to Women in the Civil Service*, 3rd edn (P. S. King and Son, Ltd, 1935).

Courtney, Janet, *Recollected in Tranquillity* (London: Heinemann, 1926).

Drake, Barbara, *Women in Trade Unions* (London: Virago, 1984, first published in 1920 by Labour Research Department).

Edgeworth, F. Y., 'Equal Pay to Men and Women for Equal Work', *The Economic Journal*, vol. 32, no. 128 (December 1922), pp.431–457.

Evans, D., *Women and the Civil Service: A History of the Development of the Employment of Women in the Civil Service, and a Guide to Present-Day Opportunities* (London: Pitman, 1934).

Fawcett, Millicent G., 'Equal Pay for Equal Work', *The Economic Journal*, vol. 28, no. 109 (March 1918), pp.1–6.

Fawcett, Millicent, *What I Remember* (London: Fisher Unwin Ltd, 1925).

Garland, Charles H., 'Women as Telegraphists', *The Economic Journal*, vol. 11, no. 42 (June 1901), pp.251–261.

Hinchy, F. S., *So Much in Life* (London and New York: Regency Press, 1971).

Hughes, D. W., *Careers for Our Daughters* (London: A & C Dent, 1936).

Hutchins, B. L. (Fabian Women's Group), *The Working Life of Women*, Fabian Tract no. 157 (London: The Fabian Society, 1911).

Kemp-Jones, E. M., *The Employment of Women in the Civil Service*, Civil Service Department Management Studies 3 (Edinburgh: HMSO, 1971).

Martindale, Hilda, *From One Generation to Another: 1839–1944: A Book of Memoirs* (London: Allen & Unwin, 1944).

Meynell, Alix, *Public Servant, Private Woman* (London: Victor Gollancz, 1988).

Morley, Edith (ed.), *Women Workers in Seven Professions* (London: Fabian Society, 1914).

Murray, G. E. P., *The Post Office* (London, 1927).

Rathbone, Eleanor, 'The Remuneration of Women's Services', *The Economic Journal*, vol. 27, no. 105 (March 1917), pp.55–68.

Scudamore, Frank, *A Sheaf of Memories* (London: Fisher Unwin Ltd, 1925).

Smith, E., *Wage-Earning Women and their Dependents* (London: The Fabian Society, 1915).

Society of Civil and Public Servants, *Equality: The Next Step. The Changing Role of Women in the Civil Service* (London: SCPS, 1982).

Stocks, Mary, *My Commonplace Book: An Autobiography* (Trowbridge and London: Redwood Press, Ltd, 1970).

Strachey, Ray, *The Cause* [1928] (London: Virago, 1979).

The Suffrage Annual and Women's Who's Who, 1913 (London: Stanley Paul and Co., 1913).

Summerskill, Edith, *A Woman's World* (London: Heinemann, 1967).

This is the Road: The Conservative and Unionist Party's Manifesto (1950).

Thompson, Flora, *Lark Rise to Candleford* [1945] (London: Penguin, 2000).

Webb, Beatrice, *The Wages of Men and Women: Should They Be Equal?* (London: Fabian Society, 1919).

Women and Work Commission, *Shaping a Fairer Future* (London: Department of Trade and Industry, 2006).

Secondary sources

Adams Carole Elizabeth, 'White Blouse and White Collar: Work, Culture and Gender' *Gender and History*, vol. 2, issue 3 (September 1990), pp.343–348.

Alberti, Johanna, *Beyond Suffrage: Feminists in War and Peace, 1914–1928* (London and Basingstoke: Macmillan, 1989).

Alexander, Sally, 'Bringing Women into Line with Men: The Women's Trade Union League, 1874–1921' in Sally Alexander (ed.), *Becoming a Woman* (London: Virago, 1994), pp.57–74.

Alexander, Sally, 'Men's Fears and Women's Work: Responses to Unemployment in London Between the Wars' *Gender and History*, vol. 12, no. 2 (July 2000), pp.401–425.

Anderson, Gregory, *Victorian Clerks* (Manchester: Manchester University Press, 1976).

Andrews, Maggie, *The Acceptable Face of Feminism: The Women's Institute as a Social Movement* (London: Lawrence & Wishart, 1997).

Bagilhole, Barbara, *Women, Work and Equal Opportunity: Underachievement in the Civil Service* (Aldershot: Ashgate, 1994).

Bain, George, *The Growth of White Collar Unionism* (Oxford: Clarendon, 1970).

Baker, Maureen and Mary-Anne Robeson, 'Trade Union Reactions to Women Workers and Their Concerns' *Canadian Journal of Sociology*, vol. 6, no. 1 (Winter, 1981), pp.19–31.

Banks, Olive, *Faces of Feminism* (London: Basil Blackwell, 1986).

Beaumont, Caitriona, 'Citizens not Feminists: The Boundary Negotiated between Citizenship and Feminism by Mainstream Women's Organisations in England, 1928–1939' *Women's History Review*, vol. 9, no. 2 (June 2000), pp.411–429.

Beaumont, Caitriona, 'The Women's Movement, Politics and Citizenship, 1918–1950s' in Ina Zweiniger-Bargielowska (ed.), *Women in Twentieth Century Britain* (Harlow: Pearson Education, 2001).

Beddoe, Deirdre, *Back to Home and Duty: Women Between the Wars* (London and San Francisco: Pandora Press, 1989).

Beechey, Veronica, *Unequal Work* (London: Verso, 1987).

Bennett, Robert, 'Gendering Cultures in Business and Labour History: Marriage Bars in Clerical Employment' in Margaret Walsh (ed.), *Working Out Gender: Perspectives from Labour History* (Aldershot: Ashgate, 1999).

Berry, Paul and Alan Bishop (eds), *Testament of a Generation: The Journalism of Vera Brittain and Winifred Holtby* (London: Virago, 1985).

Bingham, Adrian, *Gender, Modernity, and the Popular Press in Inter-War Britain* (Oxford: Oxford University Press, 2004).

Black, John, 'War, Women and Accounting: Female Staff in the UK Army Pay Department Offices, 1914–1920' *Accounting, Business & Financial History*, vol. 16, no. 2 (July 2006), pp. 195–218.

Blackburn, Robert, *Union Character and Social Class: A Study of White Collar Unionism* (London: Batsford, 1967).

Boston, Sarah, *Women Workers and the Trade Unions* (London: Lawrence & Wishart, 1987).

Boussahba-Bravard, Myriam (ed.), *Suffrage Outside Suffragism* (London: Palgrave, 2007).

Bradley, H., *Men's Work, Women's Work* (Cambridge: Polity Press, 1989).

Braithwaite, Brian, Noelle Walsh and Glyn Davies (eds), *Ragtime to Wartime: The Best of Good Housekeeping, 1922-1939* (London: Leopard Books, 1995).

Braybon, Gail, *Women Workers in the First World War* (London and New York: Routledge, 1989).

Braybon, Gail and Penny Summerfield, *Out of the Cage: Women's Experiences in Two World Wars* (London and New York: Pandora Press, 1987).

Brimelow, E., 'Women in the Civil Service', *Public Administration*, vol. LIX (1981), pp.313-335.

Brookes, Pamela, *Women at Westminster: An Account of Women in the British Parliament, 1918-1966* (London: Peter Davies, 1967).

Caine, Barbara, 'Feminism in London, circa 1850-1950' *Journal of Urban History*, vol. 27, no. 6 (September 2001), pp.765-778.

Campbell-Smith, Duncan, *Masters of the Post* (London: Penguin, 2011).

Chapman, Richard A., *Leadership in the British Civil Service* (London and Sydney: Croom Helm, 1984).

Chapman, Richard A., *The Civil Service Commission, 1855-1991: A Bureau Biography* (London: Routledge, 2004).

Clendinning, Anne, '"Deft Fingers" and "Persuasive Eloquence": The "Lady Demons" of the English Gas Industry, 1888-1918', *Women's History Review*, vol. 9, no. 3 (2000), pp.501-537.

Clifton, Gloria, 'Members and Officers of the LCC, 1889-1965' in Andrew Saint (ed.), *Politics and the People of London: The London County Council, 1889-1965* (London and Roncevert: The Hambledon Press, 1989), pp.1-26.

Clifton, Gloria, *Professionalism, Patronage and Public Service in Victorian London* (London: The Athlone Press, 1992).

Clinton, Alan, *Post Office Workers: A Trade Union and Social History* (London and Boston: Allen & Unwin, 1984).

Cohen, E. W., *The Growth of the British Civil Service 1780-1939* (London: George Allen & Unwin, 1941).

Cohn, Samuel, 'Clerical Labor Intensity and the Feminisation of Clerical Labor in Great Britain, 1857-1937' *Social Forces*, vol. 63, no. 4 (June 1985), pp.1060-1068.

Cohn, Samuel, *The Process of Occupational Sex-Typing: The Feminisation of Clerical Labour in Great Britain* (Philadelphia: Temple University Press, 1985).

Cole, Margaret (ed.), *The Road to Success: Twenty Essays on the Choice of a Career for Women* (London: Methuen & Co., 1936).

Copelman, Dina, *London's Women Teachers: Gender, Class and Feminism 1870-1930* (London and New York: Routledge, 1996).

Cowman, Krista and Louise Jackson (eds), *Women and Work Culture: Britain c. 1850-1950* (Aldershot: Ashgate, 2005).

Crawford, Elizabeth, *The Women's Suffrage Movement: A Reference Guide, 1866-1928* (Abingdon: Routledge, 2001).

Cretney, Stephen, *Family Law in the Twentieth Century* (Oxford: Oxford University Press, 2003).

Crompton, Rosemary and Kay Sanderson, *Gendered Jobs and Social Change* (London: Unwin Hyman, 1990).

Dale, H. E., *The Higher Civil Service of Great Britain* (Oxford: Oxford University Press, 1941).

Daunton, Martin, *Royal Mail: The Post Office Since 1840* (London and Dover, NH: Athlone Press, 1985).

Davies, Celia, 'The Health Visitor as Mother's Friend: A Woman's Place in Public Health, 1900–1914' *Journal of the Social History of Medicine*, vol. 1, no. 1 (1988), pp.39–59.

Davin, Anna, 'City Girls: Young Women, New Employment, and the City, London, 1880–1910' in Mary Jo Maynes, Birgitte Soland and Christina Benninghaus (eds), *Secret Gardens, Satanic Mills: Placing Girls in European History, 1750–1960* (Bloomington: Indiana University Press, 2005), pp.209–223.

Dohrn, Susanne, 'Pioneers in a Dead-End Profession: The First Women Clerks in Banks and Insurance Companies' in Gregory Anderson (ed.), *The White-Blouse Revolution: Female Office Workers since 1870* (Manchester: Manchester University Press, 1988), pp.48–66.

Dorfman, Gerald A., *Wage Politics in Britain, 1945–1967* (London: Charles Knight & Co., 1974).

Durham, John, *Telegraphs in Victorian London* (Cambridge: The Golden Head Press, 1959).

Dyhouse, Carol, *No Distinction of Sex? Women in British Universities, 1870–1939* (Oxford: Routledge, 1995).

Dyhouse, Carol, *Students: A Gendered History* (Oxford: Routledge, 2006).

Dyhouse, Carol, 'Women Students and the London Medical Schools, 1914–1939: The Anatomy of a Masculine Culture' *Gender and History*, vol. 10, issue 1 (1998), pp.110–132.

Fisher, Kate, *Birth Control, Sex and Marriage in Britain, 1918–1960* (Oxford: Oxford University Press, 2008).

Forrest, Colleen Margaret, 'Familial Poverty, Family Allowances, and the Normative Family Structure in Britain, 1917–1945', *Journal of Family History*, vol. 26, no. 4 (2001), pp.508–528.

Gamarnikow, Eva, Morgan, David, Purvis, June and Taylorson, Daphne (eds), *Gender, Class and Work* (London: Heinemann, 1983).

Geddes, J. F., 'The Doctors' Dilemma: Medical Women and the British Suffrage Movement' *Women's History Review*, vol. 18, no. 2 (April 2009), pp.203–218.

Gibbon, Gwilym and Reginald W. Bell, *History of the London County Council, 1889–1939* (London: Macmillan & Co., 1939).

Gladden, E. N., *Civil Service Staff Relationships* (London: William Hodge and Company, 1943).

Gladden, E. N. *Civil Service or Bureaucracy?* (London: Staples Press Ltd, 1956).

Glucksmann, Miriam, *Women Assemble: Women Workers and the New Industries in Inter-War Britain* (Routledge: London, 1990).

Godwin, Anne, 'Early Years in the Trade Unions' in Lucy Middleton (ed.), *Women in the Labour Movement* (London: Croom Helm, 1977), pp.94–112.

Grant, Linda, 'Women's Work and Trade Unionism in Liverpool, 1890–1914' *North West Labour History Society Bulletin*, no. 7 (1980–1981), pp.65–83.

Graves, Pamela M., *Labour Women: Women in British Working-Class Politics, 1918–1939* (Cambridge: Cambridge University Press, 1994).

Grint, Keith, 'Women and Equality: The Acquisition of Equal Pay in the Post Office, 1870–1961' *Sociology*, vol. 22, no. 1 (1988), pp.87–108.

Halsey, A. H., *British Social Trends Since 1900* (Basingstoke and London: Macmillan, 1988).

Harrison, Brian, 'Women in a Men's House: The Women M.P.s, 1919–1945' *The Historical Journal*, vol. 29, no. 3 (September 1986), pp.623–654.

Harrison, Brian, 'Class and Gender in Modern British Labour History' *Past and Present*, no. 124 (August 1989), pp.121–158.

Hede, Andrew, 'Women Managers in the Civil Service: The Long Road towards Equity in Britain' *International Review of Administrative Sciences*, vol. 61, no. 4 (1995), pp.587–600.

Hennessy, Peter, *Having It So Good: Britain in the Fifties* (London: Penguin, 2007).

Heritage, John, 'Feminisation and Unionisation: A Case Study from Banking' in Eva Gamarnikow, David Morgan, June Purvis and Daphne Taylorson (eds.), *Gender, Class and Work* (London: Heinemann, 1983), pp.131–148.

Hinton, James, *Women, Social Leadership, and the Second World War* (Oxford: Oxford University Press, 2002).

Holcombe, Lee, *Victorian Ladies at Work: Middle-Class Working Women in England and Wales, 1850–1914* (Newton Abbot: David & Charles, 1973).

Holden, Katherine, 'Imaginary Widows: Spinsters, Marriage and the "Lost Generation" in Britain after the Great War' *Journal of Family History*, vol. 30, no. 4 (2005), pp.387–412.

Holden, Katherine, *The Shadow of Marriage* (Manchester: Manchester University Press, 2007).

Hollis, Patricia, *Ladies Elect: Women in English Local Government, 1865–1914* (Oxford: Oxford University Press, 1986).

Holtzmann, Ellen, 'The Pursuit of Married Love: Women's Attitudes Towards Sexuality and Marriage in Great Britain, 1918–1939' *Journal of Social History*, vol. 16 (1982), pp.39–52.

Humphries, B. V., *Clerical Unions in the Civil Service* (Oxford: Oxford University Press, 1958).

Imlay Buckley, Elizabeth and Dorothy Usher Potter (eds), *Ida and the Eye: A Woman in British Ophthalmology: From the Autobiography of Ida Mann* (Tunbridge Wells: Parapress Ltd, 1996).

Jackson, Louise A., *Women Police* (Manchester: Manchester University Press, 2006).

Jeffrey, Keith, *The GPO and the Easter Uprising* (Dublin: Irish Academic Press Ltd, 2006).

Jeffreys, Sheila, *The Spinster and Her Enemies: Feminism and Sexuality, 1880–1930* (London: Pandora, 1985).

Jenkins, Sarah, Miguel Martinez Lucio and Mike Noon, 'Return to Gender: An Analysis of Women's Disadvantage in Postal Work' *Gender, Work and Organisation*, vol. 9, no. 1 (January 2002), pp.81–104.

Jones, Helen, *Women in British Public Life, 1914–50: Gender, Power and Social Policy* (Harlow: Pearson Education, 2000).

Jordan, Ellen, 'The Lady Clerks at the Prudential: The Beginning of Vertical Segregation by Sex in Clerical Work in Nineteenth Century Britain' *Gender and History*, vol. 8, no. 1 (April 1996), pp.65–81.

Jordan, Ellen, ' "The Great Principle of English Fair Play": Male Champions, the English Women's Movement and the Admission of Women to the Pharmaceutical Society in 1879' *Women's History Review*, vol. 7, no. 3 (1998), pp.381-410.

Jordan, Ellen, *The Women's Movement and Women's Employment in Nineteenth Century Britain* (London and New York: Routledge, 1999).

Kean, Hilda, *The Lives of Suffragette Teachers* (London: Pluto Pres, 1990).

Kean, Hilda and Alison Oram, ' "Men must be educated and Women must do it" ': The National Federation (later Union) of Women Teachers and Contemporary Feminism, 1910-30', *Gender and Education*, vol. 2, no. 2 (1990), pp.147-168.

Kelsall, R. K., *Higher Civil Servants in Britain: From 1870 to the Present Day* (London: Routledge and Kegan Paul Ltd, 1955).

Kemp-Jones, E. M., *The Employment of Women in the Civil Service*, Civil Service Department Management Studies 3 (HMSO: Edinburgh, 1971).

King, Sarah, 'Feminists in Teaching: The National Union of Women Teachers 1920-1945' in Martin Lawn and Gerald Grace (eds.), *Teachers: The Culture of Politics and Work* (Falmer Press: Lewes, 1987), pp.31-49.

Kingsley Kent, Susan, *Making Peace: The Reconstruction of Gender in Interwar Britain* (Princeton: Princeton University Press, 1993).

Klingender, Francis D., *The Condition of Clerical Labour in Britain* (London: Martin Lawrence, 1935).

Land, Hilary, 'The Family Wage' *Feminist Review*, no. 6 (1980), pp.55-77.

Langhamer, Claire, *Women's Leisure in England, 1920-1960* (Manchester: Manchester University Press, 2000).

Law, Cheryl, *Suffrage and Power: The Women's Movement, 1918-1928* (London: I. B. Tauris, 1997).

Law, Cheryl, *Women: A Modern Political Dictionary* (London: I. B. Tauris, 2000).

Laybourn, Keith, *Unemployment and Employment Policies Concerning Women in Britain, 1900-1951* (Lewiston: The Edwin Mellen Press, 2002).

Leopold, E., *In the Service of London: The Origin and Development of Council Employment from 1889* (London: Greater London Council, 1986).

Levine, Philippa, ' "Walking the Streets in a Way No Decent Woman Should": Women Police in World War I' *Journal of Modern History*, vol. 66, no. 1 (March 1994), pp.34-78.

Lewenhak, S., *Women and Trade Unions* (London and Tonbridge: Ernest Benn, 1977).

Lewis, Jane, 'In Search of Real Equality: Women Between the Wars' in Frank Gloversmith (ed.), *Class, Culture and Social Change: A New View of the 1930s* (Sussex: Harvester Press, 1980), pp.208-239.

Lewis, Jane, *Women in England, 1870-1950: Sexual Divisions and Social Change* (Sussex: Wheatsheaf Books, 1984).

Lewis, Jane E., 'Women Clerical Workers in the Late Nineteenth and Early Twentieth Centuries', in Gregory Anderson (ed.), *The White-Blouse Revolution: Female Office Workers since 1870* (Manchester: Manchester University Press, 1988), pp.27-47.

Lewis, Jane, *Women and Social Action in Late Victorian and Edwardian Britain* (Cheltenham: Edward Elgar, 1991).

Littlewood, M., 'Makers of Men: The Anti-Feminist Backlash of the National Association of Schoolmasters in the 1920s and 1930s' *Trouble and Strife*, vol. 5 (1985), pp.22–30.

Livesey, Ruth, 'The Politics of Work: Feminism, Professionalization and Women Inspectors of Factories and Workshops', *Women's History Review*, vol. 13, no. 2 (2004), pp.233–262.

Lockwood, David, *The Blackcoated Worker: A Study in Class Consciousness* (London: Allen & Unwin, 1958).

Logan, Anne, 'In Search of Equal Citizenship: The Campaign for Women Magistrates in England and Wales, 1910–1939', *Women's History Review*, vol. 16, no. 4 (September 2007), pp.501–518.

Logan, Anne, '"Building a New and Better Order"? Women and Jury Service in England and Wales, 1920–1970', *Women's History Review*, vol. 22, no. 5 (2013), pp.701–716.

MacEwen Scott, Alison (ed.), *Gender Segregation and Social Change: Men and Women in Changing Labour Markets* (Oxford: Oxford University Press, 1994).

Macnicol, J., *The Movement for Family Allowances, 1918–45* (London: Heinemann, 1980).

Marshall, C. F. D., *The British Post Office from its Beginning to the End of 1925* (London: Humphrey Milford, 1926).

Martin, Jane, *Women and the Politics of Schooling* (London: Cassell, 1999).

Martin, Nancy, *The Post Office: From Carrier Pigeon to Confravision* (London: J. M. Dent and Sons Ltd, 1969).

Martindale, Hilda, *Women Servants of the State, 1870–1938: A History of Women in the Civil Service* (London: Allen & Unwin, 1938).

Marwick, Arthur, *The Deluge* (Basingstoke: Macmillan, 1991).

McCarthy, Helen, 'Petticoat Diplomacy: The Admission of Women to the British Foreign Service, c.1919–1946' *Twentieth Century British History*, vol. 20, no. 3 (2009), pp.285–321.

McCarthy, Helen, *Women of the World: The Rise of the Female Diplomat* (London: Bloomsbury, 2014).

McClair, Elizabeth, 'Single Parenthood and the Civil Service' in Sybil Oldfield (ed.), *This Working Day World: Women's Lives and Culture(s) in Britain, 1914–1945* (London: Taylor & Francis, 1994), pp.68–72.

McGregor, O. R., *Divorce in England: A Centenary Study* (London, Heinemann: 1957).

Michaelsen, Kaarin, '"Union is Strength": The Medical Women's Federation and the Politics of Professionalism, 1917–30' in Krista Cowman and Louise Jackson (eds), *Women and Work Culture: Britain c.1850–1950* (Aldershot: Ashgate, 2005), pp.161–176.

Moran, Michael, *The Union of Post Office Workers: A Study in Political Sociology* (Basingstoke and London: Macmillan, 1974).

Mortimer, James E. and Valerie A. Ellis, *A Professional Union: The Evolution of the Institution of Professional Civil Servants* (London: George Allen & Unwin, 1980).

Newman, Bernard, *Yours For Action* (London: Herbert Jenkins, 1953).

Nicholson, Virginia, *Singled Out* (London: Penguin, 2007).

Noakes, Lucy, *Women in the British Army: War and the Gentle Sex, 1907–1948* (London: Routledge, 2006).

Oldfield, Sybil (ed.), *This Working-Day World: Women's Lives and Cultures in Britain, 1914–1945* (London: Taylor & Francis, 1994).

Oram, Alison, *Women Teachers and Feminist Politics, 1900–39* (Manchester: Manchester University Press, 1996).

Parris, Henry, *Staff Relations in the Civil Service: Fifty Years of Whitleyism* (London: George Allen & Unwin, 1973).

Pedersen, Susan, 'Gender, Welfare and Citizenship in Britain during the Great War', *The American Historical Review*, vol. 95, no. 4 (October 1990), pp.983–1006.

Pedersen, Susan, *Eleanor Rathbone and the Politics of Conscience* (New Haven and London: Yale University Press, 2004).

Pelling, Henry, *A History of British Trade Unionism*, 4th edn (Middlesex: Penguin, 1987).

Pennybacker, Susan, *A Vision for London: Labour, Everyday Life and the LCC Experiment* (London: Routledge, 1995).

Perriton, Linda, 'Forgotten Feminists: the Federation of British Professional and Business Women, 1933–1969' *Women's History Review*, vol. 16, issue 1 (2007), pp.79–97.

Pimlott, Ben (ed.), *The Political Diary of Hugh Dalton, 1918–1940, 1945–1960* (London: Jonathan Cape, Ltd/LSE, 1986).

Potter, Allen, 'The Equal Pay Campaign Committee: A Case-Study of Pressure Group' *Political Studies*, vol. 5, no. 1 (1957), pp.49–64.

Pugh, Martin, *Women and the Women's Movement in Britain, 1914–1959* (London: Macmillan, 1992).

Pugh, Martin, *The Making of Modern British Politics: 1867–1945*, 3rd edn (Oxford: Blackwell, 2002).

Pugh, Martin, *We Danced All Night: A Social History of Britain Between the Wars* (London: Vintage, 2009).

Pursell, Carroll, '"Am I a Lady or an Engineer?" The Origins of the Women's Engineering Society in Britain, 1918–1940' *Technology and Culture*, vol. 34, no. 1 (January 1993), pp.78–97.

Purvis, June, 'Jill Craigie (1914–1999)' *Women's History Review*, vol. 9, no. 1 (2000), pp.5–8.

Redmayne, Sharon, 'The Matrimonial Causes Act, 1937: A Lesson in the Art of Compromise' *Oxford Journal of Legal Studies,* vol. 13, no. 2 (1993), pp.183–200.

Roberts, E., *Women's Work 1840–1940* (Basingstoke and London: Macmillan, 1988).

Robinson, Howard, *Britain's Post Office: A History of Development from the Beginnings to the Present Day* (Oxford: Oxford University Press, 1953).

Rollyson, Carl, *To Be A Woman: The Life of Jill Craigie* (London: Aurum Press, Ltd, 2005).

Routh, Guy, 'Civil Service Pay, 1875 to 1950' *Economica*, vol. 21, no. 83 (August 1954), pp.201–223.

Sanderson, K., ' "A Pension to Look Forward To….?": Women Civil Service Clerks in London, 1925–1939' in L. Davidoff and B. Westover (eds), *Our Work, Our Lives, Our Words: Women's History and Women's Work* (Basingstoke: Macmillan Education, 1986), pp.145–160.

Savage, Gail L., 'Social Class and Social Policy: The Civil Service and Secondary Education in England during the Interwar Period' *Journal of Contemporary History*, vol. 18, no. 2 (April 1983), pp.261–280.

Savage, Gail, *The Social Construction of Expertise: The English Civil Service and Its Influence, 1919–1939* (Pittsburgh: Pittsburgh University Press, 1996).

Savage, Gail, 'Erotic Stories and Public Decency: Newspaper Reporting of Divorce Proceeedings in England' *The Historical Journal*, vol. 41, no. 2 (June 1998), pp.511–528.

Savage, M., 'Trade Unionism, Sex Segregation and the State: Women's Employment in "New Industries" in Inter-War Britain' *Social History*, vol. 13, no. 2 (1988), pp.209–230.

Savage, M., 'Gender and Career Mobility in Banking, 1880–1940' in A. Miles and D. Vincent (eds), *Building European Society* (Manchester: Manchester University Press, 1993), pp.196–216.

Savage M. and A. Witz (eds), *Gender and Bureaucracy* (Oxford: Blackwell, 1994).

Shapiro Sanders, Lise, *Consuming Fantasies: Labour, Leisure and the London Shopgirl, 1880–1920* (Columbus: Ohio State University Press, 2006).

Siltanen, J., *Locating Gender: Occupational Segregation Wages and Domestic Responsibilities* (London: UCL Press, 1994).

Silverstone, Rosalie, 'Office Work for Women: An Historical Review' *Business History*, vol. 18 (1976), pp.98–110.

Smith, Harold, 'The Issue of "Equal Pay for Equal Work" in Great Britain 1914–19' *Societas*, vol. 8, no. 1 (1978), pp.39–51.

Smith, Harold, 'The Problem of "Equal Pay for Equal Work" in Great Britain during World War II' *The Journal of Modern History*, vol. 53, no. 4 (December 1981), pp.652–672.

Smith, Harold L., 'Sex versus Class: British Feminists and the Labour Movement 1919–1929' *The Historian*, vol. 47 (1984), pp.19–37.

Smith, Harold L. (ed.), *British Feminism in the Twentieth Century* (Aldershot: Edward Elgar, 1990).

Smith, Harold L., 'The Politics of Conservative Reform: The Equal Pay for Equal Work Issue, 1945–1955' *The Historical Journal*, vol. 35, no. 2 (June 1992), pp.401–415.

Smith, Harold L. 'Gender and the Welfare State: The 1940 Old Age and Widows' Pensions Act' *History: The Journal of the Historical Association*, vol. 80, no. 260 (1995), pp.382–399.

Smith, Harold L., 'British Feminism and the Equal Pay Issue in the 1930s', *Women's History Review*, vol. 5, no. 1 (1996), pp.97–110.

Solden, Norbert C., *Women in British Trade Unions 1874–1976* (Dublin: Gill and Macmillan, 1978).

Sommerlad, H. and P. Sanderson, *Gender, Choice and Commitment: Women Solicitors in England and Wales and the Struggle for Equal Status* (Aldershot: Ashgate, 1998).

Spoor, Alec, *White Collar Union: Fifty Years of NALGO* (London: Heinemann, 1967).

Stack, Frieda, 'Civil Service Associations and the Whitley Report of 1917' *Political Quarterly*, vol. 40, no. 3 (1969), pp.283–295.

Stone, Lawrence, *Road to Divorce: England, 1530–1987* (Oxford: Oxford University Press, 1990).

Summerfield, Penny, *Women Workers in the Second World War: Production and Patriarchy in Conflict* (London: Routledge, 1989).

Summerfield, Penny, 'My Dress for an Army Uniform: Gender Instabilities in the Two World Wars', *Inaugural Lecture* (Lancaster: Lancaster University, 1997).

Summerfield, Penny and Corinna Peniston-Bird, *Contesting Home Defence* (Manchester: Manchester University Press, 2007).

Thane, Pat, 'The Women of the British Labour Party and Feminism, 1906-1945' in H. L. Smith (ed.), *British Feminism in the Twentieth Century* (Aldershot: Ashgate, 1990), pp.124-143.

Thane, Pat, 'Women's History and Labour History' *Labour History Review*, vol. 55, no. 3 (Winter 1990), pp.14-16.

Thane, Pat, *Foundations of the Welfare State*, 2nd edn (Harlow: Longman, 1996).

Thane, Pat, 'What Difference did the Vote Make? Women in Public and Private Life in Britain since 1918', *Historical Research*, vol. lxxvi (2003), pp.268-285.

Theakston, Kevin, 'Evelyn Sharp (1903-1985)', *Contemporary Record*, vol. 7, no. 1 (1993), pp.132-148.

Thom, Deborah, *Nice Girls and Rude Girls: Women Workers in World War I* (London: I. B. Tauris, 2000).

Todd, Selina, ' "Boisterous Workers": Young Women, Industrial Rationalisation and Workplace Militancy in Interwar England' *Labour History Review*, vol. 68, no. 3 (December 2003), pp.293-310.

Todd, Selina, *Young Women, Work and the Family, 1918-1950* (Oxford: Oxford University Press, 2005).

Todd, Selina, 'Domestic Servants and Social Relations in England, 1900-1950' *Past and Present*, vols 2-3, no. 1 (2009), pp.181-204.

Vallance, Elizabeth, *Women in the House* (London: Continuum, 1979).

Vicinus, Martha, *Independent Women: Work and Community for Single Women, 1850-1920* (London: Virago, 1985).

Verdon, Nicola, 'Agricultural Labour and the Contested Nature of Women's Work in Interwar England and Wales' *Historical Journal*, vol. 52, no. 1 (March 2009), pp.109-130.

Walby, Sylvia, *Patriarchy at Work* (Cambridge: Polity Press, 1986).

Weeks, Jeffrey, *Sex, Politics and Society: The Regulation of Sexuality since 1800* (London: Longman, 1981).

Whitehead, Kay, 'Concerning Images of Women in Government Offices in the Early Twentieth Century: What Difference Does Age Make?' *Australian Historical Studies*, vol. 37, no. 127 (2006), pp.25-42.

Wigham, E., *From Humble Petition to Militant Action: A History of the Civil and Public Services Association* (London: Civil & Public Services Association, 1980).

Williams, Philip M., *Hugh Gaitskell* (Oxford and New York: Oxford University Press, 1982).

Wilson, R. Guerriero, 'Women's Work in Offices and the Preservation of Men's "Breadwinning" Jobs in Early Twentieth-Century Glasgow', *Women's History Review*, vol. 10, issue 3 (2001), pp.463-482.

Witz, Anne, *Professions and Patriarchy* (London: Routledge, 1992).

Wojtczak, Helena, *Railwaywomen: Exploitation, Betrayal and Triumph in the Workplace* (Hastings: The Hastings Press, 2005).

Woodward, Nicholas, *The Management of the British Economy, 1945-2001* (Manchester: Manchester University Press, 2004).

Zimmeck, Meta, 'Strategies and Stratagems for the Employment of Women in the British Civil Service, 1919–1939', *The Historical Journal*, vol. 27, no. 4 (1984), pp.901–924.

Zimmeck, Meta, 'Jobs for the Girls: The Expansion of Clerical Work for Women, 1850–1914' in Angela V. John (ed.), *Unequal Opportunities: Women's Employment in England, 1800–1918* (Oxford and New York: Basil Blackwell, 1986), pp.153–177.

Zimmeck, Meta, '"Get Out and Get Under": The Impact of Demobilisation on the Civil Service, 1918–1932' in G. Anderson (ed.), *The White-Blouse Revolution: Female Office Workers since 1870* (Manchester: Manchester University Press, 1988), pp.88–120.

Zimmeck, Meta, 'The New Woman in the Machinery of Government: A Spanner in the Works?' in R. Macleod (ed.), *Government and Expertise in Britain, 1815–1919: Specialists, Administrators and Professionals* (Cambridge: Cambridge University Press, 1988), pp.185–202.

Zimmeck, Meta, 'Marry in Haste, Repent at Leisure: Women, Bureaucracy and the Post Office, 1870–1920' in Mike Savage and Anne Witz (eds) *Gender and Bureaucracy* (Oxford and Cambridge, MA: Blackwell Publishers, 1992), pp.65–93.

Zimmeck, Meta, '"The Mysteries of the Typewriter": Technology and Gender in the British Civil Service, 1870–1914' in Gertjan de Groot and Marlon Schrover (eds), *Women Workers and Technological Change in Europe in the Nineteenth and Twentieth Centuries* (London: Taylor & Francis, 1995), pp.67–96.

Zweiniger-Bargielowska, Ina (ed.), *Women in Twentieth Century Britain* (Harlow: Pearson Education, 2001).

Theses

Crowley, Mark, 'Women Workers in the Post Office, 1939–1945: Gender Conflict or Political Emancipation?' (unpublished PhD thesis, University of London, 2010).

Glew, Helen, 'Women's Employment in the General Post Office, 1914–1939' (unpublished PhD thesis, University of London, 2010).

Murphy, Catherine, '"On an Equal Footing with Men?": Women and Work at the BBC, 1923–1939' (unpublished PhD thesis, Goldsmiths, University of London, 2011).

Takayanagi, Mari, 'Parliament and Women, c.1900–1945' (unpublished PhD thesis, King's College, London, 2012).

Online sources

Fawcett Society, 'The Pay Gap By Occupation and Region', available at www.fawcettsociety.org.uk/index.asp?PageID=321, accessed 29 September 2009.

Fawcett Society, *What about Women?* (2013), available at www.fawcettsociety.org.uk/wp-content/uploads/2013/02/Fawcett-Society-What-About-Women-report-low-res.pdf, accessed 13 August 2014.

'Fewer Women Getting Senior Civil Service Jobs', *Guardian*, 15 July 2008, available at www.guardian.co.uk/politics/2008/jul/15/whitehall-women, accessed 27 August 2009.

The Guardian, 'MOD needs to put women in senior positions, says top civil servant', 2 December 2011, available at www.guardian.co.uk/uk/2011/dec/02/mod-needs-women-senior-positions, accessed 2 December 2011.

House of Commons Library, Parliamentary Briefing papers, *Civil Service Statistics* (2013), p.7, available at www.parliament.uk/briefing-papers/SN02224.pdf, accessed 13 August 2014.

Office of National Statistics, *Annual Survey of Hours and Earnings* (2013), available at www.ons.gov.uk/ons/dcp171778_335027.pdf, accessed 13 August 2014.

Royal Mail Annual Report for year ended 29 March 2009, p.63. Available at ftp://ftp.royal-mail.com/Downloads/public/ctf/rmg/200809RM_Group_Accounts_May_2009.pdf, accessed 1 September 2009.

'Women Graduates Step Off Fast Track for Civil Service', *The Times*, 20 June 2005, available at www.timesonline.co.uk/tol/life_and_style/education/student/news/article535357.exe, accessed 27 August 2009.

'Women "Still Fail Promotion Race": Figures Show Men's Firm Grip on Top Posts', *Independent*, 17 October 1994, available at www.independent.co.uk/news/uk/women-s till-fail-promotion-race-figures-show-mens-firm-grip-on-top-posts-1443387.html, accessed 27 August 2009.

Film

To Be A Woman, dir. by Jill Craigie (Outlook Films, 1951).

Index

EU authorised representative for GPSR:
Easy Access System Europe, Mustamäe tee 50,
10621 Tallinn, Estonia
gpsr.requests@easproject.com

www.ingramcontent.com/pod-product-compliance
Lightning Source LLC
Chambersburg PA
CBHW022304280326
41932CB00010B/979